LIFE AFTER DEATH

Remarkable changes take place in the lives of near-death survivors. Overwhelmingly, the subjects in my research sample now consider themselves to be more worthy and capable, with a strong sense of purpose in their lives. They are more at peace, and have a deeper understanding of themselves.

This change in attitude overflows into their desire to help others. Their interest in material success declines sharply, whereas their interest in spiritual matters increases. They describe their lives as more meaningful, peaceful, purposeful, and fulfilling.

Their changes in interests are equally dramatic, based on greater self-understanding, development of personal talent, and helping others.

—Cherie Sutherland

Reborn in the Light

Life After Near-Death Experiences

Cherie Sutherland, Ph.D.

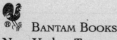
BANTAM BOOKS
New York   Toronto   London   Sydney   Auckland

REBORN IN THE LIGHT
A Bantam Book

PUBLISHING HISTORY
First published as *Transformed By the Light* in Australia and New Zealand
in 1992 by Bantam
Bantam edition/March 1995

*The author and publishers have made every effort to
acknowledge all sources used for this book. We would be
pleased to hear from anyone who has not been acknowledged.*

ISBN 0-553-56980-5

Published simultaneously in the United States and Canada

Bantam Books are published by Bantam Books, a division of Bantam Doubleday
Dell Publishing Group, Inc. Its trademark, consisting of the words "Bantam Books"
and the portrayal of a rooster, is Registered in U.S. Patent and Trademark Office and
in other countries. Marca Registrada. Bantam Books, 1540 Broadway, New York,
New York 10036.

PRINTED IN THE UNITED STATES OF AMERICA
RAD   0 9 8 7 6 5 4 3 2

Acknowledgments

This work is dedicated to:

The Light who set me on this path.

Eagle, whose wise counsel led me to begin this project.

My two sons, Laif and Eden Sutherland, who have lovingly shared my journey for many years now, through both difficult and joyful times.

Dr. Ann Daniel, whose open mind, firm encouragement and considered comments, delivered in her own gentle fashion, made our sessions together something to be valued.

All the near-death experiencers, many of whom have become dear friends, who generously shared so much of their lives with me.

My mother and father, Thelma and William Sutherland, who always believed it was possible.

Thanks are also due to:

Lyn Richards, for introducing me to the challenging world of "grounded theory."

The Australian Federation of University Women (South Australian branch) for awarding me the Jean Gilmour/ Thenie Baddams Special Grant (1990), which enabled me to purchase the computer and software required to complete my project.

The University of New South Wales Social Science li-

brarians, whose helpfulness in processing the many interli-
brary loans I required was very much appreciated.

Transforming a dissertation into a book is a fascinating
process. Special thanks are due to:

My literary agent, Rosemary Creswell, whose confidence and expertise set things going.

Susan and Nevill Drury, for their early editorial work.

The magnificent team of women at Transworld: Judith
Curr (publisher), Marie-Louise Taylor (senior editor) and
Maggie Hamilton (head of publicity), whose attention to
detail and enthusiasm have made the entire process so en-
joyable.

Contents

Foreword

The modern interest in the near-death experience (NDE) stems from the pioneering work of two American-based psychiatrists, Elisabeth Kübler-Ross and Raymond A. Moody, Jr. It was in fact the latter's best-selling book *Life after Life,* originally published in 1975 and now translated into more than thirty languages, which first named and codified this phenomenon and made so many of us aware that the passage into death apparently did not lead to oblivion after all but rather into a world of radiant, supernatural beauty and love. That book, with its enormous popularity and compelling personal testimonies, seems to have changed permanently our understanding of death and has helped to make it not a specter to be feared but a joy of supreme deliverance to be anticipated.

Cherie Sutherland's book continues this exploration of the meaning of the near-death experience but takes it into an altogether different domain from that with which Raymond Moody was chiefly concerned. Dr. Sutherland's aim is not so much to consider (though she does) the implications of the NDE for life after *death* as to determine what effects it has on life *after a near-death experience itself.* In other words, how are people changed by this experience, and what significance do those changes have for us who continue, even if temporarily, to reside on the all-too-familiar surface of our increasingly polluted planet?

Now, there have been other books that have treated this subject previously, including one of my own published some years ago, but in my personal opinion no one has conducted a more searching inquiry into this matter or written about it more superbly than Dr. Sutherland. *Reborn in the Light* is, then, a book of many virtues, not least of them the author's elegant prose, which is pellucid and a thorough pleasure to read. Other splendid features of this book are the quotes that come directly from the interviews with her near-death survivors whom Dr. Sutherland painstakingly sought out all over Australia's vast reaches. These excerpts not only illustrate the highly consistent and positive manner in which persons change following an NDE, but they have the power to move us deeply and affect us in lasting ways, as I shall make clear below. And there are still other contributions of this study that make Dr. Sutherland's book of such great value. For example, in her exploration of the aftereffects of NDEs, she has broken new ground in investigating such matters as how marriages and other personal relationships are strained by NDEs; how others' reactions to hearing about the NDE affect the experiencer; how people come to terms (or occasionally don't) with their NDE; and a whole range of lifestyle changes following NDEs that no previous researcher has bothered to look into but which add immeasurably to our understanding of the power of this experience to bring about a lasting transformation in the life of the near-death experiencer. Finally, by discovering that the principal changes described by her Australian respondents are essentially the same as those that have been reported earlier by American and English NDE researchers, Dr. Sutherland has furnished still more evidence supporting the view that the NDE is a *universal* phenomenon, both in its features and its effects on those who undergo it.

Reading this book, you will, by the time you reach its end, have no doubt that the NDE is an important phenomenon and one, furthermore, with an enormous potential to enrich, spiritually and personally, the lives of those who have experienced it. But this immediately raises a troubling question, or should, for most readers. Obviously, most people have not had this experience—only a relative handful of any population will sustain one. So any prospective reader who lacks the direct experience may very well comment in effect, "Well, it's nice that many of these people blossom so beautifully after their NDEs, but what relevance does that have for me?"

It is just here that Dr. Sutherland's book will provide a subtle, and perhaps unexpected, but definitely satisfying answer. We now know, from the latest research on NDEs, that even persons who are exposed to the literature on NDEs and come to take an interest in it, also *begin to experience changes in their lives akin to those that near-death experiencers report.* They, too, tend to find that they become more loving, more compassionate, and more spiritually oriented after gaining familiarity with these experiences and those who have them. Furthermore, in one study, it has been shown that more than 80 percent of such persons state that their own fear of death has diminished and, correspondingly, their conviction in a life after death has increased. In short, you don't personally need to have a near-death experience in order to reap some of its benefits.

Can reading a book really change your life? Try Cherie Sutherland's and see for yourself.

Kenneth Ring, Ph.D.
Professor of Psychology, University of Connecticut

Preface

Eden, my youngest son, was born on January 11, 1971. The inspired irony of my having given him such a name did not occur to me until reading Ken Wilber's book *Up From Eden* many years later. Certainly the evolution of my life moved "up" from the time of Eden's birth—if not precisely as Ken Wilber outlines. Rather than it being a movement from Eden to self-consciousness, I moved at the time of the experience, during the birth of Eden, to self-consciousness. For however long it was, I experienced the essence of who I am: selfless, egoless, bodyless, free of time and space.

This experience, which even at the time I recognized as one of death and rebirth, was to provide me with a view of reality and a consciousness of self that I had not even imagined to be a possibility, and was profoundly to alter my life.

During Eden's birth I passed from a physical experience of great pain and fear to another realm quite free of any physical discomfort—a realm of peace, calm and love. The ineffability of such an experience has often been noted. To reduce to words an experience so far removed from the construct of reality within which I had previously lived is inevitably to oversimplify and do it violence. However, in brief, I found that I was moving very quickly through a dark tunnel toward a magnificent bright light, hearing a "whooshing" sound as I went. As I approached the light, it became brighter and I saw that it was like very bright but gentle sunlight. I could see into the light where everything was bathed in a golden glow. There were gently rolling fields, flowers, an extraordinarily beautiful sight . . . joyous and peaceful. However, I stopped just short of the light, still in the tunnel. I knew I had a choice: to go on (and it was very tempting) or to go back. I reflected with great clarity that the baby I was giving birth to needed me, and my other son (still very young) also needed me, so I would go back. In addition to going back for the sake of my babies, however, I knew I was going back for me—that I would have another go at life. Once the decision was made, I found that I was traveling backward back down the tunnel away from the light and was returned to the pain of my immediate situation—giving birth to Eden.

As I soon found out, to have experienced this transcendental state did not mean that I was to be freed of my ego-bound self. The gift of this experience was to leave me with the direct knowledge that my ego-bound self was and is a part of the timeless ground of all being, integral wholeness. As Kenneth Ring notes in *Life at Death,* it is this direct knowledge that has "core near-death experiencers" (and mystics generally) speaking with such certitude about their experiences, whereas those who haven't had such direct experience are often left feeling skeptical or just indifferent.

A year later I told my mother about the experience. She was somewhat distressed, but accepting of its reality. Any later attempts I made to talk about my experience were generally greeted with skepticism. Rational, materialistic, reductionistic explanations were even "helpfully" offered to "get rid of it" for me. So, I stopped talking about it. Yet I had no doubt that it was important for me. From being fearful of everything, I now found within myself a realization that there was nothing to fear. As Ken Wilber writes in *Up From Eden*:

> Seeing that self and other are one, [we are] released
> from the fear of life; seeing that being and non-being
> are one, [we are] delivered from the fear of death.[1]

In this present study I have found that people are greatly
changed by such experiences in terms of personal
renewal—given new direction, purpose and energy. I certainly was. From my social situation as an uneducated
housebound housewife, mother of two young sons, I began
to make what now seem rather tentative forays into the
world, but at the time seemed like giant risk-taking steps.
I began to learn yoga and practiced it daily with my babies. I began to read about vegetarianism and practiced it
from then on. I read anything I could lay my hands on,
and, as time passed, began painting and writing. In essence, I continued to learn through valuing my own
experience—a theme that has evolved over the years as a
central concern of my own development. Further, against
all expectations, synchronistically, university fees were
abolished the year Eden was old enough to attend pre-
school and my application to college was accepted.

The experience I have so briefly outlined thus was to
provide the starting point for my doctoral thesis and this
book. It has remained to this day the source to which I return and from which I continue to learn so much. As Ken
Wilber writes:

> I used to think that one adopted a path just to get to
> a goal. I have learned better: The true path is itself
> the ultimate goal.[2]

The Near-Death Experience

There is a general assumption in modern Western society that death is final, that it is as Shakespeare described it in *Hamlet*: "The undiscover'd country from whose bourn, No traveller returns, . . ." Yet there have always been tales of people who have returned, to tell of realms unknown. In literature of all ages there are accounts of such journeys. Plato, in *The Republic,* recounts the story of Er, a Greek soldier killed in battle, whose body revived twelve days later on the funeral pyre. To the surprise of all present, he described the journey his soul had taken until ordered to return. In the many centuries of medieval literature, Christian "otherworld" accounts abound. For example, in the eighth century, the Venerable Bede relates the story of the vision of Drythelm, a devout Northumbrian man who died one night after a severe illness. To the amazement of all those weeping around the body, he revived suddenly the next day. He reassured his wife: "Do not be afraid, for I have indeed risen from death which held me in its bonds, and I have been permitted to live again amongst mankind; nevertheless after this I must not live as I used to, but in a very different way."[1]

Such experiences are also described in other religious and cultural traditions. For example, the theories of the Ti-

betan *Bardo Thodol,* or *Book of the Dead,* which are now
well known in the West, describe the journey of the disem-
bodied individual from the moment of death through the
after-death states. There are many similarities between
modern accounts and descriptions of Japanese death-bed
visions and the Bahá'í faith's account of the afterlife King-
dom of Light. Carl Becker argues that the near-death experience is also central to Chinese Pure-Land Buddhism, and
E. J. Hermann reveals that there is a strong affinity between the beliefs of near-death experiencers and those of
Taoist patriarch Chuang Tzu.

In the late nineteenth century, Swiss geologist Albert
Heim, having survived death himself in a mountain-
climbing accident, published his collection of accounts by
fellow climbers who had also survived near-fatal falls. At
the same time, especially in Britain and the United States,
pioneer psychic researchers had become fascinated by the
tantalizing possibility of finding a proof for "survival."
They scrutinized such phenomena as apparitions seen by a
number of people, mediumistic messages from the dead,
out-of-body experiences, and visions described by the
dying. In 1926 Sir William Barrett, published his collection of "death-bed vision" case studies, which was to become the classic work on that topic. Some thirty-five years
later, Carl Gustav Jung, in his autobiographical work,
Memories, Dreams, Reflections, described his own intense, life-changing vision precipitated by a heart attack in
1944.

In more recent times, with advances in modern resuscitation technology, even more people have been brought
back from the brink of death to recount their experiences.
However, it was not until 1975, with the publication of
Raymond Moody's *Life After Life,* that there was a more
general resurgence of interest in the phenomenon he was
to name the near-death experience.

The near-death experience is said to occur when a person is close to death (or in many cases actually clinically

dead), and yet is resuscitated or somehow survives to re-count an intense, profoundly meaningful experience. The near-death episode itself is typically characterized by a feeling of peace, an out-of-body experience, the sensa-tion of traveling very quickly through a dark tunnel, gen-erally toward a light, an encounter with the spirits of deceased relatives or friends or a "being of light," an in-stantaneous life review and for some, entrance into a world of light.

In 1983 a major survey by George Gallup, Jr., reported that eight million Americans, or approximately five per-cent of the adult American population, had had what he calls a "verge-of-death" or "temporary death" experience with some sort of mystical encounter associated with the actual death event. In 1989 an Australian survey by Allan Kellehear and Patrick Heaven found that ten percent of a sample of 173 people, when shown a vignette depicting five typical elements of a near-death experience, claimed to have had a similar experience. In a prospective hospital study in the United States, Michael Sabom found that forty-three percent reported a near-death experience fol-lowing a near-death crisis. If so many people are having this experience and if, as Drythelm suggested so long ago, their values, beliefs and life practices are indeed changed by it, this phenomenon is of considerable interest and sig-nificance.

The empirical work that has been done in this area has been carried out mostly in America during the last fifteen years and has been predominantly psychological or medi-cal in focus. Raymond Moody, in his popular first book *Life After Life,* provided an ideal or composite picture of the near-death experience that he maintained contained all the common elements of the experience. The current study, although confirming the presence of most of those ele-ments, uncovered a pattern more in accord with that found by Kenneth Ring in his scientific investigation of the phe-nomenon reported in *Life at Death.* Ring observed that in his own examination of near-death experiences, the core experience unfolds in stages, with the earlier stages being far more common than the latter. The stages are:

Peace and the sense of well-being
Body separation: leaving the body behind
Entering the darkness
Seeing the light
Entering the light

So, what is this phenomenon? How is it described by the near-death experiencers themselves?

Overwhelmingly the experience is characterized by its ineffability. Although people do in fact manage to give some sort of description, they often stress that their words can in no way do it justice or convey its awesome power. A young woman who had her experience at age sixteen during an operation for cancer of the thyroid, while trying to explain the noise she heard, said:

It was sort of like silvery moonbeams and the noise they'd make on water if they were going to make a noise. You know what I mean? A sort of brushing sound.

Later she remarked:

That's the problem I'm having, when I put it into an intellectual frame of mind, when I try to write it out on a bit of paper, I'd say well, it wasn't actually this head thinking it. It was something different, totally devoid of intellectualization, totally devoid of the little boxes that we put things into.

Peace and Well-being

All of my sample, in one way or another, described a feeling of peace and well-being. A man who as a sixteen-year-old schoolboy, undiagnosed, entered a diabetic coma remembered:

> I had an intense feeling of well-being which for me created a really strong impression because I'd never felt that, I'd never had that feeling. Since though, sometimes in meditation I've touched upon it but then I've messed it up by grasping at it too strongly. There is an intense craving to get back to that feeling.

Another man who, aged thirty-two, had his experience as the result of a suicide attempt, said:

> At the time, I accepted that this was a peace that I'd never known before, a light I'd never seen before, and it had a magnitude I can't explain and it also had its own form of magnetism on my soul . . . I've never had so much peace in all my life.

Another woman, who at ten years of age was suffering from double pneumonia and was not expected to survive the night, remembered:

> I was floating on the ceiling and I was just so, so happy. It was just complete happiness, just complete happiness. There really is no word to describe it, there really isn't. And even now all those years later I get very overwhelmed at the feeling.

LEAVING THE BODY BEHIND

Movement out of body is often the first indication that something is amiss. In general, the experience is for people to find themselves looking down on their bodies as spectator, often from a vantage point near the ceiling (as described in the previous example). They usually report that at the time it all seems perfectly natural.

A thirty-six-year-old woman had a massive hemorrhage after a home birth. She described the scene below her:

> I sort of sat up on the ceiling. I remember watching all the panic, total panic. Tina, the midwife, couldn't find a pulse, she couldn't get a needle in. I was bleeding. I couldn't work out why everyone was so fussed. I was interested when Tina said "the veins have gone flat." Then I was aware that another friend there, whose mother had just died three months before, she was really frightened. But I felt an incredible feeling of peace. . . . At one stage they were looking for elastic to make a tourniquet so they could get a vein, and I knew where it was. In the end I said where it was but they didn't hear me.

Another experiencer, a man who at fourteen had had a series of heart attacks while at school one day, recalled attempting to communicate with the people around his body and generally exploring his immediate environment:

> I was up above everything. I could still hear them talking and by that time there were six teachers there. I was out of my body and I thought to myself "I must be dead." So I went up to Miss Smith and told her not to bother, I was dead. She took no notice of me. I went to take her arm and my hand went right through her. I thought, something is very wrong here! I made a few more attempts to speak to

her and to Miss Breen, then I gave up. I went to open the door but my hand went through the handle. I then tried the bricks beside the door, pushed with my hand and then went straight through the bricks to the outside. I remember going through the bricks two or three times just to try it out. I noticed some girls playing hockey. Then I started to wonder where my body was and somehow or other I got back into my body.

ENTERING THE DARKNESS AND SEEING THE LIGHT

Many words have been used to describe the experience of entering the darkness. It has variously been spoken of as a channel, a valley, a trough, a void or a pipe, but most commonly it is described as a tunnel.

A twenty-seven-year-old woman who was rushed by ambulance from a country town to a city hospital with a burst appendix during pregnancy experienced the darkness as "a valley, a dark valley, with this light sort of figure coming toward me."

Another woman who had a cardiac arrest in an allergic reaction to anesthetic for a hysterectomy said:

Then there was . . . I can only describe it as total black. There was a changing level, it was like going from one level to another. It wasn't sleep, it was total black . . . And then there was the light. Yeah, but it wasn't . . . a bright light . . . it was really in the distance and it was like a fused light, and I can remember then thinking how beautiful it was.

A twenty-nine-year-old woman who was hospitalized while hemorrhaging during a miscarriage at six months remembered:

... falling down this huge, huge, huge, big tunnel or at the time, because it's falling, you feel like it's a pit, a well, a bottomless well. And you feel as if it's bottomless and you feel as if it's a well but I suppose it's like falling down a big tunnel.

As can already be seen, however convenient it might be to break up and talk about the experience in terms of common elements or stages, this is not the way it is experienced by those describing it. Although these patterns become obvious when examining the reports of a large number of people, each individual case is unique and is experienced as a whole, not as a series of discrete parts.

THE LIFE REVIEW

A woman who, aged twenty-nine, had her experience during an operation for a tubal ligation, described a "life review," entering the darkness, and seeing the light. She said:

I went into this kind of feeling of ecstasy and just started moving outward energetically. . . . And then I experienced a replay of all of my life and I'd love to know if other people have it. That was the most shocking thing of the whole experience, from my birth to the actual operation. I actually felt the operation. And it was like it was on fast-forward video. I didn't even know about videos at the time but I know in recalling it. And it was through everything, every single thing that had ever happened. It was just the most amazing experience. And people, places, everything. I reexperienced my whole life. . . . Straight after that I started . . . the darkness. I could see a light—it was like a light I could never describe—like a silver-white light. . . . It was just massive darkness and then massive light. I felt myself, just my being, move toward that, and just about three quarters of the way in the darkness and the light was beyond that, then they filled my lungs with air. I didn't even know that was going on—and suddenly I took this breath and I was back. And that was extremely shocking.

SPIRITUAL CONTACT

Many people hear the voice, or note the presence, of spiritual beings at some point during their experience. These are generally deceased relatives or friends. The man who attempted suicide, aged thirty-two, described moving toward the light, when a voice told him to go back. He said:

As I got very close to it I heard a voice distinctly sing out, a very strong voice: "Go back!" really loud, but not scary, not angry. And I thought, well, that's what I'll do. I think when I look at it now I was on the edge, nearly there. Then I just started to slide back, slowly slide back. By this time, I didn't know, but my sister had arrived and there was an old priest, I couldn't believe it, anointing me with the last rites.

A woman who was forty-four years old at the time of a fall from a ladder, when she broke several ribs and ruptured her spleen, had gone to a nearby country hospital but had been sent home with painkillers. She had been bleeding internally for seven days at the time of her experience. She said:

I could see a light all around me. But I could also see a bright tunnel of light, path or something, it was just . . . I don't know what it was exactly. But my mind was so lucid and I just felt amazingly articulate. I feel I was making contact with people I loved that had died. I think my father was there. I think my great friend and mentor, Robert, was there encouraging me not to be afraid. And I seemed to be in contact with a lot of good input from somewhere. It's hard to describe.

Another woman, who had a cardiac arrest during a hysterectomy, remembered:

I was going toward a very bright light. And as I was traveling along I could see different colored lights and then I got stopped, just stopped before I got to the light. And I felt this extreme presence of love, just absolute love. And I heard very clearly.... It shocked me somewhat but there was no problem with accepting that in essence I was being confronted with my creator. At that time I felt the presence of that extreme love but also I could hear beautiful music, wonderful music. My consciousness seemed to increase dramatically as though I just knew and understood so much more. I was told it wasn't my time to go on, that I had to come back, I had my life's work to do. At that time I remember asking what my life's work was. And I was told, you'll not know at this time but you will be shown. And I think I was still asking questions like "When?" I was always saying "When?" I was also told to come back and to tell my husband and children.

In another case, a woman remembered the experience she had as a seven-year-old child when, critically ill with pneumonia, she was left at home with her mother—the expectation being that she would die during the day.

I saw this lovely white stairway with a lot of blue around it, kind of misty, cloudy, and I saw this lovely lady coming down the stairs in a long white robe, and she had a beautiful face and I recognized her instantly. It makes me go goose bumps just to think of it even now. And, anyhow, she said: "Don't be afraid, Jennifer." And I said: "I'm not afraid, Great-grandmother." She said: "You know me?" And I said: "Yes, Great-grandmother." And she said: "Take my hand, I've come to show you the way." And she stretched out her hand to me. And I said: "Oh, I'd love to come with you, Great-grandmother, but I can't go now because Mom needs me and she's got no one to look after her but me."

ENTERING THE LIGHT

Some people actually entered the light. A woman who was in a difficult labor when she lost consciousness described what she experienced:

Suddenly I found myself in a place, it was a real place. . . . It was like, there were gently rolling hills, no crags, no sharp edges, nothing that was cruel, nothing that was other than gentle. The sky was intense blue, the scene was gently rolling, I know you've heard this before but that's what it was. And there seemed to be figures, grouped, almost a theatrical grouping, like a stage set. . . . And as I looked, one of the figures seemed to resolve itself, and I looked and I thought, oh God, it's my Aunty Hannah, who died eleven years ago, and then I saw my Uncle Abraham, who died before I was born, and I knew them. . . . They knew me even though they'd never met me. I'm going to end up crying. My granny, who I'd never met, my grandfather, just all the people I've never known and those I had known who'd died many years before, or who'd even died recently. . . . Anyway, then I turned and I looked at this figure standing next to me—it was my father. My dad died

when I was sixteen.... Dad spoke to me although
there was no speaking, his mind spoke to me. And he
said, "No, honey, you're not imagining, it's not coming from you, you're with me and this is our time to
talk." Anyway, we talked, laid the ghosts to rest. ...
And I looked down and there was my dog, Lucky. He
died when I was very young, and he was just there.
Sounds crazy, doesn't it? ... And then there was a
sense of drawing back, and I panicked and I said:
"Dad, I don't want to go!" He said: "You have to go,
you must go back, you're going to have a son, and
you have to bring this boy up, bring him up by yourself." I said: "Dad I don't want to go. I want to stay
with you." I was most distressed, I didn't want to go
back. He sent me back ... and I seemed to be moving back quickly, like, there was no sense of travel,
but just I was there ... I was there in the delivery
room again and I was crying. My husband was allowed back in and I was sobbing and sobbing and I
was exhausted. I was sobbing with the tears running
down my cheeks and I said: "I was just with my
dad." John said: "You're just imagining things."

As these examples show, some people are told to come
back, while others are given the choice. Some decide to return, for their children, their parents or for whatever reason, and others just suddenly find themselves back in their
bodies. Most people do not remember actually getting
back into their bodies, although one of my sample, a
twenty-nine-year-old who had an NDE as a result of a
bloodstream infection following the removal of a kidney,
said: "Immediately I was back in my body, fully. It was
just like somebody pushed me back in there ... and I do
remember waking up in agonizing pain."

One element that appears to be almost universal in near-
death accounts is the difficulty near-death experiencers
have in talking about the experience afterward. It needs to

be emphasized that this is not just because of their inability to describe the experience fully, although of course what is known is so different from normal "knowing" that it is almost impossible to describe to someone who has not encountered it. There is also a reluctance to describe such events, which stems from experiencers' perception of social attitudes to these phenomena. This comes from a fear of being laughed at, hushed up, thought crazy or simply presumed to be lying. A determined silence is often the result.

Response to the near-death experience has in fact been varied. Some see it as providing evidence for an afterlife, a goal earnestly sought by psychic researchers for over a century. Others take what Osis and Haraldsson so eloquently call a position of "tactical agnosticism," by which they mean that researchers deny near-death experiences can provide evidence for an afterlife, yet admit that they personally, and most of their interviewees, are convinced of it. There have also been a number of attempts at explanation that have offered physiological, pharmacological and psychological means to explain away the phenomenon. Some of these are the result not of science but "scientism." As Huston Smith writes, scientism "goes beyond the actual findings of science to deny that other approaches to knowledge are valid and other truths true."[2] Close scrutiny of the reductionistic arguments offered so far has found them less than convincing.

Although the phenomenology of the near-death experience is of intrinsic interest, it is now well recorded and well established. This study notes details of experiences by a sample of Australians, but these are examined only insofar as they form a context for the personal and social process of life after near-death experience. My starting point is that the near-death experience exists, that it is real in the minds of those who have had it and, in particular, that it is real in its consequences. This book examines these consequences.

A Review of the Literature

Although, as already suggested in Chapter 1, there have long been accounts of people returning from death, it was not until the 1970s that this phenomenon received systematic attention from the scientific community. Around the same time the concept of thanatology, or the study of dying, acquired greater focus. Elisabeth Kübler-Ross, arguably the best-known thanatologist of our time, did much to prepare the ground with her public lectures, seminars and workshops on death and dying. However, it was not until the publication of Raymond Moody's book *Life After Life* in 1975, for which she wrote the foreword, that public and scientific attention was galvanized.

In order to provide a context for the research, this chapter has as its primary aim the review of literature concerning what is known about NDEs. It has as its principal focus the literature from 1975 onward, since it is this which is most directly concerned with contemporary accounts. This literature comes from a number of fields, a minuscule proportion of it from sociology. In the first section there is a concise review of the work done to establish the phenomenology of the near-death experience within a number of populations. This is followed by a suggested typology of NDEs, within which relationship to cause of the near-death event is reviewed. Then there is a presentation of the wide-ranging debate centred on explanations and interpretations. The final section deals with the literature on aftereffects of the near-death experience, considered in both general terms and specifically in areas such as religious practices, experience of psychic phenomena and attitudes to death.

FEATURES OF THE NEAR-DEATH EXPERIENCE

Raymond Moody, philosopher and physician, states that when he was writing his first book in 1975 he knew of 150 NDE cases. However, it was on the basis of fifty detailed interviews that he outlined an ideal type, or composite picture, of a near-death experience and reported his findings in terms of common elements. This was not a systematic study and did not purport to be one. Dr. Kenneth Ring, the psychologist who produced the first scientific investigation of the NDE in 1980, largely confirmed Moody's findings but found that the experience unfolded in stages, the earliest ones being most common. By the time of Ring's book there had already been published further corroboration of Moody's prototypical description by Ring himself and a number of other authors, for example, Karlis Osis and Erlendur Haraldsson, Michael Sabom and Sarah Kreutziger, Craig Lundahl, Bruce Greyson and Ian Stevenson. In addition, in an article in *Anabiosis,* Fred Schoonmaker was revealed to have gathered over 2300 cases since 1961 of "persons who have survived acute life-threatening situations," of which he maintained over sixty percent reported an NDE of Moody's description.[1] It must be noted, however, that he has still not published his findings.

There have also been a number of studies examining the phenomenology of NDEs in various geographically and

demographically distributed populations throughout the
world. They include, for example, the interviews of James
Lindley, Sethyn Bryan and Bob Conley with near-death
experiencers in the Pacific Northwest, Timothy Green and
Penelope Friedman's study of NDEs in a southern Californian population, Margot Grey's study of English NDEs
and Paola Giovetti's Italian survey of NDEs and death-bed
visions. There have been reports from other cultures, such
as Dorothy Counts' Melanesian study, Satwant Pasricha
and Ian Stevenson's Indian research, and C. E. Schorer's
record of two Chippewa tales from the 1820s. There have
been studies done of "special" populations, such as that by
Richard Kohr using a sample of members from the Association for Research and Enlightenment, Robert Sullivan's
study of combat-related NDEs and David Royse's survey
of clergy. There have even been reports of individual cases
as diverse as that of physician George Ritchie, cultural anthropologist Patrick Gallagher, writer Katherine Anne
Porter, NDE researcher Barbara Harris and "Robert," currently serving a life sentence for murder in Australia.[2]
Many of these are considered later.

CLASSIFICATION OF NEAR-DEATH
EXPERIENCES

Some researchers and theorists have made an attempt at
classifying near-death experiences into unambiguous types
in order to facilitate description and comparison, and to
enable more detailed analysis of such things as the relationship of individual types of NDE to specific causes.

Michael Sabom in his medical investigation of the phenomenon has proposed the clearest typology to date. He
suggests two main types of near-death experience—
"autoscopic" (self-visualizing) and "transcendental" (involving passage of consciousness into a dimension quite
apart from the immediate surrounds of the physical body).

He also includes a third category of experiences that is a combination of the two.

Bruce Greyson, writing in the *American Journal of Psychiatry,* sought to discover whether discrete types of near-death experiences result from different mechanisms. He differentiated near-death experiences into three distinct types on the basis of a cluster analysis of eighty-nine NDEs. These were "transcendental" (comprising such features as encounters with an apparently unearthly realm), "affective" (involving feelings of peace, joy and cosmic unity) and "cognitive" (characterized by time distortion, thought acceleration, life review and sudden understanding). Although NDEs can be made up of elements from any or all of these categories, he suggests that with such a typology it is possible to say whether an NDE is *predominantly* transcendental, affective or cognitive, which can be important when comparing NDE reports with physiological or psychological variables.

Greyson found no correlation between the type of NDE and the specific cause of the near-death event. He did note, however, that those near-death crises which could be *anticipated* were rarely associated with a cognitive NDE and yet were frequently associated with transcendental and affective ones.

The least satisfying typology is provided by Michael Grosso, a philosopher who suggested in 1981 that there were two types of near-death experience: the death-bed vision and the NDE of Moody's prototype. He describes the death-bed vision as occurring in a person already ill, usually bedridden, who suddenly at the hour of death experiences a vision, often of a deceased relative or friend. There is usually a marked elevation of mood as the person views or interacts with the apparition.

As already noted, there have been a number of studies of this phenomenon predating the modern (post-1975) interest in NDEs. Although certainly associated with being close to death, I would normally consider death-bed vi-

sions to form a separate set of events. They differ from
near-death experience phenomenology in a number of obvious ways, not the least of which is that the experiencer
regains rather than loses consciousness at the time of the
experience and observes the vision from the vantage point
of the bed (or wherever he or she is physically situated)
rather than from out of body, and I do not believe that it
is useful to consider the two experiences as two types of
the one class of phenomena.

SUGGESTED EXPLANATIONS AND
INTERPRETATIONS

Many explanations have been proposed by researchers and
theorists from a number of different fields. Overall they
tend to be more evaluative than descriptive, and so far they
can be considered only speculative at best. At one end of
the spectrum are those who are dismissive, attempting to
explain away a phenomenon that cannot be accommodated
in a materialistic belief system. Glen Gabbard and Stuart
Twemlow write:

> It comes as no surprise, then, that many of the stan-
> dard interpretations of near-death experiences are ul-
> timately reductionistic because of this need to make
> the data fit a pre-existing and narcissistically in-
> vested paradigm.[3]

In his book *Recollections of Death,* Michael Sabom, a cardiologist, quotes Dr. Richard Blacher, who wrote in the
Journal of the American Medical Association:

> We are dealing here with the fantasy of death. . . .
> That it answers so many puzzles of mankind and cre-
> ates a bridge between science and religion makes it
> a tempting concept for speculation. It is for this very

reason that the physician must be especially wary of accepting religious belief as scientific data.[4]

Michael Sabom responds in the same journal:

Dr. Blacher points out that "the physician must be especially wary of accepting religious belief as scientific data." I might add that equal caution should be exercised in accepting *scientific belief as scientific data.*[5]

It is important to keep this caution in mind since the fallacy of "scientism" is that empiric-analytical science, grounded in the five senses, is the only path to knowledge.

Psychological Explanations

As early as 1952, Carl Gustav Jung admitted how puzzling such a phenomenon was to him. In his essay "Synchronicity: An Acausal Connecting Principle" in *The Interpretation of Nature and the Psyche,* he recounted what we can now recognize as a classic NDE experienced by a woman in childbirth. Following this he wrote:

Indeed it is not easy to explain how such unusually intense psychic processes can take place and be remembered, in a state of severe collapse, and how the patient could observe actual events in concrete detail with closed eyes.[6]

He concludes:

We must ask ourselves whether there is some other nervous substrate in us, apart from the cerebrum, that can think and perceive, or whether the psychic processes that go on in us during loss of conscious-

ness are synchronistic phenomena, i.e., events which
have no causal connection with organic processes.[7]

More recently, the debate has covered many other possibilities, some of them much more mundane. For example,
even Michael Sabom admits that before his own investigation he had felt sure that reported NDEs must be "conscious fabrications" either on the part of those reporting
them or by the author writing about them. Others have
considered the "subconscious fabrication" hypothesis,
which is based on Freud's belief that we are all convinced
of our own immortality and therefore have a need to deny
or defy death. Jan Ehrenwald suggested this explanation
for the out-of-body experience, but Glen Gabbard and Stuart Twemlow have countered with their finding that out-of-
body experiencers are no more likely to suffer from high
death anxiety than nonexperiencers. Somewhat related to
these are the "religious-belief-fulfillment" and romanti-
cized "wish-fulfillment" hypotheses, which suggested that
if someone has a prior belief in an afterlife, this will be
what is experienced during an NDE. Ring, Sabom and
Grosso have all shown, however, that this is not always the
case.

Bruce Greyson considers three psychological mechanisms thought to explain NDEs: depersonalization, birth
memories and regression in the service of the ego. Uri
Lowental, for example, believes NDEs to be a form of regression in the face of death. He considers NDEs to be a
preverbal memory of the birth experience—the birth canal
being represented by the "tunnel" and the "light" in fact
being the mother's radiant face.

Based on the work of Stanislav Grof on birth memories,
Carl Sagan further speculates that the universality of the
NDE is due to nothing other than a vivid reliving of the
birth process. However, there are many problems with such
an explanatory hypothesis. Grof himself strongly rejects
Sagan's misinterpretation of his work. Susan Blackmore

tested a similar hypothesis by Barbara Honegger that
maintains that out-of-body experiences are lucid dreams
relying heavily on birth imagery, and also found it to be an
unhelpful analogy.

"Depersonalization in the face of life-threatening danger" has been put forward as an explanation by Roy Kletti
and Russell Noyes, who write:

> It was first proposed by Oskar Pfister, that persons
> faced with extreme danger exclude reality from their
> perceptions and lapse into pleasurable fantasies that
> constitute a form of psychic protection against the
> threat of destruction. He noted that depersonalization
> developing under such circumstances not only pre-
> vents the conscious experience of fear but is accom-
> panied by the idea that the threat does not concern
> the person experiencing it.[8]

This hypothesis has been much discussed in the literature,
even though it is a theory based on study of people *psychologically* rather than *physically* near death. In addition,
its characteristics have been shown by several commentators to differ in a number of significant ways from the phenomenology of NDEs. For example, Gabbard and
Twemlow state that "all aspects of the depersonalization
experience are so thoroughly unpleasant that the patient often fears he is losing his mind."[9] As Grosso suggests, depersonalization tends toward a flattening affect and
shriveling mental capacities in contrast to the heightened
affect and expanded awareness of an NDE. Finally, in
sharp contrast to the wide age range of near-death experiencers, it has been noted by Gabbard and Twemlow that
depersonalization usually occurs in those between the ages
of fifteen and thirty but is virtually unheard of in persons
over forty years of age.

Stanislav Grof and Joan Halifax and Michael Grosso
have proposed an explanation of NDEs in terms of Jungian

archetypes, in Grosso's case, more specifically "the archetype of a healthy death" or "the archetype of death and enlightenment." Grosso does, however, acknowledge that this
approach needs the support of findings from parapsychology.

Physiological Explanations

It has been suggested by Nathan Schnaper that NDEs can
be explained as altered states of consciousness and that
these tend to be either physiological, pharmacological or
psychological in cause. In the physiological grouping, the
explanation most frequently offered is cerebral anoxia or
hypoxia, indicating insufficient oxygen flow to the brain.

Many researchers have argued against this hypothesis.
From the studies he examined, Sabom concluded that "as
oxygen supply to the brain decreases, there is a progressive
muddling and confusion of cognitive abilities," in sharp
contrast to the clarity reported by near-death experiencers.[10] Hypercarbia, or elevated levels of carbon dioxide in
the brain, said to produce the feeling of traveling down a
tunnel or being surrounded by lights, is another explanation considered by some. In an often quoted case, a patient
is said to have observed (while out of body during an
NDE) the taking of blood from his femoral artery for
blood gas analysis. Since his arterial carbon dioxide level
was actually found to be lower than normal, this is said to
show the implausibility of the hypercarbia explanation.

It has also been proposed that NDEs are nothing but autoscopic hallucinations, the term autoscopic referring to
the self-visualizing component of NDE phenomenology.
This hypothesis is based on the work of Dr. A. Luki-
anowicz, according to whom the autoscopic hallucination
is a rare psychiatric disorder. Both Sabom and the researchers Gabbard and Twemlow compared descriptions of
autoscopic hallucinations with NDEs and found it to be an
implausible suggestion on the basis of a number of signif-

icant differences. For example, in autoscopic hallucinations the "projected image" or "double," of which only the face and torso would be seen, is perceived from the physical body rather than, as in NDEs, the whole body being perceived from a vantage point outside it. In addition, and in contrast to NDEs, sadness is the most common affect.

It has often been suggested that NDEs can be explained as drug-induced hallucinations or delusions. Ketamine, a dissociative anaesthetic used both in medical and recreational settings, is one such drug, and both ether and morphine have also been proposed. Quite apart from the difference in character of the two kinds of experience, the fact that many NDEs occur in people who are drug free seems to be ignored. It has also been noted that drugs may actually *inhibit* the occurrence and certainly the recollection of NDEs.

Neurophysiological Explanations

Ronald Siegel believes that NDEs are "subjective hallucinatory phenomena" and also claims they may have a neurophysiological basis. His view is carefully questioned by John Gibbs, and he is sharply criticized for his reductionism by Gabbard and Twemlow. Daniel Carr suggests an explanation of NDEs in terms of stress-induced limbic lobe dysfunction. He notes:

> The hyperactivity of limbic lobe neurons giving rise to clinical symptoms resembling NDEs may be spontaneous, as in temporal lobe epilepsy, or iatrogenic, as in cases of electrical brain stimulation.[11]

After examining the typical characteristics of temporal lobe seizures, however, Michael Sabom concludes that they do not fit with NDEs, and Kenneth Ring summarizes neurological hypotheses as follows:

It is not difficult—in fact, it is easy—to propose naturalistic interpretations that could conceivably explain some aspect of the core experience. . . . A
neurological interpretation, to be acceptable, should
be able to provide a *comprehensive* explanation of *all*
the various aspects. . . .[12]

"Global" versus "Mini" Theories

Michael Grosso supports Ring's view, claiming that any
explanation of NDEs must take into account the phenomenon as a whole, with its three puzzling components—its
universality, the psi, or paranormal, aspects and the
changes in attitudes and behavior of experiencers that
follow. Bruce Greyson suggests, however, that we do not
need to "restrict our consideration of explanatory hypotheses until we have the data to support a unitary concep-
tion of the near-death experience," that it is conceivable
that the various components may in fact have different
causes and functions. This is a view supported by Kevin
Drab, who believes that there could be considerable value
in moving emphasis from the "cumbersome global" theories to "mini" theories concerning the various aspects of
NDEs.

There is no shortage of mini-theories, as can already be
seen. For example, there have been a number of attempts
to explain the out-of-body aspect of the experience, the
tunnel, the light, the "panoramic memory," the meeting
with deceased relatives or friends and the enhancement of
the near-death experiencer's sense of personal identity during the NDE.

In addition, the NDE has variously been "explained" as
"hypnagogic sleep," "hypnopompic sleep" or as a "dream"
or "dreamlike" image, while Maurice Rawlings has quoted
Biblical scripture (2 Corinthians 11:14), warning that the
"being of light" is in fact a satanic deception.

Cultural Conditioning

The "cultural conditioning" hypothesis is one that in fact is often referred to in the NDE literature yet is seldom discussed in any detail. It maintains simply that the content of NDEs is strongly related to the after-death beliefs of near-death experiencers. That is, what people expect to happen after death will in fact occur during their NDE. This view tends to be in sharp contrast with the universality argument which maintains that the NDE is in fact a universal experience with strong cross-cultural agreement.

As Stanislav and Christina Grof note, there are striking parallels between modern accounts of NDEs and descriptions from eschatological literature. Frederick Holck, a historian of religion, located evidence of experiences in the canonical literature and other writings of religious movements and folklore. He found examples from Bolivia and Argentina, Lithuania, Vietnam, Borneo, Siberia, India and China, from New Zealand Maoris and North American Indians, in Jewish and Islamic traditions and in Zoroastrianism. He concludes that these phenomena are found universally and therefore can be considered part of the experience of the human race.

Of the numerous descriptions of NDEs to be found in other cultures, two such accounts were heard from Chippewa Indians in Michigan and recorded by H. R. Schoolcraft in the 1820s.[13] Dorothy Counts, an anthropologist who has been doing fieldwork in New Guinea since 1966, reports three near-death experiences from the Kaliai area of West New Britain Province, Papua New Guinea. And Satwant Pasricha and Ian Stevenson present four cases and the main features of another twelve cases located in India.

In each of these three studies, culturally specific details are obvious. For example, in the Chippewa accounts, Native American elements feature, such as bows and arrows, painted paddles and animals such as the deer and moose, moccasin snake and eagle. In the three New Guinea accounts, each experiencer followed a wide path or road, two of them to a village, accompanied by ancestors or deceased fellow villagers. It is interesting that one of them, the most highly educated and acculturated, saw a "being of light" which he described as a white man with long white robes, a beard and long hair, brightly lit as though by a flashlight. Another saw, in the village, a house where there were men working with steel, some men building ships, and another group building cars—a desirable scene in terms of the cargo belief. There were also a number of other culturally specific details such as the presence of sorcerers, the chewing of betel nuts, the gathering of areca nuts and the traditional healing practice of spitting ginger on a wound infected by sorcery.

In the Indian accounts the most outstanding feature is the presence of Yamraj (the god of death), the Yamdoots (his messengers) and Chitragupta, who has a book in which are recorded everyone's good and bad deeds from the life just ended. A fascinating feature of the accounts recorded by Pasricha and Stevenson is that each of the individuals had died and been brought to the after-death world by a mistake on the part of the Yamdoots. In all four of the cases cited, the "right" person is said to have died soon after the revival of the one who was sent back to life.

Although it has been suggested that such cross-cultural examples demonstrate that the content of a near-death experience is strongly related to the after-death beliefs of the person having it, it would be premature to make such an assumption on the basis of these nine cases alone, widely separated as they are by time and culture, method of collection and interview. Nevertheless, it is a suggestion worthy of further examination, especially since it often appears that the *interpretation* of the experience is colored by embeddedness in a particular cultural context. That is, it appears that the ineffable is described in culturally specific or meaningful terms.

However, Pasricha and Stevenson put forward quite a

different view. In their Indian/American study they question why we should find it so surprising that the after-death world could be described so differently by different people. They write:

> If we survive death and live in an after-death realm, we should expect to find variations in that world, just as we find them in the different parts of the familiar world of the living. . . . In the same way, there may be different receptionists and different modes of reception. . . .[14]

However, in the Tibetan *Bardo Thodol,* it is written that "the essential point is to recognize with certainty that whatever appears . . . is your own projection." Evans-Wentz, in his classic commentary on the *Bardo Thodol,* writes:

> For a Buddhist . . . as for a Hindu, or a Moslem, or a Christian, the *Bardo* experiences would be appropriately different: the Buddhist's or the Hindu's thought forms . . . would give rise to corresponding visions of the deities of the Buddhist or Hindu pantheon; a Moslem's, to visions of the Moslem Paradise; a Christian's, to visions of the Christian Heaven; or an American Indian's, to visions of the Happy Hunting Ground. And, similarly, the materialist will experience after-death visions as negative and as empty and as deityless as any he ever dreamt while in the human body.[15]

It should be noted that although it is unlikely that an American Indian would report a vision of Krishna, or a Hindu would report a vision of Buddha, the reports from near-death experiencers do not so easily fall into Evans-Wentz's picture. Pasricha and Stevenson, for example, cite cases of people born into one culture who have subse-

quently become deeply involved in another, and have had
NDEs featuring imagery associated with their culture of
adoption. In addition, although some near-death experiencers do report seeing a "being of light," most of these,
whether religious or not, do not in fact personify this being
as a deity identifiable within their religious belief or cultural background. On the other hand, atheists or agnostics
have claimed to have seen Jesus.

Harold Widdison questions whether culture actually
produces the experience or simply attaches culturally specific meanings to it. He cautions against seeing the NDE
as nothing more than a reflection of an individual's culture,
and suggests that it is the individual and his or her efforts
to articulate the experience rather than the experience itself
that is culture bound. Yet in the majority of cases so far reported, the efforts at articulation by near-death experiencers show remarkable consistency. Cultural anthropologist
Patrick Gallagher notes:

> Virtually all the reports ... recorded by researchers
> from NDErs show practically identical perceptions
> and descriptions of the event—despite vast differ-
> ences in the witnesses' cultures, languages, educa-
> tions, ages, religious beliefs, and occupations—and
> these accounts are all independent. Sound anthropo-
> logical reports of similar events are seldom identical,
> or even similar, no matter how alike the reporters
> may be.[16]

The argument that the NDE is only a culturally conditioned response to a threat of death has made the collection of NDE accounts from young children of particular
interest. A number of researchers, including Melvin Morse
and William Serdahely, have had a particular interest in
recording such cases. However, unfortunately the reports
of childhood NDEs that actually have been related by the
children themselves are still very few in number.

At this point it is perhaps worth exposing the assumption implicit in the "cultural conditioning" hypothesis, namely, that we learn what to expect of the after-death state within our culture and then apply this directly when we personally come close to death. But the question arises, how did our culture come to invent such a scenario in the first place?

Rather than assuming that our cultural expectations determine the content of a near-death experience, it could equally be argued that accounts of near-death experiencers have determined the content of our cultural expectations. This can be seen, for example, in cases such as that of Drythelm in the Middle Ages, whose account was taken up and adapted by the medieval Christian church for its own instructive purposes. Carol Zaleski writes that the otherworld journey narrative is valued "primarily for its power as a model for conversion and its usefulness in advertising the cause of particular religious institutions and ideas . . ."[17] For example, Bede's account of Drythelm's vision "can be read as a manifesto for Benedictine monasticism, ascetic discipline, and intercessory masses for the dead."

Glenn Roberts and John Owen, writing in the *British Journal of Psychiatry,* see the relationship as somewhat reciprocal. They write of the

. . . intriguing possibility that some and perhaps much of the folk-law [*sic*] imagery of the after-life could be derived from NDEs, and that cultural expectations not only determine NDE imagery but are themselves also derived from it.[18]

Just such a phenomenon is to be found in Irving Hallowell's anthropological study of the Salteaux Indians of the Berens River north of Winnipeg, published in 1940, long before this contemporary debate. The following quotation comes from Ian Wilson's book, *The After-Death Experience.*

Hallowell found that the Salteaux's beliefs in life after death derived largely from the apparent experiences of those thought to have been dead yet who
revived. Among the descriptions given by these individuals were feelings of extraordinary bliss; the
sensation of being out of, or separated from the
physical body; and, not least, the meeting with deceased loved ones and friends in some form of
"spirit realm."[19]

Overall, when reading the above studies, or listening to the
tapes collected for the present study, it is the similarity
rather than the difference that emerges most strongly. I believe it could be said that the deep structures of the experience are the same, and yet the surface structures are
unique to each case. That is, during a near-death experience people can leave their bodies, pass into an area of
darkness, move toward a light, enter a world of preternat-
ural beauty and encounter beings such as deceased loved
ones or friends who communicate with them before they
return. Yet in individual cases there could be differences in
the particular constellation of elements reported. In addition there could be differences in what is observed while
out of body; in the experience of the darkness as a tunnel,
a valley, a culvert or a void; whether they find themselves
immediately immersed in the light or whether they move
toward it, whether they move quickly or float slowly; what
they encounter in the "world of light," its geography,
who they interact with, what is communicated to them;
whether they choose to return, are persuaded to or are
forced. The fact that they have been to another realm could
be said to form part of the deep structure of the experience, whereas their description or interpretation of what
they encountered could be said to form part of the surface
structure. I would argue that it is in terms of these surface
structures that cultural conditioning *could* have an influence.

Survival

The critique of NDE interpretations frequently focuses on claims that NDEs indicate that there is survival after bodily death. This claim is rarely made by researchers—except, for example, Elisabeth Kübler-Ross. However, most near-death experiencers, as will be shown, in fact believe this to be the case. This position is indulgently explained by some as a failure on the part of NDErs to discern the difference between objective and subjective reality. Others simply explain it as wishful thinking, and James Alcock concludes that "faith is the *only* basis for such a belief." Although there is strong opposition to the survival hypothesis by a number of researchers, there is also cautious support from others, with some maintaining that at the very least it would be premature to dismiss it as a possibility. V. Krishnan in an early paper postulates that transcendence feelings and out-of-body experiences (OBEs) might be protective mechanisms with survival value rather than actual evidence of a postmortem world, but later concedes that he would prefer to keep the survival question open. Others actively encourage its continued investigation.

There often seems to be an ambivalence behind some of the statements made on the subject of survival. For example, Stephen Vicchio writes: "The issue of survival after death may in principle be one that is clouded in obscurity and possibility."[20] And Raymond Moody, who, as a researcher, denies that he is trying to prove there is life after death, as an individual writes: "I have come to accept as a matter of religious faith that there is a life after death, and I believe that the phenomenon we have been examining is a manifestation of that life."[21]

Philosophically speaking, the opposing lines appear to be drawn in terms of objectivist and subjectivist interpretations. The majority of the explanations discussed above have been subjectivist in approach; that is, their proponents seek a material cause for the subjective experience near-death experiencers describe. They do not believe that people *in fact* leave their bodies, go down a tunnel toward a light, encounter deceased relatives, etc.

However, a problem with most of the explanations is that even if they are not as Gabbard and Twemlow suggest, simply an exercise in propping up an ailing belief system, they are often being discussed at second or third remove from the actual experience. As has been demonstrated by their critics, many of these hypotheses simply could not be maintained in the face of real experiences and real experiencers.

Since near-death experiencers are not often given voice in such a debate, it should perhaps be noted that they tend to take the objectivist stance and support the survival hypothesis. They believe that they *did in fact* leave their bodies, go down a tunnel toward a light and encounter deceased relatives. For the fifty I have personally interviewed there is no dispute or doubt—the experience is real, there is an afterlife.

This position goes beyond the domain of belief—for them it is a self-evident fact. As cultural anthropologist and near-death experiencer Patrick Gallagher writes: "Like other NDErs I no longer tremble. Now I *know* that our current life is merely an interlude."[22]

A number of researchers admit to being as much puzzled now by the NDE as Jung was in 1952. Despite a vigorous involvement in the explanation debate, Bruce Greyson notes in the introduction to a book by near-death experiencer Barbara Harris: "I find the scientific perspective so much harder to provide now than before I knew so much."[23] He later writes:

I believe the NDE is one of those puzzles that just might force scientists to develop a new scientific method, one that will incorporate all sources of knowledge, not only logical deductions of the intellect, and empirical observations of the physical, but also direct experience of the mystical.[24]

And finally, Kenneth Ring notes:

The irony is that this entire question may well prove to be entirely irrelevant to the issue of its importance to humanity at large.

The larger significance of the near-death experience turns not so much on either the phenomenology or the parameters of the experience but on its *transformative* effects.[25]

THE AFTEREFFECTS OF THE NEAR-DEATH EXPERIENCE

Bruce Greyson notes that study of the aftereffects of near-death experiences has proven to be the most fertile area of near-death research for two main reasons. The first is that, unlike the experience itself, aftereffects can be observed by others. The second is that this is the most meaningful area of research. He writes that the aftereffects of the NDE are

... uniquely profound, pervasive, and permanent, totally unlike the after-effects of any phenomenologically comparable experience. NDEs are seed experiences, and it is only by studying the fruits that eventually grow from those seeds that we can understand their full meaning.[26]

Overwhelmingly the aftereffects appear to be positive and beneficial to the near-death experiencer. Certainly those aftereffects referred to in the literature are generally the positive ones. However, Phyllis Atwater, herself a near-death experiencer, notes that there can be many difficulties encountered by experiencers in the process of integrating their experience into their daily lives. She writes that coming back means facing your belief system and everything you ever knew about yourself and the world around you.

For some near-death experiencers, the early stages of recovery can be a disconcerting and even painful time. Patrick Gallagher likens the "re-view" of the familiar to "counter shock," a process commonly experienced by anthropologists when they return to their own culture after a period of fieldwork in a foreign society. Raymond Moody notes that this problem has been dubbed "reentry syndrome" by some researchers. He also reminds us that over two thousand years ago it was described in Plato's *The Republic* in the simile of the cave. There Plato invited us to imagine an underground world where prisoners spent their lives facing the back wall of a cavern, fastened so they could not turn their heads. Behind them a fire burned and all they could see of the activity going on in their world was the shadow play on the wall in front of them. This was their reality.

Plato asked us to imagine what would happen if one of them was suddenly released from these bonds and delusions and taken out into the sunlight for the first time. If, after adjusting to the light and beauty of the new surroundings, this person was then forced back down into the cave, we are asked to imagine how difficult it would be for him comfortably to fit back into his previous life and reality.

Many near-death experiencers would identify with this situation. Atwater writes that after the NDE "the familiar is now foreign, and vice versa. The world is the same but you aren't."[27] She asks: "Once you have experienced a Greater Reality, how do you return to what now seem petty comings and goings?"[28]

The very real difficulty some near-death experiencers have in adapting to the "living world" is a matter touched upon by a handful of researchers and writers. Carl Jung in *Memories, Dreams, Reflections* noted how unhappy he was in the early weeks after his NDE. He wrote:

> Disappointed, I thought, "Now I must return to the 'box system' again." For it seemed to me as if behind the horizon of the cosmos a three-dimensional world had been artificially built up, in which each person sat by himself in a little box. And now I should have to convince myself all over again that this was important! Life and the whole world struck me as a prison, and it bothered me beyond measure that I should again be finding all that quite in order.[29]

Steve Straight, in his *Anabiosis* article published in 1984, describes Katherine Anne Porter's NDE and its re-creation in her work of fiction *Pale Horse, Pale Rider*. After her NDE, Miranda (Porter's principal character) compares the two worlds she has experienced. Porter writes:

> Miranda looked about her with the covertly hostile eyes of an alien who does not like the country in which he finds himself, does not understand the language nor wish to learn it, does not mean to live there and yet is helpless, unable to leave it at his will. . . . She saw with a new anguish the dull world to which she was condemned, where the light seemed filmed over with cobwebs.[30]

Katherine Anne Porter, in an interview many years later, described how she had tried to live like others after her NDE but found that she couldn't. She said: "You are no longer like other people, and there's no use deceiving yourself that you are."[31]

Atwater suggests that there are other aftereffects that can cause problems for near-death experiencers. She cites as major stumbling blocks an inability to personalize emotions or feelings, especially those of love and belonging to anyone; inability to recognize and comprehend boundaries, rules or limits; naivety and difficulty in understanding time sense. Just how widespread these problems actually are is impossible to discern from Atwater's book alone. Apart from the related issue of "unconditional love," most of these difficulties are not considered elsewhere in the literature.

A number of researchers have noted that the changes in near-death experiencers can have a disturbing effect on family and friends. Barbara Harris describes the way in which the changes she underwent made continuation of her marriage impossible. She writes:

> I couldn't go back to the way I was. I was the proper mother, the proper wife, an active member of many, many community organizations. These things are important and I am not putting them down, but they couldn't take up all my time anymore. I needed to be with sick people, I wanted to be with dying people. I went back to school and became a respiratory therapist. And then, as this evolution of my own being became stronger and stronger, it did not fit into my own marriage anymore, so it had to end.[32]

Charles Flynn also remarked that value clashes and changes in attitude could lead to broken engagements and divorce for near-death experiencers. Others have also noticed that this could happen; however, there has as yet been no empirical study of the incidence of breakdown of primary relationships among experiencers.

Although the above aftereffects have been grouped together as negative or at the very least problematic, they are not without paradox. Who is to say that a change in life direction or the breakup of a marriage is not a positive step in the lives of those concerned, however painful the transition may be? Who is to say that a profound review of one's life situation, attitudes and beliefs, however confronting and uncomfortable, will not lead in a positive new direction? For example, Carl Jung, who earlier described the unutterable disappointment he felt during the early weeks after his NDE, wrote:

> After the illness a fruitful period of work began for me. A good many of my principal works were written only then. The insight I had had, or the vision of the end of all things, gave me the courage to undertake new formulations. I no longer attempted to put across my own opinion, but surrendered myself to the current of my thoughts. Thus one problem after the other revealed itself to me and took shape.[33]

David Raft and Jeffry Andresen later noted this receptivity to spontaneous thoughts or unbidden mental activity in one of their own patients. They were particularly fascinated by this "free-association"-type method that near-death experiencers used in their pursuit of self-knowledge, and noted with some amazement how the changes generally reported by them bore a striking resemblance to certain changes experienced by people in psychoanalysis. Harris also had the same thought. She wrote that the healing effect of her NDE was like years of psychotherapy, yet it happened in an instant.

Raft and Andresen detected a sharp contrast between the positive attitude of NDErs and the distress and anxiety that commonly afflicted the majority of other survivors of a close brush with death. Russell Noyes also writes that accustomed as he was to seeing patients suffering from post-traumatic disorders in the psychiatric clinic, he was most surprised to come across positive aftereffects in near-death experiencers.

Yet even in the earliest studies some positive aftereffects had been discerned. Raymond Moody wrote:

Many [NDErs] have told me that they felt that their lives were broadened and deepened by their experience, that because of it they became more reflective and more concerned with ultimate philosophical issues.[34]

Although by 1984 aftereffects had also been reported in other publications, Kenneth Ring's *Heading Toward Omega* provided the results of the first major empirical study of these wide-ranging phenomena. He writes:

All the transformations in the life of an NDEr—the changes in personality, relations with others, values and beliefs—take place and are given meaning within the context of a spiritual understanding that is born in death but that requires everyday life to be realized.[35]

To family and friends, some near-death experiencers appear to be changed from the very moment of their "return." However, in fact it may take many years for the transformation to become fully manifest. This renewal is, as already suggested, evident in many areas of their lives. Martin Bauer explored generally the association between NDEs and positive attitude change by response to the LAP (Life Attitude Profile) questionnaire, and found significant positive changes in all twenty-eight of his respondents. Glenn Roberts and John Owen note that NDEs promote a general "re-evaluation of personal meaning, values and beliefs, leading to enduring changes."

One of the most compelling features of NDE aftereffects is a major change in priorities. A near-death experiencer quoted in Flynn's study says: "You really see what's important in your life." One of Ring's respondents writes:

I was transformed from a man who was lost and wandering aimlessly, with no goal in life other than

a desire for material wealth, to someone who had a
deep motivation, a purpose in life, a definite direction.[36]

Such profound personality changes have been noted by
other researchers and authors. Noyes reports that twenty
percent of his sample of people who survived an encounter
with life-threatening danger (including near-death experiencers) spoke of their lives taking on a sense of mission.
Raft and Andresen comment on the changed motivations
of their subjects, and Moody remarks on the way they feel
more in control and responsible for their lives. Inherent
gifts and talents that have lain dormant are often awakened
in near-death experiencers, and inner potentials actualized
to an astonishing degree.

Changes in self-concept are marked, according to Ring.
Other researchers have commented on the near-death
experiencers' acceptance of themselves, their growth in
self-confidence, enhanced self-esteem and drive to self-
understanding. They are said to have become less judgmental and less self-righteous, less prejudiced and less in
need of others' approval or social success. As Ring notes:

In short, one of the strongest findings of this research with respect to personality changes is that after their experience, NDErs like themselves more.[37]

Some writers note that near-death experiencers often abandon typical cultural patterns. Ring remarks that after an
NDE, no longer can a person take refuge in the comfort of
the conventional views and values of society.[38] Gallagher
writes that "continual anxiety and concern over quite brief
events and imagined statuses . . . living for urgent goals,
roles, dreams, or schemes now seem to be of little rhyme
or reason."[39] In addition they have been found to have little
sense of rivalry and an indifference to competition. There

is also often a marked distaste for violence resulting in, for instance, an aversion to hunting and television watching.

They are said to demonstrate an acceptance of life, an intensified appreciation and even a reverence for life that carries over not only into their response to nature and beauty but into their links with all things, and especially in their relations with others.

Much attention has been paid to this greater acceptance and appreciation of others by near-death experiencers. As Moody notes, an overriding love for humanity is often reported. He writes:

> Upon their return, almost all [NDErs] say that love is the most important thing in life. Many say it is why we are here. Most find it the hallmark of happiness and fulfillment, with other values paling beside it.[40]

Comparing it to Martin Buber's concept of the I-Thou relationship, Flynn describes the *agape* that NDErs experience, which "gives them the capacity to look beneath the surface of others and relate to their deepest essences, and to affirm and love others unconditionally."[41]

Altruistic attitudes develop and concern for others becomes a focus for post-NDE activity in many cases. Near-death experiencers have been found to develop compassion, patience, tolerance, love, acceptance, insight and understanding, and have been described as evolved human beings showing unusual serenity.

Many of them feel the need to work with the sick and dying. One of Raft and Andresen's patients felt that he had been "reborn with a mission in life" to help those less fortunate than himself. Pennachio reveals the case of a woman who during one of her experiences "made a promise to care for children." He writes that "this has been realized as her home has been opened to nearly 100 homeless and unwanted children during the past seventeen years." She is quoted as saying that during the experience

"I was being turned completely around; I was being made over. I was made different; I'm not the person I was."[42] This theme of rebirth often emerges quite strongly in the literature. Grey likens the transformation in values to a spiritual rebirth, and Harris quite simply says: "I met my real self during the experience in the hospital. It was the most important incident of my life. I had really been born again."[43]

A powerful longing for knowledge is another feature of NDE aftereffects. Ring writes that

> ... the NDE appears to trigger a strong inner drive for understanding as a result of which one's prior value orientation shifts away from the acquisition of conventional sources of self-esteem and moves toward the attainment of knowledge.[44]

To learn and to love appear to be the two most important tasks for near-death experiencers. Most writers on this subject make at least some mention of this drive to learn. Harris writes:

> I became a seeker. I started to read all kinds of books on quantum physics, Buddhism, all the major religions, psychology, and finally psychiatry. I was given information about myself during my NDE that I couldn't integrate. It took me years of looking and searching.[45]

In addition to a change in values there has also been shown to be a definite change in beliefs among those who've had an NDE. For example, Sabom and Ring both found a dramatic increase in belief in an afterlife, Grey discussed changes in belief about heaven and hell and in a recent paper that recorded the changes in belief experienced by those in my own sample I reported that belief in reincarnation was also found to be noticeably strengthened.

A strong decrease in fear of death among near-death experiencers has also been noted by a number of researchers and commented upon by most people writing in this area. Sabom, in a comparison with a sample who had been close to death but not had an NDE, found that in contrast to most who had (who reported a marked decrease in fear of death), most of those who had not had an NDE reported no change in attitude, and five out of forty-five actually reported an increase in fear. This change in attitude on the part of those who've had an NDE has important implications not only for their own future lives but for society in general since, as Flynn notes:

> Psychologists and sociologists have traced many of our individual, as well as societal, problems to anxieties related to death. . . . Such freedom from fear leads to indifference to negative kinds of immortality striving.[46]

Freedom from a drive for material success, with all that that entails, is one such change frequently noted. An intuitive acceptance of both life and death and a focus of attention on the here and now are further outcomes of this change in attitude to death.

An increase in the incidence of psychic phenomena has also been reported in studies of near-death experiencers over recent years. Richard Kohr compared their psychic and psi-related experiences with two other groups, and a small number of other projects has focused on a comparison between incidence of psychic phenomena both before and after NDEs. Overall a statistically significant increase was shown to occur. The form that this has generally taken and the impact it has had on the lives of NDErs has been recorded by several researchers and my own results are fully presented in a later chapter of this book.

Change in religious beliefs, attitudes and practices has also been reported in recent research. Steven McLaughlin and Newton Maloney gave questionnaires to a sample of forty near-death experiencers to measure religious orientation and religious change. They found an increase in importance of religion and religious activity, and Sabom similarly found that religious views were strengthened. In studies such as those of Ring, Grey, Flynn and Atwater, where aftereffects were specifically investigated, consideration was given in each case to the religiousness of near-death experiencers. They all concluded that experiencers became more religious after their NDEs. However, as Ring notes: "The thrust of the spiritual development of NDErs is very clearly in accord with a general spiritual—rather than religious—orientation toward life."[47]

In a foreword to Kenneth Ring's book *Heading Toward Omega*, Elisabeth Kübler-Ross writes that the near-death experience is "a spiritual, sacred experience, which leaves the person profoundly transformed." As has been seen, it can take many years for that transformation to take place. But, as Flynn notes, NDEs also have a wider significance:

The meaning of the NDE lies not only in the effect it has on experiencers themselves but in the effects they have on those of us who haven't had any sort of transcendent experience and, ultimately, in their effect on the world as a whole.[48]

The Process of the Method

DEFINITION OF A NEAR-DEATH EXPERIENCE

In this book a near-death experience is defined in terms of both content and circumstance. In terms of content it is defined as having a number of the components described by Raymond Moody in *Life After Life*. These are: a sense of peace, a noise, an out-of-body experience, travel down a dark "tunnel" toward a bright light, experiencing a "life review," encountering deceased relatives or friends or a "being of light," "entering the world of light," coming to a "border" beyond which it is not possible to pass and returning to the body. In terms of circumstance, an additional criterion for this study is that this experience should have taken place when the person was *physically* close to death, not just psychologically preparing for it.

Physical closeness to death is often judged by onlookers to be represented by one or more episodes of apparent unconsciousness as a result of extreme physiological trauma. In some cases, such as during an operation, bodily signs can be monitored at the time of the NDE, whereas in others, such as drownings or car accidents, only the outward signs can be noted. In general, a person can be said to have been near death if they could have died, and if they have been believed to be dead or actually pronounced clinically dead and yet recovered. Since my study was not conducted within a hospital setting (for a number of reasons), the measurement of closeness to death is not possible to determine apart from a reliance on the truthfulness of accounts given by the people interviewed. It should be noted, however, that the definition of death is problematic anyway, even for the medical profession, which uses such terms as clinical death, biological death and brain death to describe it.

Although the phenomenon in question is called a *near-death* experience, it is necessary to note the controversy concerning whether near-death experiencers have actually died before being resuscitated or reviving. In most studies, including my own, there are many cases of people who were declared to be clinically dead—some for considerable periods of time. One of my subjects actually awoke when a relative came to view her body in the morgue, and Sabom cites the case of an American soldier "killed" in Vietnam who was believed dead by everyone who had anything to do with his body until a mortician found blood oozing from the incision he had made to inject embalming fluid. Moody notes that clinical death is said to occur if a person stops breathing, the heart stops beating, blood pressure drops below the possibility of measurement, the pupils dilate and body temperature falls. He writes that "most people who have ever been pronounced dead were adjudged so on the basis of this criterion." Yet many near-death experiencers have revived from this state.

With advances in technology, the concept of brain death has also been introduced as a measure of "real" death. This is based on the absence of electrical activity in the brain as measured by an EEG—a flat line. Yet Audette and Moody report that Fred Schoonmaker has collected over 1400 cases of NDEs, of which fifty-five had flat EEG's, lacking brain activity in blocks ranging from thirty minutes to three hours.

According to Professor Negovskii, a Russian scientist quoted by Michael Sabom, biological death is the irreversible state that follows clinical death if it is allowed to follow its natural course. However, he does note that the transition from clinical death to biological death is itself a process.

Several other commentators and researchers, such as Sabom, and Roberts and Owen, have also noted that death does not take place at a certain instant but rather is a process that takes time. How far in the dying process near-death experiencers go appears to vary widely. In terms of our normal measurement of time, periods of apparent unconsciousness and absence of bodily signs can vary from minutes to hours and in rarer cases even days. And in terms of the NDEs themselves, they can range from an experience of peace, freedom from pain and an out-of-body experience to an extensive experience through all the NDE components, including a long, detailed set of interactions in the "world of light." I agree with Raymond Moody, who notes that at present it seems to be impossible

> ... to determine exactly what the point of no return is. It may well vary with the individual, and it is likely not a fixed point but rather a shifting range on a continuum.... All I ultimately want to claim is this: Whatever that point of irretrievable death is said to be ... those with whom I have talked have been much closer to it than have the vast majority of their fellow human beings. For this reason alone, I am quite willing to listen to what they have to say.[1]

The Near-Death Experience Scales

In an effort to provide an external measure of whether or not a person has had an NDE of the Moody type, Kenneth

Ring devised what he called the Weighted Core Experience Index (WCEI). This provides, in effect, a weighted measure of the depth of the experience. This scale assigns a weighted score to each of ten elements of the NDE. For example, a subjective sense of being dead is given 1 point, a clear out-of-body experience is given 4 and encountering visible "spirits" is given 3. Scores can range from a possible 0, indicating the absence of any kind of NDE, to 29, indicating the deepest type of NDE. Ring further suggested certain cutoff points in order to use the scores for classification. For example, he suggests that if someone has a score of less than 6, that person has not had enough of the experience to be considered a core experiencer. If someone scores between 6 and 9, that person is considered to be a moderate experiencer, and those whose scores range from 10 to 29 are considered deep experiencers.

My first response to such a scheme was dismay. Attempting to measure such unmeasurables seemed an affront to the near-death experiencers, and the apparent arbitrariness of the scheme was most unappealing. Ring himself acknowledges the somewhat arbitrary nature of both the weightings and the cutoff marks, but points out that the scheme tends to err on the conservative side, possibly excluding some Moody-type experiences with few elements rather than including any about which there was any doubt. Since my own research was focused on the aftereffects of NDEs, it was important to ensure that the people whose aftereffects I was to study had indeed had an NDE to begin with. If that meant eliminating a few possibles from the study, that was unfortunate yet preferable to examining the aftereffects of something that was not an NDE to begin with. In fact, when confronted with a number of doubtful NDEs in my own sample, I was driven to reexamine the WCEI and found it ultimately to be a reliable, if rough, guide to the depth of an NDE.

Each transcript was rated by myself and another person familiar with the study. If there was any disagreement about the presence of a particular element, we reexamined the case concerned and either came to agreement or did not score it as being present. Overall this resulted in WCEI scores ranging from 6 to 24, of which 15 were moderate experiences scoring between 6 and 9 and 35 were deep experiences scoring between 10 and 24. These assessments were confirmed as accurate throughout the analysis and were useful in a number of ways that will become clear in later chapters.

In 1983 Bruce Greyson devised another scale, which he called the NDE scale. He writes that when tested, this scale was found to be consistent, reliable and highly correlated with Ring's Weighted Core Experience Index. In addition, it differentiated those with questionable claims from those with soundly based claims to have had NDEs.

The NDE scale takes the form of a set of sixteen questions clustered in four component areas (each of four questions): cognitive, affective, paranormal and transcendental, which can be either interviewer- or self-scored. The highest possible score is 32, and Greyson suggests that a score of 7 or higher would be required to establish the presence of an NDE.

The purpose of the development of this scale was to enable researchers to test hypotheses relating to causal factors and aftereffects, and also to assist clinicians in distinguishing between NDEs and what Greyson describes as "organic brain syndromes and non-specific stress responses following close brushes with death."[2] In addition, Greyson notes that it can be helpful in categorizing NDEs into types according to whether there is a predominance of cognitive, affective, paranormal or transcendental features.

In the present study, since interviews had already been completed, an effort was made to score interview transcripts on the NDE scale. It was found that there was insufficient information to do so reliably and therefore the attempt was abandoned. I concur with Greyson's judgment that while Ring's WCEI can be useful to measure the depth of already gathered NDE reports, the NDE scale is more suited to identifying NDEs in an unscreened population.

SAMPLE CONSTRUCTION

At the beginning of the project I was often warned that my greatest problem would be to get any sample of near-death experiencers at all, let alone the number I sought. Keith Basterfield had already reported his difficulty in collecting NDE accounts over a three-year period (finally publishing the results of a small questionnaire mailed to twelve subjects). In early American studies, use was often made of hospital facilities to locate people who had just undergone such an experience. Such recent experiencers were not appropriate for my purposes since this project was to focus on aftereffects rather than on the experience itself. Later studies, especially in the United States, made frequent use of members of the International Association for Near-Death Studies (IANDS). However, as there was no such organization in Australia at the time, I had to look elsewhere.

It seemed obvious that the usual sampling procedures would not be possible. Notwithstanding the research suggesting that many people have had such an experience, there was no organization, central register or available list within Australia to provide a suitable source for probability sampling. Thus, since a sampling frame was unavailable and I believed the population to be widely distributed, a probability sample was out of the question. "Availability sampling" seemed the most appropriate course.

It was decided to use the first available sampling units that met certain limiting criteria appropriate to the study: a near-death episode over two years ago; reasonable geographical accessibility (within the eastern states of Australia) and English-speaking subjects. Apart from these few limiting criteria, a wide variety of demographic features was seen as advantageous for the analysis.

Finding the Subjects

Some researchers believe it is difficult to interest people in a study that probes their private affairs. However, in retrospect, it seems that once the near-death experiencers were convinced that what they had to tell would be understood and accepted, they appeared relieved to be able to speak about their experience and its profound aftereffects. For some this was their first opportunity ever. For this reason, the manner of approach to these people was critical in obtaining their cooperation. It is not evident from other studies just how eager to talk, or how withholding, people in the United States or Britain are about their experiences. However, in Australia, up until the beginning of this study there had been little mention of the phenomenon in the media, and although people generally had heard of it, they did not seem to have very much information. Consequently near-death experiencers tended to be rather hidden from view and generally kept their experiences to themselves—a tendency that was confirmed by responses in later interviews.

Over the three years of the study, contact was made with over two hundred near-death experiencers from all states of Australia. However, the final sample was made up of fifty subjects, located by a variety of means:

- Two people who responded to my published articles on the subject;
- Five people who responded to public talks given during the first year of the project;
- Two people who responded to media interviews;
- Twelve people who were recruited from a sample

of experiencers already obtained by another researcher;

· Twenty-nine people who were referred to me by third parties who had read my articles, heard me speak or met me in some other context.

The fifty respondents included fifteen men and thirty-five women. Their ages at the time of the NDE ranged from seven to seventy-six years. Of the total, twenty percent were nineteen years old or younger, fifty-eight percent were twenty to thirty-nine years, twenty percent were forty to fifty-nine years and two percent were sixty to seventy-nine years. The number of years since their experience ranged from two to fifty-two.

Geographically the sample was widely distributed. In all I traveled over 6,200 miles. As a result, the sample comprised people from farms, small rural towns and large provincial centers as well as suburban and inner-city dwellers.

The near-death experiences in this sample occurred as a result of illness in sixteen cases; surgery or postoperative complications in twelve cases; miscarriage, childbirth or post-childbirth in ten cases; serious injury in six cases; drowning in two cases; poisoning in one case and attempted suicide in three cases. Details of the individual cases are outlined in the next chapter.

This process of gathering a sample revealed two salient features of the near-death experience: its widespread but well-hidden nature, and the necessity of gaining the trust of the experiencer before beginning the data collection.

DATA COLLECTION

As already noted, the research is in large part exploratory. At the outset it was believed important to be able to compare responses across the sample to reveal the pattern of aftereffects and measure the degree of their establishment. Yet it was also believed important to allow for a wide-ranging discussion of any issues raised to enable, in addition, a qualitative analysis. Therefore, because of its flexibility and comparability, the instrument form chosen was the semi-structured or "focused" interview.

On the interview schedule there was provision for detailed questioning in all the areas to be investigated. Depending on the actual experience of the interviewees and how wide-ranging their responses, these questions could be asked or omitted, as appropriate. This style of interview allowed for unanticipated answers by the interviewees and provided sufficient freedom to explore further any areas thought to be fruitful at the time. This was one of the advantages in being the only interviewer. Another was the direct relationship between the early interviews and the development of the project as a whole.

The Interview Schedule

Early preparation of the interview schedule was somewhat influenced by Kenneth Ring's brief interview schedule and more detailed Omega questionnaires (featured in his book *Heading Toward Omega*), although his emphasis on psychological testing and the format of a self-administered questionnaire was not considered appropriate for this project. The content of the schedule sought to test some of his results, but was also influenced by insights gained from other reading on the subject and questions raised by my own NDE. Before starting this project I had never met another experiencer and had many queries about the experience and its aftereffects. Although Ring's results were tantalizing, I had no idea what to expect from an Australian population.

After pilot-testing on six near-death experiencers (three men and three women), the initial interview schedule was found to be too exhaustive. There was also some ambiguity, considerable repetition and an occasional drafting error. In addition, the respondents themselves had raised issues that needed to be pursued in the next draft for future interviews. Overall, I found in this early testing that the level of detail in the first draft was superfluous, since once the respondents felt secure and relaxed, much of what was to be questioned was usually covered with little prompting on my part. Subsequently the modified interview schedule (see Appendix II) was used as a guide to ensure comparability across the sample. Checklists could be consulted, but the questions were not read out to the interviewee in a formal fashion.

Nonetheless, all interviews covered eight main areas:

- demographic information (at the NDE and at the interview);
- details of the NDE itself, including the circumstances within which it occurred;
- attitudes to death (before and since NDE);
- religious/spiritual affiliations, beliefs and practices (before and since NDE);
- psychic sensitivities (before and since NDE);
- life direction (before and since NDE), including attitudes to self, relationships, and interests, study, work;
- present lifestyle priorities;
- attitudes to social issues.

Interviews were usually conducted within the home of the respondent, an element that was to provide an unanticipated richness to the data. Contact was always made be-

fore the interview and ongoing contact to the present day
became common. Interviews were taped and there were no
objections raised except in one case, where the person concerned asked for the tape to be turned off before revealing
sensitive information that she did not want recorded. The
recorded part of the interviews generally lasted about
ninety minutes and the post-interview discussion often ex-
tended for a further sixty to ninety minutes.

Interviewee Attitudes

In general the interviewees tended to be highly sensitive to
the reception of their information. It soon became clear
that the changes they had undergone involved many private
and sometimes painful matters, for example, those concerning primary relationships, the death of close loved
ones and deeply felt spiritual beliefs. Despite the fact that
many of their life changes were already in the public domain, for example, changes in social relationships such as
divorce, career changes, interaction with social institutions
such as the Church and interaction with health-care professionals, I believe that many of these concerns would never
have been revealed had the interviewer not been suffi-
ciently trusted.

Other Sources of Data

In addition to the initial interviews there have been a
number of other sources of data for this project. For example, halfway through the project I responded to a desire on
the part of many near-death experiencers to meet one another by initiating the setting up of a local chapter of the
International Association for Near-Death Studies. As a result, there have been several meetings that were very well
attended by experiencers from very far afield. Within the
context of these meetings (the first of which was held in
my own home) I taped discussions as the participants in-

troduced themselves to the group and spoke of the most significant changes to come about in their lives as a result of their NDEs. The opportunity for corroboration and elaboration of the formal interviews was significant. In addition, informal contact at these gatherings further enabled enrichment of the data—genuine friendships developed and even more revelations were made.

It has been suggested that different settings are likely to induce and constrain talk of particular kinds. One of the rare original interviews that was not conducted in the home of the experiencer took place in an office. Whenever someone passed through, the topic was changed or the interviewee stopped talking altogether. In another example, the interviewee was from another state and we met in a hotel room. At one stage the husband, who had never been told of his wife's NDE, returned and was sent away on an errand so that we could complete the interview in privacy. As a marked contrast, at the local IANDS meetings, almost everyone present had had an NDE, and those who hadn't were the partners of someone who had. People were talking freely in a social setting for the first time ever—comparing NDEs and later experiences without any fear of ridicule or censure.

The IANDS newsletter, which is published quarterly, has also provided data in the form of short articles or letters written by the experiencers. Occasional calls were a further source of information as they phoned to talk about recent events, to discuss their ideas or feelings about incidents related to their NDEs or life changes or hopes for the future. In addition, I have hundreds of letters written by both my own sample and others about their experiences, attitudes and beliefs. Those who were interviewed still occasionally write to keep in touch.

Finally, at the close of this project I sent a letter to all respondents asking whether their participation in the research (my coming to see them and any subsequent contact) had affected their perception of the experience in any way, or precipitated any changes in their lives. The responses to this final letter are examined in the next chapter.

Apart from the near-death experiencers themselves, I have also been invited to give a number of talks to doctors, psychiatrists, nurses and nursing students, following which there were often lengthy discussions. Intrigued by their apparent lack of knowledge on the subject, I prepared a simple ten-item questionnaire (see Appendix III) that was distributed to nurses and nursing students to determine not only their level of knowledge about NDEs but also its source. These results are presented in a later chapter since they are particularly relevant to the question of why people tend to keep quiet about their experience.

DATA ANALYSIS

Two years into the project, with the quantitative analysis largely completed, a clear picture was emerging of the types of life changes experienced by near-death experiencers, and the degree of their commonality. Yet, however convincing this analysis, and it was convincing, it seemed that there were "noises" in the data, another underlying story that was not being revealed by this approach. There was a messiness in the lives of experiencers, comprised of such diverse feelings as puzzlement, wonder, loss, nervousness, fear, anticipation, trust and hope, that was being skated over since it was difficult to hook into from the perspective of the precise areas I had set up to examine. What I wanted was to be able to move these clear areas to the background and move the messiness forward to have a better look at it. While worrying about this dilemma, I attended an interstate conference and was introduced to the "grounded theory" approach to qualitative research. Although rather late in the project, I could see that it indeed provided the possibility of seeing the data as a whole through different eyes. With the initial analysis in the background, unlimited by categories of aftereffects, I could seek to understand how experiencers actually dealt with such an experience in their post-NDE lives.

Although it is clearly not the best way to approach a grounded theory study, Anselm Strauss writes that it is possible to use a body of collected data to do grounded theory. Much data had in fact already been collected in preparation for a qualitative analysis, and it was felt that any further data required by the exigencies of theoretical sampling could be generated by return to the near-death experiencers. The results of this belated but conceptually important excursion into the unknown appear in Chapter 10.

Theory of the Method

Readers interested in the theoretical underpinning of the method can refer to Appendix I: A Further Note on Method.

The People of the Study

There is a strong commitment in this study to the recognition of the researcher as an integral part of the research process. The result, from the viewpoint of the researcher, can be observed throughout this book. Yet there is inevitably another result—from the viewpoint of the "researched." As already noted, at the close of the project a letter was sent to all participant near-death experiencers soliciting their views concerning the impact of the research process on their perceptions of the NDE and their lives in general.

In this chapter, after an initial presentation of some basic information about each of the people in the study, including the researcher, there is a review of their responses. The names of the participants are pseudonyms.

REVIEW OF THE PARTICIPANTS
IN THE STUDY

The table on the following pages is arranged in alphabetical order for easy reference. It summarizes information about all participants in the study with regard to their age (at the NDE and at the interview), the circumstances within which their NDE occurred, their score on Ring's

Weighted Core Experience Index and their level of education and occupation at the time of their NDE.

AFTEREFFECTS OF THE RESEARCH PROCESS

The researcher is unavoidably a part of the study. As this study proceeded, it seemed obvious that I was being changed by the research process, by the contact with the near-death experiencers and the new meanings that were woven from those interactions. I was intrigued by the possibility that participation in the research process might also have touched *their* lives in some meaningful way. In January 1991 a letter asking about this was sent to most of the experiencers who had been interviewed. Not all could be contacted because four had since died, at least two were overseas and there were five who were no longer at the same addresses. Excluding these, the response rate of about eighty-seven percent was very high, considering that most of the interviews had been done from eighteen months to three years earlier. The responses were generally lengthy and detailed.

Perception of NDE Since the Interview

Only two people noted that they hardly give their NDE a thought these days. Charlotte wrote that talking about it now "has no particular significance" for her, but that what it has done is to make her "feel better about the ultimate state of death." She added that her mother had recently died and she felt no grief, knowing that she was now "in a safe and lovely place." Daphne wrote that she had spent a stressful two years during which the NDE seemed to fade away, although acknowledging that the stress was due to leaving her husband, which she did in large part because he had never understood her NDE and had always "knocked" it.

Name	Age at NDE	Age at Interview	Circumstance of NDE	WCEI Score	Education at NDE	Occupation at NDE
Cherie	23	43	childbirth	16	biology certificate	housewife
Al	35	66	perforated ulcer	9	university post-grad.	captain U.S. Air Force
Albert	53	63	heart attack	8	management certificate	buyer (department store)
Alexandra	29	49	peritonitis after removal of kidney	21	university	doctor
Anthea	32	43	hysterectomy	20	teachers college	teacher/librarian
Barbara	10	62	pneumonia	9	some primary school	student
Barry	45	65	hemorrhage after heart surgery	12	trade certificate	stores officer
Ben	14	58	explosion	7	some high school	student

Name	Age at NDE	Age at interview	Circumstance of NDE	WCEI Score	Education at NDE	Occupation at NDE
Bill	32	42	drug/alcohol overdose	18	some high school	welfare officer
Bronwyn	36	39	childbirth	11	some university	housewife
Cass	47	49	spinal fusion operation	12	some high school/ secretarial	TV associate producer
Charlotte	44	49	ruptured spleen/internal bleeding	17	some high school/ secretarial	housewife
Christina	39	54	poisoning	11	art school	commercial artist
Claire	14	31	drowning	6	some high school	student
Cora	29	41	tubal ligation (allergy to anaesthetic)	14	high school	housewife

Cherie Sutherland

Name	Age at NDE	Age at interview	Circumstance of NDE	WCEI Score	Education at NDE	Occupation at NDE
Daphne	29	44	miscarriage	6	secretarial	housewife
Denise	17	41	car accident	21	high school	student
Edwina	16	25	operation for cancer of thyroid	19	some high school	student
Eileen	34	53	heart attack/stroke	13	nursing certificate	nurse
Evan	41	50	heart attack	8	high school	federal police
Gary	16	33	diabetic crisis	17	some high school	student
Grace	30	44	childbirth	19	art certificate	housewife
Greta	37	43	hysterectomy	8	secretarial	clerk
Hal	14	56	heart attack	22	some high school	student

Name	Age at NDE	Age at interview	Circumstance of NDE	WCEI Score	Education at NDE	Occupation at NDE
Harriet	27	61	burst appendix during pregnancy	10	some high school	housewife
Helen	26	46	prolapse repair after premature birth	20	some high school	housewife
Janet	34	42	hysterectomy	22	some nursing	shop attendant
Jennifer	7	52	pneumonia	13	some primary school	student
Juliet	46	53	bladder repair	19	some high school	healer
Kate	31	49	miscarriage	19	teachers college	housewife
Lorenzo	49	55	heart attack	9	some high school	musician

Cherie Sutherland

Name	Age at NDE	Age at interview	Circumstance of NDE	WCEI Score	Education at NDE	Occupation at NDE
Lou	17	29	water-ski accident	8	some high school	apprentice spraypainter
Martine	33	65	peritonitis after childbirth	11	high school	housewife
Mary	58	65	heart attack	24	high school	healer
Mel	33	52	buried alive	14	high school	field man in geological exploration
Michael	15	19	drowning	15	some high school	student
Moira	29	63	kidney infection	14	high school	teacher of ballroom dancing
Morris	55	71	heart operation	24	some high school	retired

Name	Age at NDE	Age at interview	Circumstance of NDE	WCEI Score	Education at NDE	Occupation at NDE
Nerida	27	39	childbirth.	14	some high school	housewife
Olivia	25	50	childbirth	17	high school	housewife
Patrick	23	71	rheumatic fever/nervous breakdown	16	some high school	apprentice heating engineer
Paula	27	34	medication overdose	16	some high school	housewife
Robert	44	53	suicide attempt (shooting)	14	welfare course	residential child care worker
Ruby	25	55	heart attack	8	geology/mineralogy course	geophysical surveyor
Shana	23	44	kidney operation	22	nursing	nurse
Stella	76	80	pneumonia	7	some high school	housewife

Name	Age at NDE	Age at interview	Circumstance of NDE	WCEI Score	Education at NDE	Occupation at NDE
Sue	23	43	hysterectomy	7	nursing	housewife
Tessa	24	52	car accident	12	secretarial	office worker
Ursula	37	49	post-childbirth	7	high school	housewife
Victoria	22	43	childbirth	6	some technical college	housewife
Virginia	24	44	suicide attempt (drug overdose)	17	some university	public relations officer

Most people emphasized that there had been no change in their perception of the NDE itself. For example, Mary noted that "it couldn't be deeper or more meaningful." Alexandra wrote that since her experience had always felt "so pivotal and crucial for all later developments, it would be hard to say it had changed in being of central importance." And Ruby was unequivocal in her statement that her experience

> ... is as vivid as this moment, and I can think no differently about it. It's rather like the blue sky—it's there, it's blue and it'll always be there.

However, several noted a change in attitude toward their NDE since the interview, generally in terms of feeling more comfortable and gaining more clarity about it. For example, Virginia wrote that she now felt clearer about the NDE and noted that she had gained greater insight into its spiritual teaching. Denise had found that since her participation in the research the experience had been legitimated in her mind and now she was able to accept it as normal, whereas before she had tended to deny its reality and never talked about it. Paula wrote that her perception of the NDE had changed "very much for the better" since becoming involved in the research. In a long, detailed letter she described these changes and what they had meant to her. She wrote:

> Yes, I do think about it very differently these days. I feel so much more comfortable with the experience, having had the chance to have someone like yourself tape and listen to me in a serious manner. I feel more confident when the need requires me to discuss it with others and I have now been able to accept it within myself and use it as a positive turning point in my life. The experience means more and more to me as time goes on. It shows me that there is so much of God's and the Universal love and teachings

waiting to be given to us providing we *love ourselves* enough to *accept* it all.

This feeling that the experience meant more once it had been legitimated was often expressed. The means by which they had previously sought this legitimation is considered in a later chapter.

Attitude to the Research

Gratitude was the most frequently articulated attitude to the research process. For example, Mary wrote:

> Yes! Your coming to visit me, our subsequent meetings and coming together with other "experiencers" has meant more to me than words can convey. . . . Your research is filling a very large gap in the general understanding of NDEs—bless you! And thank you for having the understanding, courage and tenacity for carrying out this research.

Others, for example, Helen, Victoria, Evan and Michael, were grateful particularly for being able to talk openly about their experiences for the first time. Michael wrote that before the interview he very rarely mentioned his NDE to anyone, yet now he finds he is able "to talk about the experience to family and friends without feeling too uncomfortable." He ascribes this both to "getting it off my chest and talking honestly about it to someone who was interested, and finding out and realizing that many other people had had similar experiences."

This relief and pleasure in finding out that others had had similar experiences was expressed by many. Shana noted that this knowledge gave her great comfort and a sense of stability. Moira wrote that it had "confirmed the experience" for her and convinced her that it was "a valid experience."

Other Changes Since the Interview

Michael and Paula were not alone in feeling able to talk about their experience more freely since the interview. Both Hal and Denise also wrote of their confidence that now allows them to "spread the word" and Bill remarked that he now feels like a stronger person because he can discuss it. However, this newfound confidence and ability to talk about their NDE is not only of personal benefit, since several noted that it helped them in their work, and as Denise wrote, it enabled her "to be more effective with counseling the grieving and being generally more "healing."

Several remarked that they had thought about their NDE a lot since the interview. Patrick wrote that he'd reflected on our meeting and that it had crystalized his thinking on the matter. Michael even revealed that he'd had a few very vivid dreams relating to the experience and concluded that this had been because he had been thinking about it more often. The interview had stimulated others to seek out more information. I received numerous requests for a reading list, and Ruby noted that our discussion had given her the motivation to question others—find comparisons, similarities and then isolate each part of the NDE and analyze it. Alexandra wrote that since the interview she had become much more interested in NDE research and studies, to the point where she had even begun collecting data among other health-care professionals. Hal wrote that since our meeting he had read several books and pamphlets and now felt less unsettled by these experiences. This is particularly interesting, since in a letter written two years earlier he had noted:

I think I have psychic advantages, and I try to repress them. I want to be ordinary and normal, not extraordinary. I don't like these excursions away from "worldly reality."

Some described their different attitudes to life in recent times. Martine wrote that her life was "making sense at last" and Mel wrote that he now found life to be a playground for lessons in loving and joyful learning. And Cass reported: "My life is full and rich, and gifts of life come to me in abundance."

There were a number of other individual changes noted. For example, Mel reported that "there has been a real change in my recent history which has to do with a speeding up of my quest for a real connection with my spiritual self." Martine wrote: "I am touching more and more often this feeling of Peace that passeth all understanding and I do not fight it anymore." And Paula noted that she was working more and more on "becoming in tune with guidance and psychic abilities" so that she could help others.

All who had attended the IANDS meetings commented in their letters about how important the contact with other near-death experiencers had been for them. Mary wrote of how strengthening and supportive it had been for her, and Denise referred to her feeling that it had been a real "coming out." There were numerous requests for me to arrange another meeting soon. Finally, Martine wrote:

> You started it all—the contacts we had together made me feel "normal," although I didn't talk about this experience with other people. . . . Before we talked to each other I really felt something was wrong with me and my feelings. . . . Now I feel *new*, as if I am starting another lifetime in this lifetime. I am back to the time I was a young girl dreaming of what could be and *it is*!

This chapter, in taking a wider view, exploring the impact of the research process on its participants, has leapt somewhat ahead of the main story. Chapter 5 returns its focus to the first results of this interaction—the immediate aftereffects of the near-death experience.

In the Wake of the Near-Death Experience

TELLING OTHERS

One recurring theme in near-death accounts is the difficulty near-death experiencers have in talking about the experience afterward. They quickly discover that prevalent social and medical attitudes make general acceptance of such phenomena extremely problematic. Chronologically, as early as the moment of return to their body, they can get their first indication that talk of their NDE will not always, if ever, receive the kind of response they would like. Initially, while still in the afterglow of the experience, this can come as quite a shock to the experiencer. This section examines *who* exactly they did tell about the experience, and the response is noted.

The following table gives the response of people told about an NDE. The fifty interviewees each nominated whom they told about their experience (which could include more than one person), and in each case, what the response was. The response columns indicate for each category of person told the number of positive or negative responses.

Person told	Positive response	Negative response
family member	18	17
friend	16	5
nurse	4	2
doctor	2	9
psychiatrist	5	5
counselor	3	0
minister/priest	0	2
teacher	0	2

To place this table in context, it should be noted that there were three people who, after getting a very negative response when they told of their NDE, did not tell anyone else for many years. For example, Hal (aged fourteen) initially told three people of his experience—his mother, who told him not to be silly, his minister, who was embarrassed, and his teacher, who did not want to hear about it. After that he told nobody for over thirty years, until he saw Elisabeth Kübler-Ross on television. There were also thirteen near-death experiencers who didn't tell anyone at all about their experience for many years, and then were extremely cautious about whom they did tell. Finally, there were three people who had never told anybody about their experience before speaking to me.

In all, thirty-five told family members of their experience. Among these family members the most common responses deemed positive by experiencers were those of simple belief and acceptance. Occasionally a family member would be very interested and want to talk about the experience, but in most cases the response was basically one of relief to have the person safely alive, and a preparedness to believe what was recounted. Of negative responses, the most commonly cited were cynicism, no comment, disinterest and impatience, all of which were experienced as hurtful by the experiencer. For example, Anthea noted that when she told her husband about her NDE, he said he thought she was "a bit strange . . . you know, like, you were pretty sick at the time, probably suffering from delusions or something." And Sue remarked that her husband didn't want to hear about it: "He thinks it's quite scary and wants no part of it."

Twenty-one told friends of their experience. The overwhelmingly positive response should not be surprising since many experiencers noted that they told their experience only to those friends they thought would be interested or accepting. Nevertheless there were five negative responses, from people who didn't take the NDE seriously, or laughed. Lorenzo said that the friend he told didn't believe him and thought he was spooky. And Cass said she told various friends, but "people are inclined to laugh at you." Patrick found similarly that his story "was poohpoohed in many ways. I thought, until I met a brother in the experience, I can't talk about it."

Only six of the thirty-six who had their NDE in a hospital told nurses of their experience. Four of the six nurses who were told gave a positive response. Two of them seemed to know that something had happened. Juliet recounted:

> The next morning, one of the nurses was walking past—she'd just come on duty—she was walking past the door and then she came back and looked in. She came over to me and said, "What's happened to you?" She said, "I was walking past and when I looked in I could see this glow around you." I told her what happened and she said, "Yes, I believe you—it happens." And she said, "You just looked different," and she talked with me.

Olivia found that the nurse she told also believed her. She said:

I tried to talk about it with the theater nurse. She said it was something a lot of people had experienced. She said she couldn't explain it but she said she had no doubt that it had happened because too many people had spoken to her about it.

The two nurses who responded negatively seemed to have done so because of their inability to cope with being observed by the experiencer while out of body. For example, Victoria had watched attempts to revive her during her NDE. She said:

Later in the day, when I was strong enough to talk ... I mentioned it to one of the staff and she freaked out. I said to one of them: "You were doing such and such last night, weren't you?" And she said: "How did you know that, your eyes were closed?" I said: "I was up at the ceiling, watching you." She wouldn't talk about it, she just freaked. I thought, "Oh, well, I'm obviously not meant to say anything to anybody," but I was extremely intrigued by the whole thing, I was fascinated.

During the nine days that Eileen was in a coma, many friends sent her flowers. One day while out of body she observed two nurses come into her room with more flowers. They discussed how stupid it was to have a room full of flowers for someone who was unconscious and decided to take the flowers into some of the other wards. Some days later when she came out of the coma she asked the nurses why they had taken her flowers away. They were shocked to have been found out in such a way and would not talk about it with her.

Only two of the eleven NDErs who told doctors were met with a positive response. Juliet told her GP about it after she returned home from the hospital, and he accepted it. Robert, who had attempted suicide by shooting himself with a shotgun, recounted:

> Then I remember coming around in the intensive care unit sometime later. I even spoke to the doctor about it later and he said, "There must be some purpose. We were amazed that you lived because technically you should have died with the injuries you had." He said, "You must have been given another chance to do something."

However, doctors were far more likely to respond negatively. In fact, a number of experiencers remarked that they purposely did *not* tell their doctor. Morris, who was fifty-five at the time of his NDE during a heart operation, said he didn't tell his doctor because "they can't handle things like that!"

One doctor appeared startled when Eileen told him of her NDE and, soon after, sent a psychiatrist to visit her. Fortunately the psychiatrist was able to reassure her that they were quite common. The most frequent responses by the doctors were cynicism or dismissal. Cora was so overwhelmed by her experience that she attempted to share it with her doctor. His response was cynical. I asked her how she felt after receiving such a response, and she answered: "Oh . . . completely alone, burdened and exhausted." Although Paula and Robert both reported that their psychiatrist laughed when told of their NDEs, Albert remarked that when he described the experience to his psychiatrist, there was no comment at all. He added: "That minimized it [the NDE] in my mind."

The counselors who were told of the experience were in each case chosen because it was thought they would accept the experience and be helpful. Thus, the positive responses were not surprising. On the other hand, the teachers and ministers of religion who were consulted soon after the experience in each case responded with discomfort, dismissing it, or warning that such matters should not be pursued. Janet recounted that she went to see three Protestant ministers and

> ... without failure they all said you shouldn't delve into things like that, you'll go mad, if you're not already mad. And, it's satanic and you're not meant to know about things like that, just leave it aside. And one of them did recommend I go seek psychiatric help.... But I *knew* I wasn't going mad, I knew that there *was* total love.

As must be obvious from the above, most experiencers have difficulty in communicating their experience, whether because of their own reticence or because the person they confide in does not want to hear what they have to say. Remaining silent about it, while privately holding it as a focus, seems to be their most common solution to this problem. It is also clear from the interviews, as earlier noted, that they are highly sensitive to the response they receive—a disbelieving look is enough to silence them for years. On the other hand, very little is needed to give them the corroboration they so often seek in the early days.

Quite apart from the medical crisis during which it occurs, it seems that the NDE should be seen as a major life crisis that can take many years to integrate. An effective response by someone in health care can do much to assist in the early stages of this process, although, as is clear from the above, this is not often forthcoming.

If one is charitable, it appears that the inappropriate response by health-care professionals could be due to ignorance of the phenomenon. To test this hypothesis, a short ten-item questionnaire was administered to trained nurses and nursing students. The results of this survey and a discussion follow, concerning some possible implications for the health-care profession—such as the need for recognition of potential near-death experiencers and the development of a more appropriate post-NDE response.

KNOWLEDGE OF THE NEAR-DEATH EXPERIENCE

In 1977 Michael Sabom and Sarah Kreutziger reported in an informal survey that they found that few professionals who cared for critically ill patients were aware of NDEs. By 1983 Roberta Orne found that the level of awareness among the 912 nurses she surveyed was high (seventy percent) but that the level of knowledge was still low. During 1990 a survey was conducted for the present study among fifteen second-year and twenty-one third-year nursing students, and twenty registered nurses whose years of experience since graduation ranged from two to forty. A simple ten-item questionnaire (see Appendix III) was completed by each participant in the survey. My aim was to determine not only the level of knowledge of NDEs among this population, but also its source.

Of the total sample (fifty-six persons) only four respondents—all of them students—had not heard about NDEs either directly or from another source such as television, radio or books. The level of general awareness therefore appeared to be high. However, when examined more closely it was clear that the most common source of knowledge was secondary, for example, the media. Seventeen of the twenty registered nurses and thirty-one of the thirty-six students had heard about NDEs from secondary sources. For eleven of the registered nurses and twenty-one of the students this was in fact their only source of information. Only nine of the twenty registered nurses and eleven of the thirty-six students had actually heard about NDEs from a patient, family member or friend. Perhaps most significantly of all, not one of the fifty-six respondents had heard about NDEs during their training.

In view of their sources of knowledge about NDEs, it is perhaps not surprising that fifteen registered nurses and thirty-three student nurses assessed their level of knowledge as being low or very limited. Only one person considered her knowledge of the subject to be high and seven thought theirs was medium.

It is clear that nurses generally do not consider themselves to be adequately informed with regard to NDEs. Many of my sample (particularly among the students) wrote on the questionnaires that they would like to learn more about this phenomenon. There is now a considerable body of literature on NDEs which could fill some of this need, but there is no real substitute for an encounter with a genuine near-death experiencer.

IMPLICATIONS FOR HEALTH-CARE PROFESSIONALS

The need for appropriate training is a primary implication. Health-care professionals need to know what a near-death experience is, what pattern it generally follows, and when it is likely to occur. As already noted, Michael Sabom found that forty-three percent of people who undergo a near-death crisis (for example, cardiac arrest) have an NDE. Thus, although NDEs *can* occur during any near-death crisis situation in any area of medicine, they are more frequently to be found in areas such as cardiac and intensive care units.

As would already be evident from my sample, NDEs are just as likely to occur in children in a near-death situation as adults. The impact of an NDE on an adult is immense, as will increasingly be revealed throughout this study. In the case of children, it is no less dramatic, as seen in my example in Chapter 1 of the ten-year-old girl, Barbara, who had such a joyous out-of-body experience. At the time of the interview, fifty-two years later, she said:

"Even now, all these years later, I get very overwhelmed at the feeling [of joy]."

In Barbara's particular case the scene she observed while out of body was a peaceful one, with her mother and father sitting silently on either side of her bed. She recounts that she was about to go down the tunnel toward the light when she caught sight of her mother's anguished face, and realized that as much as she wanted to go, she could not do that to her mother. And so she chose to return.

On the other hand, David Herzog and John Herrin cite the case of a seven-year-old boy who witnessed a chaotic scene while out of body—that of his own emergency resuscitation. The next day he asked his doctor:

> Why did everyone beat me up last night? I was being good and the doctors ran in here, held me down and started hitting me on the chest and sticking needles into me.[1]

In cases of near-death crises in children, it is important to be aware that the child may have had an NDE. This can be very helpful after the event, since a simple explanation of the procedures the child has undergone during the crisis could save much of the confusion and distress evident in this boy's question.

Over the last decade there have been a few attempts in the American literature to address the problems raised by the possible occurrence of NDEs, especially in emergency situations. Anthony Lee questioned in 1978 whether nurses should change what they do during and after a "code," and provided suggestions for cardiopulmonary resuscitation both during near-death events and post-resuscitation. Annalee Oakes, who conducted a survey between 1975 and 1978, examined the responses of thirty practicing critical-care and emergency nurses to NDE reports and found them to vary widely. In addition, she found them to disagree as to the appropriate way to utilize a patient's

NDE report in nursing care. She proposed nursing care guidelines for potential experiencers, but also suggested appropriate post-CPR care, including follow-through and referral care for experiencers and their families. Kimberly Clark, a social worker in a critical-care unit of a five-state trauma center, whose role includes the training of staff to deal with NDErs, also suggests a number of appropriate clinical interventions with both conscious and unconscious patients. In a 1986 edition of the *American Journal of Nursing* there were articles by three nurses, Louise Papowitz, Roberta Orne and Joyce Strom-Paikin, all of whom wrote of their experiences with near-death experiencers and made suggestions as to their care. Following an interdisciplinary conference in 1984 titled Clinical Approaches to the Near-Death Experience, Bruce Greyson and Barbara Harris reported guidelines and interventions that were developed to assist experiencers in coping with psychological difficulties resulting from their experiences. And Bette Furn suggested the use of cross-cultural counseling techniques as a means of helping them readjust to their environment. Whether they *should* readjust to their environment, is, of course, another question.

Both of the above implications for health-care workers—that is, early identification of near-death experiencers and an appropriate program of care—can be handled with little difficulty. It appears that overall there is a primary need for sound information concerning NDEs to be introduced into formal training programs for health-care professionals. After that, a little interest, awareness and sensitivity can go a long way in giving support to recent experiencers, thereby facilitating the integration of the NDE into their future lives.

Changes in Attitude to Death

WHAT HAPPENS AT DEATH?

It has often been reported that there is a marked increase in belief in an afterlife following a near-death experience. This was certainly the case with my sample of near-death experiencers, where twenty-one of the fifty (forty-two percent) said that before their NDE they had no belief in an afterlife. These people generally expressed the view that at death they just died and that was that. For example, Edwina said that she'd thought of death "as a big black wall, no continuity, and that was the end." Denise said, "I had the community attitude that death was final, very final, very black." And Tessa reported: "I just thought you didn't go anywhere. You were buried or cremated and that was the end."

On the other hand, nineteen of the fifty NDErs (thirty-eight percent) said they already believed in life after death before their NDE. Although this is a small sample, this agrees, within the usual standard error allowance for statistical errors, with the fifty-nine percent of the general Australian population, estimated by the Australian Values Study Survey (1983) to believe in an afterlife. It should be noted that within my sample, this belief in life after death

tended to be a legacy of their childhood religious training.
For example, twelve of the nineteen, before their NDE, believed in a notion of heaven and hell. For some, this was
mixed in with doubts, as Cora said:

> Consciously I thought that at death we might just ex-
> pire and you were nothing, but deep underlying that
> was a true belief that if you were good you went to
> heaven and if you were bad you went to hell.

However, for most, although they might not have felt comfortable with it, their belief was strong. Eileen recounted:

> I did believe in heaven and hell. I always dreaded
> this hell business. I didn't like the fire. As much as
> I feel the cold, I didn't like the fire. Because coming
> from Ireland it was pumped into our heads about this
> dreadful fire, the fires of hell, and we did really be-
> lieve in it. I did really think there was such a thing
> as the fires of hell. And it took me to be a grown
> adult to find out that there's no such a place. . . . I
> think that is the reason why we have a near-death ex-
> perience, to show us that it's not dreadful, that it's
> not awful, that it's nice to die.

Bill said:

> Well, by my religious conditioning I thought that if
> I left the church or committed adultery, you name it,
> I'd burn in hell. Or if I was lucky I'd go to purgatory,
> and they'd cook me for a while. Or if I was a goody-
> goody, went to church every Sunday and wore the
> halo, I'd be going straight up to heaven.

After the experience all fifty of my sample believed in life
after death. The belief they now hold is based on their own

experience and in many cases explicity rejects the view earlier held. Since his NDE Bill now believes:

> I'll go into another sphere, for untold time (since there is no time) and when my number comes up maybe I'll end up in Boston somewhere, or I'll end up in Russia, I'll come back as a Russian, or whatever. I tend to believe that more than anything.

Hal noted that although he'd had a strict Methodist upbringing, he didn't accept the teachings of the Church at all. He said: "I thought at fourteen years of age that when you died that was it, you were dead. But my experience has changed my ideas entirely." And Janet said that before her NDE she also thought you just died and that was it. Now she says:

> I see death purely as a homecoming, it's just a total reunion, so much love and happiness. I have this sort of intuitive sense of the fact that we go on and continue to keep learning, and we continue to grow on another level.

There are a number of views of what happens at death expressed by the experiencers, but they are uniformly positive. Paula noted that before her NDE she believed just what the Church had taught her but felt quite lost in the world.

> I didn't know whether God existed or not. But row I know you don't die—you just pass onto another plane. You leave the physical body and the spirit body passes on to another plane.

Moira remarked that her upbringing in the Church of England had told her that there was a heaven, but she'd also heard about hell—which she couldn't equate with a loving

God. But now she says, "I believe we just move into another stage of consciousness. There is no death, we go on
for eternity." Nerida, who is still a committed Christian (in
the Kelly-Low Brethren), nevertheless has altered her belief since her NDE. She said:

> I hold to the biblical interpretation of death. But hav-
> ing a firsthand experience like that has changed me
> in the way that I view possible judgment. The Chris-
> tian Church teaches that there will be a judgment
> and an accounting. But now I don't fear judgment
> and I've come more to the view that judgment is
> something we do ourselves.

The implications of such an experience for religious beliefs in general are many and varied and are dealt with in
the next chapter. Meanwhile, Barbara, who had her experience as a child, had not thought about what happened at
death at all before her NDE, but now she says:

> To me death is not to be feared, nothing to be feared.
> And I think it's something to be really anticipated
> because I believe that this is not the only life I've
> had and it's not going to be the last one either. I've
> read a few books on reincarnation and it seems to
> me to be the only thing that fits. It seems to me to
> be the only answer.

Belief in Reincarnation

When talking with near-death experiencers about death
generally, or the possibility of life after death, the issue of
reincarnation is often spontaneously raised. Nevertheless,
during the interview all respondents were specifically
asked whether or not they believed in reincarnation.

Seventeen of the fifty (thirty-four percent) said they already believed in reincarnation before their NDE. This is

in line with the thirty-two percent of the general Australian population, estimated by the Australian Values Study Survey, to hold that belief. However, some of these respondents had only a tentative belief before their NDE and were much more certain after it. For example, Olivia said that before the NDE:

> I was aware of reincarnation, but didn't have the firm belief that I have now, nor did I have the understanding of it, but I felt that that's where I was heading. And now I definitely believe in reincarnation, I have no doubt about it at all.

And Alexandra said that before the NDE:

> I thought it was possible. Intellectually I do have a few doubts as to whether what we in the West talk about reincarnation is so literally true. But I would say I live it as if it is a truth—it seems to me to be a very useful concept to have.

After the NDE, the total of those who believed in reincarnation increased from seventeen to thirty-nine. Of those who definitely did not believe in it before their NDE (fifty percent), many claimed to be quite convinced afterward. For example, Ruby said that before the NDE "I couldn't accept it at all, but I believe it absolutely now." Paula noted: "Before I never gave it a thought but now I believe it definitely." And Moira said: "I had no belief before at all—I thought it was a whole lot of Eastern rubbish—but now I think it's a good hypothesis."

However, some (twenty percent) felt just as uncomfortable with the notion of reincarnation after their NDE as they did before. Nerida said:

> I was not convinced in reincarnation before the NDE and I'm not now either. It's illogical to me that that

would be so. I'd hate to think we had to come back
and do it all again.

The NDE did force people to consider their beliefs. While
eight of the fifty had not thought about reincarnation before their NDE, only one of these still had no opinion after
the experience.

ATTITUDE TO SUICIDE

As part of the formal interview all respondents were asked
about their attitude to suicide. As the question was not
specific, some respondents answered in terms of attitudes
to their own possible suicide, some answered only in terms
of the suicide of others and some mentioned both.

A surprisingly high number, twenty-one, of near-death
experiencers had either tried suicide or thought of suicide
for themselves at some time before their NDE. This generally occurred at times of great stress or tragedy in their
lives. However, since their NDE, twenty-six felt strongly
opposed to suicide and not one thought they would ever
commit suicide now. For example, Paula noted that she had
spent twelve years wanting to commit suicide. She said:

> I had it planned but didn't actually get to attempt it.
> Now I can't see any point in it, I think you've got to
> stay here and keep hoping, keep struggling. Al-
> though when I think back to that time I still under-
> stand why I wanted to go.

Shana, who had thought of committing suicide because of
intense pain, recounted that during her NDE:

> The one thing I got when I was up there was that I
> would never get back there by committing suicide,
> and that my task was to serve. But that was for me

personally, it wasn't a general statement for every person. There are some people I knew who've committed suicide. It's a path for some people. It's just not my path, it was definitely not my path.

The NDE seems to cause a definite shift in attitude when it comes to the suicide of others. Although strongly against suicide for themselves, several of the near-death experiencers felt compassion and sadness for those who do commit suicide. They claim they have learned from their own NDE that there is no point in suicide, but realize that, as Shana said: "It is a path for some." Eight people suggested suicide was a matter for the individual to decide, whereas none claimed to have thought this before their NDE. As Victoria said: "I think of it as an individual's decision what they do with their lives, whether they continue to live or choose to die." And Michael said: "I wouldn't do it myself, but if they have a reason to do it, it's their choice." Janet, who was adamant she would never commit suicide herself, said: "I feel that if a person did commit suicide, they would be met with total love and compassion, as I was. God is just total love."

This was certainly the experience of the three people in my sample who had their NDE as a result of a suicide attempt. Now all three of them maintain they would never attempt suicide again, and they each feel compassion for anyone who does so. For example, Robert said:

Now I feel that if someone wants to commit suicide they must be deeply depressed, because I was. I feel very sorry for people who do it. They must have a very deep reason and we haven't found the right way of helping these people. Now I'm glad I didn't die. The vision helped me to come back to myself again afterward.

Researchers have shown interest in this change of attitude

among suicide attempters who have had near-death experiences. Although it is sometimes suggested that people who have had such an experience or know about them would be more likely to take their own lives in order to reenter the bliss of the "world of light," the above results demonstrate that the opposite is the case. People who have had a near-death experience do not take their own lives, and my data support recent studies that indicate that even repeated suicide attempters do not generally attempt to take their lives again once they have had an NDE. It has also been suggested that knowledge about NDEs can be used in a therapeutic setting and that suicidal patients who read NDE accounts were less likely to make further suicide attempts.

FEAR OF DEATH

One of the most widely noted changes reported by near-death experiencers concerns fear of death. Michael Sabom found that there was a marked decrease in fear of death among his sample of experiencers, whereas among a sample of forty-five nonexperiencers (those who had been close to death but not had an NDE), only one person claimed a decrease in fear while thirty-nine reported no change and the remaining five actually reported an *increase* in fear of death. Kenneth Ring also noted similar findings. He wrote:

> The data . . . clearly demonstrate that core experiencers, as a group, tend to show a sharp decline in fear where no such pattern is evident for nonexperiencers.[1]

The present study asked each respondent whether they had any fear of death before their NDE and whether there was any change afterward. Of the fifty respondents, thirty-three (sixty-six percent) noted that they had a fear of death before their NDE. This fear was sometimes connected with early religious beliefs concerning the nature of life after death, as already outlined. Eight respondents (sixteen percent) said they already had no fear of death before their NDE. For example, Alexandra noted that:

> As a little kid I used to trot around with my mom while she laid out what I'd call "the stiffs." She was a district nurse and I saw death at a young age. Death was not a strange thing at all. It did upset me a little but not in a conventional sense. I was very curious about it.

And Ben, who as a child during the war had seen a lot of death, said: "I had never been overimpressed with death—I had no fear of it. I just accepted it as natural."

Nine respondents (eighteen percent) said they had not thought about death before their NDE at all. Most of these were the children of the sample, but one of the adults, Morris, said: "I didn't think about it before so I wasn't really afraid. But now I'm not afraid at all."

The most striking observation is that after the NDE, forty-nine of the respondents (ninety-eight percent) said they now had no fear of death at all. For example, Charlotte recounted:

> After it was all over, when I eventually recovered in hospital, even when all the pain came back I had just completely lost my fear of dying. I don't fear it at all!

Christina said:

> Now I have no fear of death! Now I know that I'm not the body therefore it's possible to take another body. When you die it's not the whole of you that dies.

And Córa, who did fear death before her NDE, when asked if she had a fear of death now, answered:

> No! And even straight afterward, even though I hadn't come to any understanding, I didn't fear it. That's something I didn't lose. It's so important!

The implications of such a change in attitude, in what has been called our "death-denying" society, are highly significant. To begin with, by perceiving that one's true being is transcendent, timeless and part of the whole, it is possible to accept and even welcome death, as so many near-death experiencers have shown. There is no longer a need to deny or defy death by engaging in immortality projects. The desire to leave something behind can be abandoned as no longer relevant. Immortality vehicles such as money, fame, heroism, the building of monuments and the founding and maintenance of family dynasties can be seen for what they are—symbolic substitutes—and put into perspective. The cutthroat competitive spirit for getting ahead in the world (at the expense of others) can no longer be supported.

However, it is one thing to record that experiencers have no fear of death, and it is quite another to show how it manifests in their lives. Their change in attitude to immortality projects is further examined in a later chapter.

On a personal level, the loss of the fear of death for oneself can also be transferred to others. Several of the respondents spoke of not grieving, even at the death of a close relative or friend. For example, Tessa told of being at the funeral of a very dear friend. She said:

> Everyone was crying, but I felt at peace for him. I thought, I know where you are and I know what you're experiencing. And I felt happy for him, not sad.

Shortly after the death of her mother, Christina sent me a letter describing her feelings about it. She wrote:

> My mother died two weeks ago after suffering a massive stroke six weeks before. She was paralyzed and almost blind and could not speak very much and didn't really recognize individuals (so they said!). I tried to give her support, and help her "over" from here. I like to think I succeeded. She was mostly in a kind of coma—and finally let the body go on July 17th. She passed over peacefully and suffered no pain. What joy she must have felt dropping the poor old body!

Another implication of having no fear of death is not only the ability, but the *desire* to work with the elderly, the grieving and the dying. The next section examines this change in attitude on the part of near-death experiencers.

INTEREST IN ISSUES RELATED TO DEATH AND DYING

Only thirty-one of the respondents were asked if they had any particular interest in issues related to death and dying. Most of these said they either had not thought about or had no particular interest in issues related to death or dying before their NDE. There were, however, four of them who did. Barry said that he had always thought of death as a part of life, and was interested in it on those terms. Alexandra saw a lot of death with her mother, a district nurse, as has already been noted. Shana had been a children's nurse and had already become interested in reincarnation because, she said, "That was the only thing that made any sense of children suffering and dying." And Edwina related:

I had a maudlin fascination with death as a child, absolutely maudlin. I used to hang around in graveyards. My family still teases me about it because from the time I was about three till I was about eleven, I used to spend hours looking at old gravestones. You know, total fascination, totally morbid. My mother used to sort of cope with it and take me off to graveyards.

On the other hand, after the NDE, twenty-one of the thirty-one NDErs asked said they now did have an interest in death and dying. Five of them were interested in reading about it and several mentioned an interest in contemporary debates about euthanasia and hospice care. However, sixteen of them actively participate, either in a voluntary or paid capacity, in the care or counseling of the frail elderly, the dying and the grieving. For example, Sue said:

I now have a second job nursing old people. I love old people, I feel totally devoted to them. My husband says, "I don't know why you do it," but I love it. I really relate well to them.

Several of them work in a voluntary capacity in a hospital or hospice setting. Mary feels that the main reason she had to "come back" from her NDE was that she had to do her hospice work. She also works as a healer with cancer patients. She said:

That experience [the NDE] meant a lot. When you're dealing with people who are dying, it helps them to know that you know what you're talking about, because you've been there.

Others are simply aware of the dying in the community and attempt to help in any way they can. Juliet said that in her work she tries to help people by lessening their fear of death. And Kate said:

> I try to visit people who have someone dying. Subsequently I have gotten cancer myself, so I'm sort of aware of people who are dying and I try to help them through this time. People are so afraid, whereas for me that's something I'm not.

Five of them do a lot of work professionally with the grieving. Alexandra said:

> The single most frequent issue to come up in my practice is that someone in the family is dying, or they haven't gotten over someone's death.

She said that she feels her NDE as well as the experience of personal loss after the death of her daughter in 1984 are a great help in this work. Olivia also notes that she often works with people having difficulty getting over the loss of someone close. She said: "I find that by sharing the near-death experience with them, I can make them feel better, so I do use it that way."

Finally, since her son committed suicide three years ago, Victoria has become very involved in a self-help group for those grieving the loss of children—Compassionate Friends. She actually had her NDE during the birth of that son, and said she doesn't know how she would have coped if she had not known what she now does from her own NDE. Being able to share this knowledge with others in similar circumstances is now very important to her.

This sort of concern for others is a feature of post-NDE life and is further discussed in a later chapter.

Changes in Religious Beliefs, Attitudes, Practices

An increase in religiousness following a near-death experience is frequently reported in the literature. This chapter examines the incidence of change in religious beliefs, attitudes and practices in the lives of fifty near-death experiencers. Overall an attempt will be made to clarify whether these changes were indeed to greater religiousness or rather to a deeper spirituality. Firstly, the religious affiliation of respondents (before and after their NDE) is summarized, followed by an examination of their perception of themselves as predominantly religious or spiritual. Attention then turns to their perception of the experience itself as either a religious or spiritual one. The presence of six experiences, activities or beliefs is scrutinized. Finally, there is a discussion of whether religiousness or spirituality figures as one of the most significant changes to come about as a result of their NDE.

Where the connections between religion and NDEs have been explored at all, this has been done from a variety of directions. David Royse conducted a questionnaire survey of 174 clergy to determine their attitudes and knowledge of near-death experiences. Michael Sabom made note not only of the religion but of the regularity of church attendance of each of the respondents to his medical investigation of NDEs. Carl Becker took a cross-cultural approach with a historical look at the centrality of near-death experience to Chinese Pure-Land Buddhism and later explored the similarities between modern near-death accounts and both ancient Japanese death-bed visions and the theories of the Tibetan *Bardo Thodol,* or *Book of the Dead.* Steven McLaughlin and Newton Malony administered tests to a sample of forty NDErs to measure religious orientation and religious change. As Ring had earlier found, they detected no relationship between prior religiousness and depth of NDE. However, an increase in importance of religion and religious activity was noted. It has been suggested by Ring and others that although prior religiousness does not affect the occurrence or depth of NDE, it can color its interpretation. This is particularly evident in Carol Zaleski's medieval Christian accounts and in the findings of Craig Lundahl concerning the perceived "otherworld" in Mormon NDEs.

Ring concluded that experiencers became more religious after their NDE, but it should be noted that this so-called religiousness was ambiguous in its manifestations. It tended more toward inward spiritual transformation than toward outward demonstrations of faith such as a greater involvement in organized religion. In the present study, an effort was made to clarify this point. For example, in a question concerning the experience itself, I asked: "Would you describe your experience as a religious or spiritual experience or would you describe it in some other way?" In another question I asked: "Would you have described yourself as a religious or spiritual person before this experience? Now would you describe yourself as a religious or spiritual person?"

I found, as could have been anticipated from the previous research cited, that the respondents in large numbers rejected the "religious" label (often vehemently) and availed themselves of the "spiritual" alternative, making clear the reason for their choice in most cases without any further prompting on my part.

In order to determine whether my sample could be considered normal or whether the participants were already unusually religious or spiritually inclined before their NDE, a comparison was made with a general population sample. Although not all areas of my inquiry were covered, the Australian Values Study Survey provided some of the data on the religious and spiritual practices and associated beliefs among a general Australian population required for this comparison.

RELIGIOUS DENOMINATION

Changes in religious affiliation of fifty near-death experiencers are noted below, and a comparison is made with the general population.

Religion at NDE	*NDErs (%)*	*General pop. (%)*	*Religion at interview*	*NDErs (%)*
No religion	46	16	No religion	84
Church of England	24	28.3	Church of England	4
Roman Catholic	12	25.6	Roman Catholic	8
Methodist	4	4.3	Methodist	0
Presbyterian	2	7.2	Presbyterian	0
Jewish	2	0.4	Jewish	0
Baptist	2	2.1	Baptist	0
Lutheran	2	1.3	Lutheran	0
Calvinist	2	n.a.	Calvinist	0
Brethren	4	n.a.	Brethren	2
Buddhist	0	0.2	Buddhist	2

In terms of religious affiliation, about half of the sample (forty-six percent) claimed to have no religion at the time of their NDE. However, after their experience, eighty-four percent claimed to have no religion. With respect to this category "no religion," there could appear to be a major discrepancy, with forty-six percent of my sample claiming to have no religion compared with the general population sample of sixteen percent. However, two-thirds of this group mentioned that they had had some religious training as children (in a variety of denominations) but had abandoned this before their NDE. For example, Alexandra said:

> I broke away very quickly from the organized kind of religion, I guess before I even left primary school. But you see I was lucky because my family were not strict in that sense, they were Quakers, and my dad was linked with a Protestant church, and my mother said you ought to study other religions. So my parents were pretty broad-minded.

And Stella said:

> I was Church of England as a child, but nothing since. I realized very young that people went to church to show off their new hat. That wasn't to me what it should be, so I didn't go.

And Virginia recounted:

> I was baptized a Roman Catholic. At the age of seven I was sent along to have instruction in taking my first Holy Communion. They said something good was going to happen, and I was really looking forward to this. I remember it so distinctly—I went up to the altar and innocently put out my tongue, and nothing happened! I couldn't believe it. Before that I used to be taken to church by my grandmother. I

used to just sit there and look around and I used to
think how ridiculous it all was. This continued right
up to my teens, I could see the hypocrisy, particularly of the Roman Catholic religion, where you can
do anything you like, you go along on a Saturday to
confess the sins and all of a sudden on the Sunday
it's all forgotten and you can start again. Today I ex-
cuse it away as the difference between Christian activity and church activity. But there was always that
belief within in God.

Evan said that he was brought up Roman Catholic in a
boys' home

> . . . and came across cruel times. We were held up to
> ridicule. . . . The head warder used to go through
> into the shower and he'd have the cat-o'-nine-tails
> and whip you, and that used to hurt so much, and es-
> pecially when you were wet it used to sting you
> more. You see, religion was stern in those days, early
> fifties. It was drummed into us, we had no choice. I
> know I didn't like it.

This same group further volunteered that at that time (before their NDE), had they been asked about religion in a
survey, they would normally have said Church of England,
Roman Catholic or whatever, just out of habit, although
they were no longer affiliated with any denomination.
Therefore, although the forty-six percent is accurate for
this sample, it is not necessarily in disagreement with the
Australian Values Study Survey results.

Unlike Sabom, this study found a dramatic change in
religious affiliation, especially from organized religion (of
whatever denomination) to no religion. For example, although Anthea identified herself as a Protestant before her
NDE, since then she said: "I don't believe in any religion,
I believe more in spirituality and I don't feel that it has to

be labeled." Denise noted that she had been High Church of England before her NDE. She said:

> There was a lot of hellfire and damnation stuff. After the NDE I rejected that. I just felt that previously, to me, God was a very alien God, and after [the NDE] that just didn't hold water anymore. To me it was almost as if the slate was wiped clean at that point of arrival and everything starts afresh after that. To me God is no longer a judgmental being. After [the NDE] there was an anger and rejecting of religion, and I've never really gone back to that. I don't attend church. It's almost as though I feel I've got the answers. I know that sounds very superior—it's not meant to come over that way. It's just that when some ministers stand up there and preach their sermon, I can't accept that now. So that's why I separate religion and spirituality. I feel that some people just haven't got it right.

Only two respondents changed from no religion, one to Buddhism and the other to Roman Catholicism. Eileen said that she felt her conversion to Catholicism five years ago had nothing to do with her NDE. She said it was "just something I have always felt I would do one day, but never got around to it, but the one day come round and I done it."

Gary noted that he'd been brought up as a Baptist but had stopped going to church before his NDE and "had never had much of a feeling for God or things like that." He said:

> The reason I got into Buddhism was because of the NDE. After it I'd gone around to churches, gone to this Jewish synagogue in Carlton, and really sort of investigated various religions, the Bible, whatever. I tried to sort out the meaning of life. And one day

there was a book sale going on and I opened a copy of *Teachings of the Compassionate Buddha,* and it hit me like a 10-ton brick. I'm not joking. I just thought this is amazing, this is it! And here I was only sixteen, and never heard of Buddhism in my life.

RELIGION OR SPIRITUALITY?

As can already be seen, the near-death experiencers of the sample often make a distinction between religion and spirituality, the religious and the spiritual. This especially arises in terms of their perception of themselves. For example, Daphne said:

I don't like the word "religious" because it has church connotations. I think "spiritual" is the stronger because it's only between me and the Higher Intelligence. "Religious" concerns religion, whereas "spiritual" concerns your own spirit and your own will and soul environment.

And Ben said:

A religious person is one who believes in a particular dogma, who takes sides. After the experience I studied religions and I found that at the basis of all religions there is an almost identical principle, so all these factions and schisms were to me an absolute nonsense. Whether you believe in one religion or another is like barracking for one football team or for the other. Why take sides? So looking at this—I'm not at all religious. I would describe myself as spiritual.

Thirty of the fifty respondents claimed to be neither religious nor spiritual in orientation before their NDE. Since their WCEI scores ranged from six to twenty-four, this confirms Ring's finding that prior religiousness has no apparent bearing on either occurrence or depth of NDE. The remaining twenty included twelve who claimed to be religious and eight who claimed to be spiritual. After their NDE only three experiencers claimed to be religious. This is interesting since there were eight respondents who claimed to be affiliated with a particular denomination. That is, five of these eight churchgoers did not consider themselves religious. Four claimed to be spiritual rather than religious, and Albert said he was still neither one nor the other.

In all, after their NDE, thirty-eight of the fifty experiencers now claimed to be spiritually inclined rather than religious. In this category are three groups of people: those who already considered themselves to be spiritual before their NDE; those who were religious before their NDE; and those who considered themselves to be neither. For example, Anthea thought of herself as spiritual before her NDE. She said:

> I'd say that before [the NDE] I believed firmly in God but I wouldn't say I was a religious person. And now I would say I am a spiritual person and still don't see myself as a religious person. But certainly a very spiritual person.

And Martine said that although before the NDE she was quite religious, now she describes herself as

> ... spiritual because I don't go to churches anymore. I don't belong to any denomination. I even have fixed my life up that everybody is from a different religion. I was a Calvinist and I married a Jew, and I have Catholic son-in-laws and Church of England daughters! And it's quite all right. I feel much more

at ease in that big vast spiritual thing than to have to
be in the rules. I hate that sort of thing. I can't stand
little boxes. And a religion is for me "you can't do
this" and "you have to do that," and "God is there to
punish you." I don't believe that.

Michael said:

I was not at all religious before. Now I am more
spiritual. I disagree with the church. I went for a
while, one of my friends is a Christian. I went with
him for a while but some of the sermons I disagreed
with completely. They were wrong as far as I was
concerned.

And Janet noted that she considered herself to be neither
religious nor spiritual before her NDE. She said:

When I was young I was sent to the Methodist
Church. When I got into my teenage years I really
questioned what it was all about and I stopped going.
Now I would say I am spiritual. I have some problems
with the word "religious." "Religious" to me means
someone who is steeped in dogma, whereas someone
who is coming from a spiritual aspect is one who has
had an actual experience of God. And it's been a very
intimate experience with God so therefore that person
doesn't doubt God exists, and lives a life of example
rather than preaches at people.

In terms of the experience itself, over two-thirds of respondents perceived the NDE to be a spiritual experience, not
one perceived it to be religious, but fourteen of them perceived it to be neither religious nor spiritual. For example,
Helen described it as "a life experience," Jennifer, who had
encountered her deceased great-grandmother during her
NDE, described it as "a loving experience between Great-

grandmother and myself," and Nerida described it as "a personal experience."

When asked whether he would describe his NDE as a religious or spiritual experience, or in some other way, Ben said:

> I would describe it as a spiritual experience— something that perhaps some religions are aiming at, but never, ever come anywhere close to it.

And Anthea described her NDE as "absolutely totally spiritual. Not religious but spiritual."

RELIGIOUS OR SPIRITUAL EXPERIENCES, ACTIVITIES OR BELIEFS

The percentage of subjects who responded positively to questions concerning each of six religious or spiritual activities and associated beliefs both before and after their NDE is summarized below. Comparisons are made wherever possible with a general population.

The following table summarizes the positive responses of fifty near-death experiencers to questions concerning six experiences, activities or beliefs. Since comparison is made with a general population, the number of experiencers is expressed as a percentage.

Type of experience, activity or belief	General population (%)	Before NDE (%)	After NDE (%)
value of organized religion	56	36	20
church attendance	34	38	20
prayer	56	48	74
meditation	n.a.	12	60
quest for spiritual values	n.a.	20	88
guidance	44	32	86

The above results show an established shift on all six items away from organized religion and church attendance and toward private nonformula prayer, meditation and a general quest for spiritual values. When making comparisons with a general population in terms of belief in the value of organized religion, church attendance, tendency to pray and having a sense of being guided, there is agreement with my sample before their NDE, within the statistical errors.

Among this sample of experiencers there appears to have been considerable doubt about the value of organized religion even before the NDE, but following the NDE only ten people (twenty percent) still believed there was any value in it. For example, Anthea remarked that her ideas about organized religion changed after her NDE because, as she said: "I felt less that they have the answers. I feel more that the answers come from within your own being." And Edwina described her attitude:

I now have a very strong view that church and religion are totally divorced from spirituality. It doesn't matter what sort of religion you get involved with. It just doesn't help each individual along the path to understanding or spirituality. The only way people do it is by looking in themselves, and looking in and in and further and further, and most religions I feel take people away from that. I do believe in God but not in a traditional church God. I mean I believe that all that light is what we call God.

And Cora described her ambivalence. She said:

First, I have a feeling of anger and rage at the indoctrination of organized religion. I think the actual experience has given me a strength in my personal spiritual growth. I tend not to need the church yet I love the input of other religions or spiritual paths or teachings. But I tend in a way to have my own and it's very much based in the traveling through the dark into the light.

Of the small number (twenty percent) who still attend church after their NDE, Tessa goes only to take her massively brain-damaged son, who enjoys the service. She says that she can't accept the sermons being preached.

They say if you're not a Christian none of you will be able to come in through the eye of the needle, and all that sort of thing. And I think, well, I went up there and I saw it and I certainly wasn't a Christian at the time. So how do they know? So I can't accept it. I've got my own beliefs and I try to live my way.

Kate enjoys going to church but claims she is "a believer" rather than a Roman Catholic and that her beliefs are not necessarily those of the Catholic Church. After describing her strong belief in reincarnation she laughed and said "the Roman Catholic Church would be horrified if they knew what I believed."

A few others who attend church regularly, although

nominally attached to a particular denomination, are happy
in any church. For example, Helen said:

> I feel that church is a bit of a sham. Not God but the
> people. They seem to fuss over stupid little things
> that are really political. But I belong to a lot of
> churches. I play the guitar in the Roman Catholic
> folk group, I'm in the musical group of the Church
> of Christ and I play with the Salvation Army. I'm
> probably Anglican but it doesn't worry me where I
> am—it's all God inside me.

And Harriet said:

> I grew up Church of England but I don't put so
> much importance on going to church. I'd rather *do*
> something than go to church. It's what you do with
> your life and what you do for people that matters
> more than going to church.

Martine described an experience she had a couple of years
ago when she wanted to see if there was anything for her
in organized religion. She said:

> I went to St. Mary's Cathedral because I thought I'd
> choose the biggest place where I can get the whole
> Catholic Mass. And so I went there and I have never
> been so disappointed in my life. I couldn't believe it.
> It was so cold. They couldn't go fast enough through
> the whole thing. There was no feeling whatsoever.
> People were like automatons and there were four
> priests taking the communion and they were just
> shoveling them in like choo, choo, choo. I came out
> of there and I said, the churches, that's finished for
> me. I can get the feeling of the spiritual in meditat-
> ing. I get more glow and it's direct! That's another
> thing, the direct line. I always feel they want to put

somebody in between. When I can go direct to the
Light. I don't have to say, "Please will you get me up
there if I'm good enough, will you?" I can go direct.
And some people don't understand that—you can go
direct!

In terms of prayer, Janet expressed a commonly held view
when she said:

I find that my whole life is always a prayer or a chat
to God or whatever. I just talk to God like he's just
there all the time. You know if I need to know something I'll just sit down and I'll tune in and ask what
I should be doing. It's always there, that information.
I just put myself into that quiet space and listen. You
see, I pray and meditate—for me the two can't be
separated. I think when you pray you talk to God,
and just on that level of being close to a friend, and
when I meditate, to me, that's quietly listening.

Many of the NDErs took up meditation after their NDE.
Only six of them meditated before their experience,
whereas now thirty of them claimed to meditate regularly. Kate noted that since her NDE her spiritual practices
had been very much affected. She said:

The big thing is that instead of, you know, "I believe
in God," now I *know*! And it's sort of not a hassle.
If you're praying or meditating, you really know God
is there. God is *real* to me. So it's very easy for me
now.

It should also be clear that the figures in the table regarding a "quest for spiritual values" are reflected in almost
every aspect of the various areas already discussed in this
chapter. Before their NDE only ten people said they were
already engaged in a quest for spiritual values, whereas af-

ter their experience forty-four of the fifty near-death experiencers claimed this as a major preoccupation in their lives.

A similarly well-established shift can be seen in terms of their sense of being guided. Before the NDE only sixteen people said they had a sense of being guided, whereas "guidance" was one of the most commonly reported features of the post-NDE lives of forty-three respondents. As Janet said: "I feel that my whole life is totally guided by God." And Denise answered:

> Yes, I feel very much guided. It's not that I seek it out, it just happens. I feel that that's just how it is—these things just seem to happen, but I always feel that my life is directed.

Juliet noted:

> I ask, and say, you know, "I don't know what to do" and then I try not to worry about it. As you know, the universal provider always provides, if you allow it.

And Martine said:

> I do get guidance, yes. When I let it flow I do the right thing. As long as I don't resist, as long as I don't put my mind, which is very strong, in the way. If I just flow with that guidance, good things happen.

Finally, it was through guidance that Janet and her husband were led to give up their secure middle-class lives and business in an affluent suburb of Sydney to establish a retreat center in the Snowy Mountains. The story of the steps that led to this move is so remarkable and complex that it is not possible to include it here. Suffice it to say that over a nine-month period following Janet's NDE their lives were turned upside down as they learned to trust and follow the guidance Janet received. During the interview, which was conducted at the now well-established retreat center, Janet said:

> We've virtually reached the stage now, we were told by inner guidance, that we had to teach by example and we were to be teaching what faith in God could do. We were asked to give up personal income, so Oakdale functions on donations—it's a nonprofit center. We've made it into a trust, we've handed it all over so we don't own it anymore. We were told not to have any income but we were to take whatever Oakdale could afford to pay us, if and when. And now for the last twelve months we've lived that way and that was pretty scary at first. I went through tantrums and told God off over that one. And here we are, twelve months later, and all has been flowing just so smoothly and all our needs are met abundantly. And I realize that we're having to do it purely as an example to show people that there is a power beyond ourselves that is controlling and planning. To me it was a case of total surrender and total freedom.

Although Janet's case is perhaps the most remarkable because of its complexity and detail, it is not at all unusual for NDErs to experience guidance in many aspects of their everyday lives, from the most mundane to the most important. Some "lifesaving" examples are given in the next chapter.

THE MOST SIGNIFICANT CHANGE

My final question concerned the most significant change to come about as the result of the NDE. This was a totally open question with no suggestions given for their responses. Fourteen people nominated spiritual growth as the most meaningful change, six suggested an increase in love and a further six said they now had no fear of death. Another five spoke of a feeling of inner peace and four of knowing God. Others considered they were now more responsible and caring, had greater understanding of themselves and others, had developed a thirst for knowledge, a desire to serve others and a lack of interest in materialistic aims.

Edwina said:

> Love, love. Love is the most important feeling in the universe. I mean that's what's had the most impact on me as a person. I can't stress the importance of it enough. Love is the most important thing in the universe, and sometimes that feeling is so strong it makes me cry, sometimes it makes me laugh. Whichever way you look at it, it's just fantastic!

And Kate said:

> Knowing God. *Really* knowing. And that's the thing that I can't, that I feel sad I can't really share with people I know. That's the big thing that changes your whole life, there's no doubt.

Overall, there is a feeling among this sample that they now have an ongoing direct contact with God or a Higher Power that requires no mediation by institutions such as the Church or interpretation by the teachings of any denomination or tradition. If one was to assess many of the above results in isolation from the more distinguishing features of this particular population, one would have a group of people among whom eighty-four percent claim to have no religion, only six percent claim to be religious, eighty percent see no value in organized religion and eighty percent never attend church. It would be tempting to see this as further evidence of our secular society. I believe this would be a mistake and in fact it calls into question just who is included in such figures which are given as evidence of the pervasive godlessness of our times.

The next chapter explores changes in the psychic sensitivities of these same fifty near-death experiencers.

Psychic Phenomena

Most of the early studies of the near-death experience focused on its phenomenology. This chapter seeks out the presence of psychic phenomena not only in the experience itself, but also in the lives of near-death experiencers following their experience. Firstly, the experiences of the fifty respondents are surveyed for the presence of four paranormal features and these results are compared with a study by Bruce Greyson and Ian Stevenson. This is followed by a survey of the phenomena reported by experiencers both before and after their NDE. A comparison is made with general population surveys from Great Britain, the United States and Sweden.

In recent years a few researchers, such as Ring and Grey, have described a range of aftereffects of NDEs including the presence of psychic phenomena. Richard Kohr compared the psychic and psi-related experiences of near-death experiencers with two other groups within his sample, and Greyson specifically sought to compare the incidence of psychic phenomena in the lives of near-death experiencers before and after their NDE. Both Kohr and Greyson used in their studies the questionnaire developed by John Palmer for his Community Mail Survey of Psychic Experiences among a general population of townspeople and students in Charlottesville, Virginia.

When examining my own data, it soon became clear that unless it was possible to compare the incidence of psychic phenomena experienced by my sample before their NDE with the incidence in a general population, there would be no way of knowing whether they could be considered normal before their NDE or whether they were already unusually gifted psychically. In addition to Palmer's study, several others were located that reported the incidence of psychic experiences and associated beliefs among a general population.

Kohr analyzed data from an American national survey of 547 members of the Association for Research and Enlightenment, a group having interests in parapsychological phenomena, dreams and meditation. Although it is not possible to generalize from the results of that study to a wider population, it is possible to make comparisons among the three categories within that special group. Kohr's sample consisted of eighty-four near-death experiencers, 105 nonexperiencers (those who had been close to death but not had a near-death experience) and 358 others who had never been close to death. The results showed that the near-death experiencers had more psychic and psi-related experiences than the nonexperiencers and others. Overall Kohr found a substantial difference between the near-death experiencers and the other two groups, which was statistically significant for all variables.

As Kohr and Greyson suggested, there are at least three possible explanations for such differences:

- near-death experiencers are more psychically sensitive prior to their NDEs (a finding reported by Ring and Rosing in a recent paper);
- near-death experiencers tend to focus more attention on psychic and psi-related experiences;
- there is actually an increase in the incidence of

psychic and psi-related phenomena in the lives of people after an NDE.

The questions used for this part of the study were loosely based on those in Kenneth Ring's *Psychic Experience Inventory,* with a number of his questions omitted and some additional ones included. In most cases, Ring's explanation of the phenomenon was given before the question was asked. Overall, my questioning was more open-ended. For example, at the beginning of this section, a description was given of what psychic phenomena refer to, and respondents were asked whether, before their NDE, they had ever heard of such things. If so, they were asked what their attitude to psychic phenomena was before their NDE, and then, what their attitude was afterward. They were then asked whether they had ever had such an experience.

At this point the lead of the interviewee was followed, whatever experiences they spoke of were pursued and examples were recorded. Once their own examples had been exhausted, I consulted the checklist, asking about any experience not so far mentioned. As a result of this approach I added some additional topics like clairaudience, automatic writing, visions of the future, predictions made during the NDE that have since come to pass and the ability to "enter" the body of another person.

It should be noted here that no effort was made to verify the claims of psychic phenomena either before or since the near-death experience, apart from asking for explanations and examples of reports as outlined above.

PSYCHIC PHENOMENA DURING THE NEAR-DEATH EXPERIENCE

Descriptions of psychic phenomena associated with the near-death experience itself were taken from the accounts of the experience given during the interviews.

Out-of-body experiences were reported by forty-five respondents (ninety percent of my sample). Of these, thirty-five (seventy-eight percent) claimed to have realized they were outside of their bodies when they saw their own physical body below them. Greyson and Stevenson record that seventy-five percent of their sample of seventy-eight near-death experiencers similarly reported feeling or seeing themselves to be outside the physical body.

Of my sample, twenty-six respondents (fifty-two percent) reported meeting some person, spirit or presence either known or unknown to them. Almost half (forty-nine percent) of Greyson and Stevenson's sample reported seeming to meet some person or persons not physically present.

Eight of my respondents encountered a deceased relative. The others reported seeing friends, angels, luminous beings, beautiful people or a "being of light." Grace reported encountering numerous relatives who had died before her birth, her father and a dog who had been a childhood pet. Anthea said she met three angels who gave her the choice of going further with them, or returning to her body. And Hal, whose experience was so long and detailed that it took him about ninety minutes to relate, encountered many spirits, relatives and friends, as well as the "being of light," during his NDE. For example, when he left his body for the second time he went through the wall of the school building, where his body was lying after a second heart attack, and went into the playground. He said:

> While I was out of my body I went over to one of
> the girls near the hockey field. She had a lot of spir-

its moving about her. They were all up at about six feet in height, they were going straight through trees and straight through the tennis court surrounds. But there was one old lady spirit and she was trying to communicate with the girl. I watched this for a while and then I went up to her and said, "It's no good, you can't talk to them." And she said, "But I have to." This must have been the girl's grandmother.

After that excursion he returned to his body, but soon had another attack and found himself out of the body again. This time he was met by a teacher from the same school, who had been killed during the war. He was told that this teacher was there to reassure him, and to help him. Finally, after travel through the tunnel he found himself in the "world of light," where he met many relatives, two school friends who had drowned and the "being of light."

Twenty-five respondents (fifty percent of my sample) reported receiving some communication during the time they were out of their bodies. This ranged from simple messages such as "Go back" or "You are too early," to quite lengthy telepathic interchanges. Helen, whose experience occurred during a repair operation after childbirth, said:

It was beautiful where I was going, actually very beautiful. And I'm sure I saw people, my grandmother. I was really happy to go, but then I thought of my little children—two little boys plus the baby— and I really felt that I should be a mother to them and bring them up. So I discussed it with the "being of light." It was really beautiful, but he said I could come back and fulfill my life as a mother. And it was just lovely.

Grace, whose experience occurred during childbirth, was told (telepathically) that she had to go back since she was going to give birth to a son and would need to bring him up alone. Despite her wish to stay, she did go back, did give birth to a son, and one year later was deserted by her husband. Greyson and Stevenson report that thirty-nine percent of their sample reported apparent extrasensory experiences.

Finally, nineteen respondents (thirty-eight percent of my sample) described a transcendental environment that they had visited. The most common description was of a very beautiful place—a garden, gentle rolling hills, green pastures or a magnificent forest. Martine and Hal both saw a stream and Hal reported being taken through beautiful countryside past the stream, to a city, and finally into a building called the "archives," which held all knowledge. He said:

I came tumbling out onto a lovely place, with green grass, and right in the middle there was a stream and on the other side of the stream there were departed relatives that I knew, and they were playing there. I stood and looked around and there were female relatives and they said, "Oh, Hal, we've been waiting for you, come on over." They looked so nice, but I couldn't get over the stream. It seemed I was in another dimension. [Soon after] I saw there were two boys coming toward me and I recognized them. . . . They said, "You'd better not go across the stream, you'd better come with us, we've got some people for you to meet . . . . before you go back you've got to meet the Light." I said, "Who's the Light?" And he said, "Oh, that's the Supreme Being." I said, "You mean God?" He said, "Oh, if you like." He seemed a little vague about that. [Some time later his friend] said, "Look, the Light's coming now." I could see in the distance a pinpoint of light and it was coming toward me. It seemed to be coming from hundreds of

miles away, coming at immense speed, and it just kept
getting brighter and brighter. But I could look at it
and be not at all worried about looking at this bright
light. It was perhaps the brightest light I've ever seen.
I told you that I still had the feelings of peace about
me, but as the Light got closer, the feelings of peace
got even greater. It was a wondrous feeling. . . . And
then the Light got closer and I said to [my friend]
"What am I supposed to do? Do I have to get down
on my knees and pray, or something?" He said, "No,
you don't have to do anything like that. Don't worry,
he'll start to talk to you. You just answer anything he
asks you." . . . The Light came up to me and he spoke
to me. He said, "Hello, and how are things down
there?" I think that's what he said to me. I said, "I
don't know, I'm only a fourteen-year-old schoolboy. I
don't know how things are."

As earlier noted, Hal's experience continued for a lot
longer. He asked a lot of questions while he was with the
Light and was later taken to the "archives," the site of all
knowledge.

For all of those who reached this transcendental environment, the wish to stay far outweighed any other consid-
erations. However, one way or another, they were all either
forced to return or more gently persuaded to do so.

INCREASE IN PSYCHIC PHENOMENA AFTER A NEAR-DEATH EXPERIENCE

Respondents were asked whether they believed in psychic
phenomena before their NDE and whether their attitude
had changed afterward. They were also questioned about
their experience of particular psychic phenomena. It
should be noted that in the following table the number of
subjects varies slightly for individual items. This is be-

cause those respondents who had not heard of, or thought about, various phenomena by the time of their NDE were eliminated from the analysis.

This table summarizes the percentage of near-death experiencers who responded positively to questions regarding psychic experiences and associated belief before and after their NDE. Comparison is made with results from a

Experience	General population	Before NDE (% NDErs)	After NDE (% NDErs)
clairvoyance	38(USA)	38	71
telepathy	58(USA) 36(GB)	42	86
precognition	n.a.	49	86
déjà vu	n.a.	73	85
supernatural rescue	n.a.	25	73
intuition	n.a.	54	92
dream awareness	42(USA)	44	79
out-of-body experience	14(USA) 12(GB)	8	49
spirits	27(USA) 26(GB)	22	65
healing ability	n.a.	8	65
perception of auras	5(USA)	13	47
Belief			
psychic phenomena	39(Sweden)	55	98

Note: *All differences between percentages before and after NDE are significant at p<.001 except for déjà vu.*

number of general population studies. The country of origin of the particular general population survey quoted is noted in brackets where appropriate.

The results presented above show that percentages of the general population answering positively to these items are comparable to percentages of my subjects before their NDE, evidence of the "normality" of my sample in this regard. Significant increases following NDEs were found for all items except déjà vu. Greyson also found the increase in déjà vu not to be statistically significant. A number of respondents noted that the incidence of déjà vu was greater when they were children, although they still experienced the phenomenon now.

Before their NDE only twenty-four people had a general belief in psychic phenomena. This means, of course, that twenty-six of the sample did not believe that psychic phenomena could happen. This figure is not entirely surprising since ten of the respondents had had no experience of psychic phenomena at all, and another six had had no experience apart from déjà vu before their NDE. For example, Mel said that had I asked him such a question before his experience he would have been outraged and said: "No, certainly not! What are you talking about, lady? What do you think I am, queer or something? Certainly not!" Yet after his experience, Mel now says: "I do it all the time, I live there."

Since the NDE, all but Albert believe psychic phenomena can happen. In Albert's case this disbelief is interesting, since later in the interview he reported experiences of telepathy with his wife, déjà vu and even a remarkable supernatural rescue. Yet this sort of ambivalence is not isolated to his case. For example, Mel later said, when talking about auras, "I have seen them but can't draw them up on order. I have trouble believing that stuff but I have actually seen them."

CLAIRVOYANCE

Among this sample of near-death experiencers, eighteen people had had at least one experience of clairvoyance before their NDE, but afterward, thirty-four of them reported such experiences. For example, Anthea reported a very early experience:

> As a child I had what I realize now were clairvoyant experiences, although at the time I couldn't label them. I was aware very much of my own "third eye." And also when I was about two years of age I had an experience when I was told that when I grew up and got married I was going to have a baby girl and she would die. [She did have a baby girl and she did die.] I also saw my husband when I was a child and when I saw him in real life I recognized him straightaway.

Since her NDE, Anthea says that her episodes of clairvoyance have increased markedly. In fact, she now uses her ability in her work as a psychic healer. She gives psychic readings, works with doctors in healing and was even involved in a project with historians getting information on the early foundations of Australian history, which led them to archives and manuscripts for confirmation.

Harriet noted that before her NDE she had never had any psychic experiences but since then she had had quite a few. An example of clairvoyance that she gave had occurred about ten years before. She said:

> I was visiting my son and his wife and there was a friend of theirs there. I'd never met her, she was a foreign lady, and apparently she could read jewelry. And she asked if I would like her to read mine. I said, "No thanks," and then my daughter said, "Mom's a bit—!" And this lady laughed and said,

"That's interesting, can you tell me anything about myself?" I'd never met the girl or heard anything about her. And I told her that I could see a number 9. "That's all I can see when I look at you." And she said, "That's strange, I've just bought a house and it's number 9, I haven't moved into it yet. Can you tell me anything about it?" I said, "It's a single-fronted with a long hall. It's red brick with green paint around the windows and doors." And she said, "That's right." You know, it's only ever happened a couple of times, for some reason. I don't know why.

TELEPATHY

Before their NDE, twenty-one respondents said they had had an experience of telepathy. However, following their NDE, forty-three of them claimed to have experienced telepathy. This ranged from telepathic exchange between people who were close, such as spouses or children, to being able to "read the minds" of strangers. This was a facility that several respondents said they found burdensome. For example, Ben found soon after his experience that he could read people's minds but, when, as a naive teenager, he demonstrated his skill, he soon found that it was socially unacceptable. For his own peace of mind he has since worked at suppressing it. He said:

I try to shield myself from the mental noise of other people. To hear someone else's mental chatter is a rather painful experience, because often their mind's in such a mess, it's such an unholy noise. I'd rather listen to a jackhammer.

PRECOGNITION

Twenty-four respondents (forty-nine percent) said they had had at least one experience of precognition before their NDE, whereas forty-two of them (eighty-six percent) experienced precognition after their NDE. Michael gave an example that is reminiscent of an interchange between the queen and Alice in Lewis Carroll's *Through the Looking-Glass,* when the queen began screaming *before* she pricked her finger.

Michael related that:

Sometimes I'll jump before I hear a loud bang. I've done it at work heaps. There'll be a really loud bang and I'll finish my jump before it actually happens. People sort of look at you and go "ooh!" Sometimes I just know things are going to happen and they do.

Barry noted that his precognitive episodes usually had to do with natural disasters. For example, he said:

Yes, earthquakes used to bother me a tremendous lot. They haven't lately but I used to know there was going to be an earthquake somehow. Sure enough, the morning after, I'd hear there'd been an earthquake in San Francisco or somewhere.

Some experiences are very commonly reported. For example, Bill noted that he often knows that a certain person is going to call him, and then the telephone rings. Others said they might have been thinking of someone they hadn't seen for a long time, and then receive a letter or a visit from that person. Harriet mentioned an often-expressed feeling that is somewhat related to precognition. She said:

I never worry about having lots of money, I never worry about thinking that I'll need something be-

cause I know it will be there anyway. Somehow or
other it always is.

She also told of a frightening precognitive episode that
came to her during a dream. She said:

> The worst one I had was about my grandson. He was
> up here for the school holidays. He was about eight
> and his mother was going away to the coast and tak-
> ing the children with her. And for some reason I had
> had this terrible dream a couple of nights before about
> Dean drowning and it was so vivid, I saw the face and
> everything. . . . I didn't know what to say to her. I just
> said to her, "Watch Dean near the water, be careful
> near the water." And I worried the whole time they
> were away. And two weeks later, when they came
> home, the phone rang, and it was Dean. "Nana, we're
> home!" And I said, "Did you have a nice holiday?"
> He burst into tears and he said, "I nearly drowned!"
> And then a couple of weeks later, the mother came
> around to show me the photos, and there it was ex-
> actly as I'd seen it. And she said to me, "That's the
> spot where Dean nearly drowned." And I said, "I
> know." And I told her what had happened. A couple
> of other things have happened, and yet they'd never
> happened to me before I was near-death.

In some cases precognitive flashes or visions are among
the most difficult of phenomena to deal with. For example,
in Harriet's case above, what could she do about what she
foresaw? Olivia said that she had often wondered why she
had to experience such events, especially the more har-
rowing ones. She recounted her precognitive vision of the
Mount Erebus disaster:

> I was at a circle meeting and the whole evening every
> time I tried to go into meditation all I could get was

a plane floundering through white, which was snow. And right at the end of the evening I went very deeply in and it was all white. For a moment I saw the tail of the plane with the symbol for Air New Zealand. . . . And for a moment, and this wasn't very pleasant, this is where I broke off from it, I think I was depressing everybody else there. For a moment there was the wreckage of the plane, the jagged metal and what have you. And a hand came up, reached up just above his face, and it was a man's hand with a ring with a black stone . . . and as it reached up it just fell down again, and there was blood trickling down between his fingers. This wasn't very pleasant, and it was a little bit too much for me at that time, and I wasn't really happy with it so I broke off. All that night every time I closed my eyes the whole thing came rushing back in again. The woman who ran the circle actually rang Air New Zealand to tell them, and they absolutely pooh-poohed it. In the morning my husband phoned me and said I've just heard the news, and the details fit in exactly. There have been a lot more since then, but they're not pleasant because you can't do anything.

SUPERNATURAL RESCUES

Supernatural rescues are phenomena, by contrast, that are usually welcomed. Before their NDEs only twelve of my sample had experienced such an event. However, since their NDEs, thirty-five of them (seventy-three percent) had now had one or more of these experiences. Some respondents spoke of rescues as though they were a simple extension of the guidance discussed in the previous chapter. That is, they saw them in an everyday context as well as in the more dramatic moments of life. Helen said that she has them "all the time, incredibly so, my boys can't believe it at times, you know, the things that happen." She recounted a rescue from a disastrous bus accident, when the whole side of a bus she was traveling in with two of her sons was wiped off by a semi-trailer. She and her boys were the only ones to escape uninjured. Another rescue was of the financial variety. She was divorced, living on a pension with her four sons and struggling financially, when a relative of her ex-husband whom she had not seen for twenty years died and left her a considerable sum of money.

Several respondents described hearing a voice ordering them to do something that ultimately saved them. For example, Martine recounted that she was driving back to Sydney from Byron Bay. There was a lot of traffic in both directions. She said:

> I was in a whole row of cars going this way and the other row was going toward Brisbane. And I saw from the corner of my eye a car coming toward me. And I heard that booming voice saying behind me: *"Stay in alignment!"* And I felt like I was in a capsule. I was in this sort of capsule, completely encased in it. And within seconds he gave me all sorts of instructions. And the other car came toward me and bounced back. It came straight for me, got my door, just scratched the back door and went back. And I didn't even feel a shudder. Nothing whatsoever. It could have been a whole big accident if I'd lost my head. And I didn't! I found it extraordinary that I could bounce that car back just through being completely aligned. We have to be just there and not worry about it. And I was in a capsule completely.

Juliet recounted that some years ago she had gone for a drive with a male friend. They were sitting in the car talking, overlooking the water:

And suddenly this voice screamed at me, *"Go Juliet, go!"* And I didn't question it, I just said, "We've got to go!" And Geoff immediately turned the ignition on and I looked through the window, and coming across, from four panel vans, were a group of guys with chains, tire levers, all that sort of stuff. Luckily Geoff didn't say, "Why, what's wrong," you know, he just immediately reacted and we took off. And then they chased us and they ran back to the panel vans and chased us in the vans. It was a hell of a drive out because they followed and tried to cut us off. It would have been death, I imagine. I feel I didn't have to go that way, you know. I was told to get moving and we moved! . . . It proves that if we listen, we'll be guided. This voice was like you sitting there and screaming at me, it was just so loud and it saved our lives.

DREAMS

Awareness of dreams was reported by twenty-one near-death experiencers before their experience, whereas thirty-eight of them reported a greater awareness and understanding of their dreams afterward. As already noted, dreams are sometimes the vehicle for precognitive visions. They can also provide answers to questions. For example, Anthea said she "gets direction" in her dreams. And Olivia said:

I've got to this stage where if I really have questions about something, I can go to bed, send the question out and ask for the answer to come to me during the night, and then go to sleep. And it will cut through a dream I'm having, and it will be symbolic or realistic, but the answer is there for me. And I wake up and I know that that's the answer. The answers are always nitty-gritty truths, they're not always what we want to hear . . . but they are always right.

Jennifer reported that she was also more aware of her dreams since her NDE, and that over the years she had often received warnings in her dreams. But in recent times she had become irritated by frequent episodes of "hearing strangers' conversations" in her dreams. She said:

> It annoys me really because I don't know them from a crow and they yab, yab, yabber away in my dreams, and I'm getting all their conversation, and I wish they'd just all go away. They're having very earnest conversations and I don't really want to be in them at all . . . cluttered with these strangers.

OUT-OF-BODY EXPERIENCES

Before their NDE, only four people had already had an out-of-body experience. Since their NDE, twenty-four of them claim to have been out of body at least once. These out-of-body experiences can happen either spontaneously or voluntarily. For example, Mel noted that he has out-of-body experiences a lot. He said:

> I call it third position. I can come out [of my body], go to your position and get some of your experience from there. Or I can put myself up there and observe the dance between us, and gather information. Then I can come back here with that new information. But that's not the same as that other out-of-body experience [during the NDE] because that was much more profound and powerful. This is something I contrive to do. But if you take it lightly, it's gonna bite, you're gonna get remorse. If you're not working from absolute personal integrity, you're gonna get problems.

Several others also spoke of doing it voluntarily. For example, Edwina said:

> I can sometimes, when I'm very in tune, push myself out to go and visit people, not just by telepathy, but actually sort of be there. But I do that only when it's very important, because I'm in trouble, or something like that. . . . Sometimes it'll happen without me even sort of expecting it, probably about once a month.

Cora, although she did not have an out-of-body experience during her NDE, said that since that time she has them "all the time." She said:

> Well, I can actually consciously take myself out of my body, so I can do that. And I'll do that for particular exercises. But say I've done a long yoga session and I relax, I actually leave my body, I can see my body and all sorts of things . . . I'm always still a bit surprised.

And Christina said:

> I have had out-of-body experiences since the NDE but not in the same way. If I meditate I can consciously move out of the body—but without the whooshing sound and the whiteness. It's very different.

Moira said that it happens to her when it is least expected. She described one episode:

> I know this sounds stupid. In real life I was walking down the street one day and I suddenly found myself out of my body. And I was thinking, how can this be, I'm still walking down the street, but I was a couple of paces behind. And I looked at myself from behind . . . and I saw every bit of myself and I thought, "Oh,

so that's how she looks" [laughs]. And it was as if I
was looking at somebody else, even though it was
myself, because I said "she." I didn't say "So that's
how *I* look." I was very aware then that the real
"me" was the "me" outside.

Janet described an important episode in her post-NDE life:

I lifted off out of my body and I actually flew up this
valley, and saw this huge cliff face, and I was thinking all sorts of things like, what am I being shown?
Then I saw the eucalypt trees, then I saw these oak
trees down here near the river, and I knew they
weren't Australian, so I was fairly confused what it
was about. And just when I started to get really
afraid of it—"How am I going to get back in my
body?" I was, zoom, back in. As soon as the fear set
in, that limited the whole experience and I was back
in my body really fast. And I said to Joe, "I don't
know where this place is but I'm sure I've just been
shown the place we're going to." It wasn't till No-
vember that the guidance told us it was up in the
mountains near Tumut. . . . When we came to Tumut
on December 26, 1982 we just followed our guidance and found the valley, and that's another whole
series of miracles.

Spirits

Only eleven respondents had had contact with spirits before their NDE, whereas thirty-two of them (sixty-five percent) had done so since their near-death episode. Several
of them related getting a fright when they saw or felt a
presence. Gary said that he had been walking through the
house at night when he felt that there was a presence close
to him. He said: "And then I felt this sensation of cold

down the side of my face, and I took off! I jumped about six feet and then took off!" Grace related that she had walked from the front of the house into the kitchen without turning on the lights. She said:

> As I walked in the door, my glance sort of went over toward the window and there was a man sitting there, I looked again and he was still there. And I sort of zipped into the kitchen, switched on the light and went there again, and of course there was nothing there. But it wasn't as though I'd just glanced over, I'd stood and stared. There was a big Indian vase there, so there couldn't possibly have been anyone in the window. And he had a hat on. Dad always used to wear a hat, but I thought, "Don't be stupid."

Jennifer is regularly visited by a young man she had been very close to many years ago (who died of cancer). Barry said he has a "spirit guide who is

> . . . a beautiful woman with a blue cape with a red lining, which I never made up my mind whether she was a nurse or a sister of mercy or, what the heck! She was always there when I got into trouble.

And Morris said that he is visited by a French nun

> . . . who comes in whenever there's any problems in life. She's very tall and very severe looking, but very friendly. She gives help to get out of situations. But not situations I make myself. I have to get out of those myself.

Finally, Eileen said:

> If somebody belonging to me is dying anywhere in Ireland, as you know we're 12,000 miles away, I can

tell you the exact minute they die. The minute my
father died, I knew. The second he died. He put his
hand on my shoulder, and I was in Queensland. If
somebody in Ireland dies, I hear a donkey braying.
And I can tell you exactly when they die. That's family only. With family only I can wake up and say,
"Now somebody's just died" because I can hear the
donkey braying. And yet people think I'm crazy
when I say that, but I can tell them exactly.

HEALING

Before their NDE only four people believed they had some
healing ability. However, now thirty-one of them (sixty-
five percent) claim to have a gift for healing in some form.
In many cases this is spasmodic, especially in terms of
physical healing. For example, Morris said he can heal
other people "by the laying on of hands. It amazes me. But
I can't do it always. The person has to be willing to help."
Gary, who works in a children's hospital making spinal
braces, said that he has been told that his hands emit a lot
of power. He noted that when he's fitting the braces, he
spends a lot of time close to the children. He said:

> You have to build up the trust. They'll just stand
> there and I'll talk to them and I'll rub their back. In
> actual fact some parents have told me their children
> have said that it has quite an amazing effect on them.
> It seems a natural thing to do because most of those
> children need some sort of sympathetic touch, not
> just sympathetic words, because touch is more pow-
> erful.

Mary has now worked as a healer for many years. She said:

> Well, what I do is classified as healing. People come

to me, usually when they've been given up on by the doctors. Their problems can be mental, spiritual, emotional or physical. What I do is channel healing energies that are there for anyone to use. But you can't go against the spirit of that person, it knows perfectly well what is needed and what's going to happen, but the conscious mind often doesn't. If the person is not open to healing, I just channel comfort, but if they are open to healing and there's no reason why they shouldn't be healed, I just channel the healing energy.

Ursula says that she often "picks up" other people's headaches and bad backs. She said: "When I recognize where it's coming from, it goes quickly."

A number of respondents mentioned the ability to heal themselves. Janet noted that she was rarely sick these days, whereas before her NDE she was always going to the doctor. She said: "Now if we need healing we do it ourselves. We've reached the point where we know we can ask for healing and expect to receive it."

A number of respondents mentioned their ability to heal psychologically rather than physically. They often spoke of having a knowledge of what is going on for people, a sensitivity to their needs, and an ability to counsel effectively. This capability was reported by the youngest respondent. Michael said:

I haven't had much experience healing other people's wounds or anything, but I'm very good at helping people, talking to them if they've got problems. I'm very good at that. I seem to know the right thing to say at the right time. I feel guided when I do it actually, although I don't think about it much.

Auras

Before their NDEs, only six respondents reported having
seen auras. Twenty-two of them claimed that since their
NDEs they have seen auras on one or more occasions.
Some have seen auras only once and had no clear idea of
what it meant. For example, Daphne said she saw an aura
once, many years ago, at the ballet.

Others claim to see auras regularly, or whenever they
want to. Olivia and Juliet both see auras whenever they
choose. They both described my aura during the interview.
And Ursula says she often sees auras. She gave a recent example of being with her father, who had been told there was
a problem with his heart. She said that she could see,
through the aura, that there was a problem in the head, so
she took him to a neurologist, and found there was indeed a
problem of blood not getting through the veins to the head.

Conclusion

Overall, then, it appears that there is a definite increase in
the presence of a wide range of psychic phenomena in people after a near-death experience. In response to another one
of the earlier suggested explanations for this phenomenon,
it should be noted that there was no specific question asked
to clarify whether near-death experiencers simply focused
more attention on psychic and psi-related phenomena after
their NDEs. However, it is evident from my data that there
is a great variety of responses to these psychic phenomena.
Some experiences seem to be absorbed into daily life and
accepted as normal, while others claim more recognition
due to their more disruptive nature. For example, those who
experience clairvoyant episodes (seventy-one percent) or
most kinds of precognitive flashes (eighty-six percent) seem
to take them in their stride, at times not even paying particular attention to them. On the other hand, those who have

out-of-body experiences (forty-nine percent) could be said to focus on them, since they are not easy to ignore, whether engaged in voluntarily or spontaneously.

There are, however, cases among the sample whose response to an increase in psychic sensitivity has been extreme. There are four women (aged forty-three to sixty-five) who before their NDE were respectively a school librarian, office worker and housewives, and now work with their psychic gift as healers. At the other extreme there are four men (aged fifty-six to sixty-five) who have put a brake on at least some of their psychic capabilities since they feel so uncomfortable with them. This does not mean that they have been able to eliminate them entirely from their lives, but they have managed to stop certain activities, such as going out of body and reading people's minds. The sex difference in these two extremes is worth noting and not entirely surprising considering the socialization of men and women in Western industrial settings. Almost every person I spoke to was aware of the increase in psychic phenomena in their lives, although the degree of this increase varied, and two respondents stated that they had not connected it with their NDE until the interview.

It is interesting to note that not one person mentioned the increase in psychic phenomena as the most significant change to come about as a result of their NDE. However remarkable these changes appear to have been, to focus simply on this aspect would therefore not adequately reflect the breadth of changes in the priorities of these people. Neither would it accurately reflect their principal focus, which is their focus on spiritual growth.

Changes in Life Direction

Changes in life direction following a near-death experience have frequently been noted in the literature. For example, Sabom writes that some of his respondents report that they consider the NDE to be the "peak" event, which has done more to shape the depth and direction of life goals and attitudes than any previous single experience.[1] And Ring notes that the NDE left many of his respondents feeling more positive, with a stronger sense of self-worth. Ring finds that experiencers tend to show a spiritual awareness and demonstrate a peaceful acceptance of life. He later summarizes:

> What is impressive is the power of the core experience to compel positive change. Its effect seems to be to reorganize the person's life around a new "center," which affords direction, purpose and energy. . . . [The experience] is, for many, a continuing, active force that seeks to manifest itself in life-affirming ways.[2]

The previous three chapters have largely focused on changing experiences, attitudes and beliefs with regard to death, religion and psychic phenomena. This chapter focuses on whether, and how, the various attitudes and beliefs expressed by near-death experiencers actually manifest in their daily lives. "By their fruits ye shall know them" (Matt. 7:16–20) is an apposite phrase here.

This chapter is divided into a number of sections, but it should be realized that they are all closely interrelated. For example, attitudes to self and others are considered first, but they are intimately related to changes in relationships, which follow. These three areas are also related to lifestyle choices such as smoking, drinking alcohol, exercising, choosing to seek alternative therapies or see a doctor. The experiencers make choices about a wide range of issues, including how they now wish to spend their leisure time, what they wish to study, how they wish to spend their working lives and what commitments they make to social issues. The interrelationship of all these aspects, in addition to those already discussed in previous chapters, provides a picture of who these near-death experiencers are, and gives some indication of their potential impact on many aspects of social life.

ATTITUDE TO SELF

Kenneth Ring notes that, overall, experiencers report a positive change in attitude to themselves. In the present study, a number of questions were included to test this result, loosely based on Ring's *Life Changes Questionnaire*. It should be noted that the number of respondents varies for each item. This is due to the reluctance of some to make a comparison with their pre-NDE attitudes, since they could not clearly remember. Overall, the answers showed a definite shift to a more positive view of self and strong sense of purpose and to a stronger commitment to an inner life and away from concern about what others think of them.

Self-Worth

In terms of self-worth, forty-one of the forty-seven respondents reported an increase the other six reported no change. None of my sample reported a decrease in self-worth following their NDE. Ring found a similar trend in his 1984 survey. With his smaller sample he found that there was an increase in self-worth reported by twenty-two of his respondents, no change by two, and a decrease in self-worth by the other two of the sample.[3]

An increase in self-worth had a major impact on the lives of many of the respondents in my sample. For example, Moira said:

> At the time of my experience I believed I was a nothing, that everybody else was far better educated than I. I was a very shy person in those days. Hard to believe now! [laughs] I was very shy, very diffident about my own skills. I had no skills really. I felt as if I was a downtrodden and underneath sort of person in those days, but I guess that was the way I'd been brought up. . . . But since then absolutely my whole life has changed. It's opened up and I've become more assertive and more aware of who I am.

And Mel said:

> Prior to the experience, my surface esteem was high, but that was only to cover up. But since the experience I feel myself to be more worthy.

Alexandra noted:

> I thought I had a sense of self-worth when I was a doctor, but now I can feel a sense of self-worth regardless of what I am doing. I realize I was probably pretty insecure unless I was in my doctor role. And

that didn't change overnight, but I was radically changed.

Anthea said:

I came to value myself a lot more. I felt that I was more worthy to be loved by myself.

Self-Understanding

Forty of the forty-five in my sample said that there had been an increase in self-understanding since their NDE. Ring similarly found that twenty-three of his twenty-six respondents claimed an increase in self-understanding.[4]

Bill said:

Self-understanding is never-ending work. I'm doing it all the time, same with the esteem, working at it all the time, accepting different things about myself, and doing something about it.

Lorenzo noted:

I'm more in peace with myself now. I don't plan big things anymore. Before I daydream all the time but now I happy, I do my daily chores. No more I want to do this, I want to do that. I am more resigned to what I am now.

Robert remarked:

Yes, it's taken some time to realize it but it's been for the better. It's made me more aware, and able to accept change in myself. I understand myself better these days. There's more spiritual awareness, and it seems to be getting stronger each day. It's just like growing. Now I feel I'm spiritually growing.

And Virginia explained:

> I think I have a better understanding of myself now
> and I can accept my lot. The reason why such low
> self-esteem happened was I couldn't accept my
> upbringing. I could not accept the family in which I
> was born. I could not accept it, I did not accept it, I
> rejected it completely. Now I can accept it, now I ac-
> cept my mother and have a genuine love for her,
> which of course reflects on yourself. I feel I have a
> better self-esteem than I did have. I suppose I'm
> kinder on myself than I was before. There is now an
> acceptance that I have a genuine need to contribute.
> Before, there wasn't that.

Solitude

Twelve of the seventeen NDErs who answered the next
question noted that they had an increased desire for solitude
since their experience. Alexandra noted that after her NDE

> I wanted more solitude. I didn't want to rush back
> into medicine. I mean, I never bought that whole
> medical trip ever again. That was finished for me.
> And that was pretty dramatic because I was then a
> very loyalist dyed-in-the-wool doctor. I withdrew
> from everyone, even from my mother for a time. I ac-
> tually went away for an entire year to a really weird
> guesthouse, where I lived with a mute. So I really
> withdrew. I wasn't physically very strong, and what I
> did during that year was to study comparative religion
> and feel myself hoping I could go to the Jung Insti-
> tute. I did a lot of yoga and tried to eat better.

Many years later Alexandra still values solitude, and regularly shares this with others by taking small groups of people on wilderness retreats.

Concern for Others' Opinions

Perhaps as a corollary of the higher self-esteem experienced by most respondents following their NDE, there is a decrease in concern with what others think of them. Seventeen of the twenty-one who answered the question made that claim. Ring's findings were similar, with seventeen claiming a decrease in concern, five claiming no change, and four claiming an increase.[5]

Barbara said that before her NDE she used to worry so much about what other people thought—that "it was torture"—but now that no longer happens. Cass also said that now she is not worried about it at all. Michael said:

> Yeah, I used to worry a lot. I used to have to wear the right clothes, puff out my chest for the girls, all that sort of thing. But I don't now. Vanity's gone out the window completely. You know I don't care anymore. I don't dress up or anything. I have a pretty laid-back attitude. I just sort of think that where I am now and what I'm doing now is just sort of a passing moment of time, so impressing someone else doesn't really matter, because, you know, tomorrow, it's not relevant.

Sense of Purpose

Thirty-two of the thirty-six who responded to this question said that since their NDEs they felt they had an increased sense of purpose in their lives. In Ring's sample, twenty-three of the twenty-six also made this claim.[6]

Al was one person who said that his sense of purpose had in fact "not changed in intensity" but was "much redirected." Christina, on the other hand, said that her sense of purpose had greatly increased, but she was not sure what she had to do yet. She said:

[The NDE] gave me the feeling that I had to do something but I'm still not sure what. I suppose what I'm doing is a part of that—the people I meet, the books about different subjects I read.

Greta also felt unsure of the purpose. She said: "Maybe it's to do something I haven't touched on yet. I've had a very strong urge to go back to singing. I think maybe that's it, because it's very strong."

Eileen has had a strong sense of purpose since her NDE, which has come to fruition in a remarkable way. She has established the Irish Welfare Bureau, which she runs without payment. She said:

They're my people. To me they're my people and I'm left here to do something for my people, and I'm doing it. And how long I last to do it I don't know. I've had a few heart attacks since, but I just get over them. I went to Adelaide two years ago, and ended up in Emergency, and they put an IV and everything in, and were for operating the next morning. And I said no, no, because I haven't got time, haven't got time. And the thing is, I'm not going to have something that's gonna kill me that quick because I'm not ready to go. The most important thing is what I've done for my people, what I have done for my people and what I intend to do for them. And if I ever go, and when I go, what's going to be left for them.

Grace said:

It wasn't my time, I had a mission, I was given a job to do. It's as simple as that. Up until then I was aimless, I was living for myself. I came back with a sense of purpose. I had a reason to *be*. I had a reason to do everything. Till then I'd never held a job down, I'd stuffed around and traveled all over the place and nothing meant anything. And after, it was just [click] completely different. It was like pulling up a shade, and looking outside or . . . I can't explain it.

ATTITUDE TO OTHERS

It is already clear from the voices above that changes in attitude to self can overflow quite naturally into major changes in attitudes to others.

Desire to Help Others

Twenty-nine of the thirty-seven respondents who answered the question claimed that their desire to help others had increased since their NDE. Ring found that twenty-three of his sample of twenty-six also reported an increase in helping others.[7]

Only Daphne claimed to have experienced a decrease in desire to help others after her NDE, but this was not immediate. Since her NDE she had worked for some years as a volunteer at a local hospital, but her attitude toward the patients had only recently begun to change. She said:

I used to feel compassion and want to help but lately I've changed a bit. I'd go up to the hospital and see patients who had cancer, etc. I used to look at them and feel sorry but then I'd think, and I don't want this to sound callous, but I'd think—look at you, if only you'd changed your attitude, changed your mind, and got rid of all the hate and resentment out of your body, and didn't get yourself into this helpless state, maybe you wouldn't be here with your bypasses, etc.

In contrast, as already noted above, Eileen's desire to help others has become a major feature of her life since her NDE. I asked her to describe a typical day for me. She said:

> I'm a cleaner. I get up in the morning at five o'clock and I drive three old men to work in the city. They're, well, they're in their late 60s, tippin' 70s, and I've got them working in the city on jobs and it keeps them young, you know. And then I leave them to work and I go to an old lady's flat then and I get her up and get her a cup of tea and make sure she's organized for the day. And then I start work at the hospital at six o'clock, till half past ten. I am a qualified nurse myself but to go back to nursing I have to work shift work and I can't fit the Bureau [Irish Welfare Bureau] in with that, so I am a cleaner at the hospital and I find that I get enough money just to survive on. You don't need a big position to survive. You just need enough money to survive on. And then I come back here to the Bureau at twenty to eleven, and I run this office till six, ten, twelve o'clock at night, you know, and it's a pretty busy little organization. I do Monday, Tuesday. I do the hospitals and the prisons visiting on a Wednesday, and anyone that's sick at home and needs help or things, or if I've got to go to government departments, I make sure that's all done on a Wednesday. And then Thursday, Friday and Saturday I'm here. . . . Oh, yes, and I go to an average of two or three funerals a week, and I always comfort them and tell them people that have lost their loved ones that "Never cry them back because they're gone to a better place." And this really is, this is only the waiting room. You're only passing through here anyway.

Although the example of Eileen is perhaps the most extreme, it would be possible for me to choose quotations from almost any transcript to illustrate the same level of commitment to others. For example, Denise said: "Well, most of my interests are involved in helping others, and it's not that it's deliberate, but it's just like that." And Alexandra said that although she wanted to help others after her NDE, she did not feel ready to do so for a couple of years. However, she described what she does now:

I think that people need what I call resources or knowledge. I don't call myself an analyst so much as a teacher of the ways of the psyche, because I think my job is to get people to go, study, follow their own interests, not me just tell them what to do. But you know it's a kind of a way of leading people out, like true education, you know, to draw out, but not to talk too much. You have to sometimes inspire people first, but then when they're up and going, then leave them to go for themselves.

And Harriet described her willingness to share her life with numerous homeless boys. She said:

I found that as my children grew up, it doesn't seem as if we've ever had an empty house. There always seemed to be somebody on the doorstep. My mother always said other people collect stray dogs but I collected stray boys. We always seemed to have a boy living here—one on probation, one who'd run away from home, a Chinese-Malaysian student who thought I ran a boardinghouse because he'd heard about these boys that kept coming in. I picked one up off the street one day, and he looked so wet and bedraggled. Things like that, I'm more conscious of it. Whereas perhaps before I would have driven past, or I would have said no to some of those. But now they just keep coming.

Compassion and Empathy

There was a marked increase in compassion reported by thirty-one out of forty respondents, and in empathy and understanding of others (twenty-nine out of thirty-six). Ring found an even more definite pattern with twenty-five out of twenty-six claiming to be more compassionate and twenty-four out of twenty-six claiming to be more understanding.[8]

Martine has found her compassion to be rather overwhelming at times. She said: "Now I'm learning not to be so emotional, to help people, but without me getting so into it." And Patrick said: "I feel compassion except with very hard, stiff-necked people. I feel sorry for them, mind you."

Grace related the way this sensitivity has helped her in her job. She said:

> I'm a personnel consultant and I have a reputation for being very different from other consultants—very, very empathetic. Without people telling me, I seem to understand what they're trying to say. And that's not trumpet sounding, but just an understanding. I think I get more out of what I'm doing because I'm helping. I'm doing something for other people rather than just doing something for me. Since the NDE I didn't just grow up, it was like the fabric of my being was rewoven.

And Kate said:

> Since my NDE I've wanted to help others, and I've had a real compassion. I'm sure I am so much nicer, a much nicer person. I'm sure I like myself better.

Tolerance

Twenty-three out of thirty-five respondents claimed to be more tolerant of others following their NDE, eight said there was no change in their level of tolerance and four said their tolerance had decreased. Ring's results were more definite. Of his sample of twenty-six, twenty-two claimed to be more tolerant and four said there had been no change.[9]

Tessa explained that "tolerance" was a lesson she was currently working on:

> I'm not very tolerant but I try to accept that a lot of people can't do things. I try to understand why my son drove into a semi-trailer one week after finishing high school, and gave himself massive brain damage.... If I hadn't had that experience [the NDE] I don't know how I would have coped with him unconscious for three months, paralyzed down one side, speech incoherent. I was intolerant of sickness. That's why his illness was sent to me—to make me more tolerant of disabled people.

Ruby noted: "I do lose patience at times, I believe people make things too complex." On the other hand, Anthea said: "I'm incredibly more patient and tolerant. I used to be very impatient with people but now I find myself, oh, very patient."

Expressions of Love

Twenty-two out of thirty respondents reported having an increased ability to express love since their NDE, while eight claimed there had been no change. Ring found that all twenty-six of his sample claimed an increase in love for others.[10]

Anthea said, "I'm much more loving toward people. I genuinely love people. I find it easy to express love but I find it very hard to receive love." And Edwina said:

> I have compassion for everything and everyone, and

it's like overwhelming love, but not love that needs. You know, that sort of *unconditional* love. Understanding unconditional love is one of the greatest things. That would be the most lovely thing that I could teach everybody if I could. You know, even just give them an essence of one second of the feeling of unconditional love, that's what I would like. And that one second can often be enough to make them want to go back and find out how to get there themselves.

And Bill said:

I like to have a nice attitude to people. I like to be as calm as I can around people. I like to give as much love as I can, and I like to give it to people who annoy me! And that's a real turnaround for me.

Twenty-five out of thirty-four respondents said that since their NDE they experienced an increased acceptance of others as they are. For example, Barbara said:

When I was a girl I was critical, very critical and judgmental. But now I can meet somebody and really look at them and really appreciate their beauty and see them. I've changed a lot.

Eileen gave an illustration:

I get alcoholics and drug addicts, I get people in here that nobody else would touch. And they come in smelly and dirty and filthy and I'll bring them downstairs and throw them in the shower, I'll get the toilet brush and I'll scrub them. And other people wouldn't touch them, and it doesn't bother me.

Insight into Others' Problems

Twenty-three out of thirty-two respondents claimed to have an increase in insight into the problems of others since their NDE. Ring found that twenty-two of his sample of twenty-six made a similar claim.[11]

Bronwyn said that her insight had increased noticeably since her NDE but that it was still developing. And Barbara said:

> I can easily pick up how a person feels. I pride myself that my insight on one to one in a group of people is pretty right, accurate. And that's increased.

Ben remarked that although he had insight into people's problems he had become aware that it was not possible to help anyone who was not willing to be helped. And Kate said:

> I can get very close to people, very close. And often I'll find myself just saying to someone something that is absolutely the guts of whatever it is that is happening. And suddenly the person in front of me just starts to cry, or whatever, because I'd hit that button. And I really find myself trying to be careful about that. It's not always the right thing, is it?

Thus overall, after an NDE, experiencers tend to become much more compassionate and tolerant of others. They show greater sensitivity and insight, and their commitment to helping others is demonstrated in a wide variety of ways. The next section examines their own close relationships.

Changes in Relationships

In view of their positive loving attitudes and actions toward a "generalized other," it is interesting to explore how close personal relationships work for near-death experiencers. In the literature there has hardly been a mention of this aspect of post-NDE life, although in some personal accounts there have been suggestions that fitting in pre-NDE personal relationships with post-NDE priorities can be problematic. For example, Barbara Harris wrote:

> I had two experiences that have drastically altered my sense of reality. . . . They changed my relationship with my family and to the planet. My new sense of oneness with and love for the planet became a wall in my marriage. I've spent the last nine years trying to understand what happened to me.[12]

She later quotes Elaine, who said:

> It's very difficult for your partner to understand that you become a very giving individual. Your partner is usually still in a very materialistic realm, and materialistic things just don't matter to you.[13]

At this stage it may be useful to consider the marital status of the sample population and then reports of strain in relationships with spouse/partner, family and friends following an NDE. It should be remembered that there were ten respondents in the sample under the age of seventeen at the time of the NDE (all of whom were unmarried at that time). Five of these were still single when interviewed.

Perhaps the most noticeable feature of the results is the major increase in the number of divorced people following the NDE. Twenty-six of the subjects were married when they had their NDE and only three were divorced. By the time of the interview only twenty were married and eighteen were separated or divorced. These figures, however, provide a conservative view of the number of divorces in this population since, by the time of the interview, a number of others had in fact been divorced and remarried. In fact, there was a change of status in twenty-eight cases.

To phrase it another way, there were only twenty-two people who did not change their marital status (eleven remained married to the same partner; four remained in the same de facto relationship; six remained single; and one was widowed). Of the twenty-six who were married at the time of their NDE, fourteen were subsequently divorced and one was widowed. Of the sixteen who were single at the time of their NDE, six remained single, eight were married and, of these, four were subsequently divorced.

Obviously in a general population there is always a percentage of the population who gets divorced. According to the Australian Values Study Survey, eleven percent of the Australian population has been divorced. This is much lower than the divorce rate of thirty-six percent in this population of NDErs. In addition, there are usually many different precipitating factors in a divorce. However, in this sample population almost all ascribed their divorce *primarily* to the aftereffects of their NDE.

Strain in Relationships

Twenty-three of thirty-four respondents reported a strain in the relationship with their spouse or partner following their NDE, which resulted in seventeen cases of divorce or broken engagement. Bronwyn is one person whose relationship did not break up, but she described her situation as being one of "incredible strain." She said: "I couldn't talk to him about it [NDE] even though he was there when it happened."

More commonly, however, relationships did collapse under the strain, especially when the spouse did not want, or was not able, to understand what had happened during the NDE. An additional strain was often felt when the spouse attempted to stop the experiencer from "doing what they had to do." For example, Ruby said:

> Yes, there was a lot of strain in my relationship with my husband after that. He didn't want to know about it so I withdrew and let him do his thing and I did what I wanted to do. Our marriage started to break down when he wanted to be the boss and put pressure on me not to do the things I needed to do.

Eileen described her situation:

> I found that I had outgrown my husband. I found that he was too slow for me. He wasn't moving with me, and that's exactly what I found. My life was going too fast and there was too many demands on my life. I found like I was being smothered, I was supposed to do this and that and I wasn't able to do what I had to do and I knew I had to do.

Cora said:

> I divorced probably two years after that. Not very long. And I do remember it [NDE] having a tremendous effect on our relationship. I remember looking up at him, he came home from work and he was angry because I still wasn't up and about. And I remember him looking down at me, and me just looking up and thinking: "There's no way you'll understand it and there's no way I could ever let you know." And I think in a way that was a turning point. Well, it carried on for a couple of years, pretending.

In Anthea's case, the NDE precipitated a career change, and in the ensuing upheaval her relationships were much affected. When asked if there was any strain in her relationships after her NDE, she answered:

> Oh, absolutely! That's what broke my marriage up. I knew that I had to keep growing. I knew that I had to find out more and I also knew I had to give more. The more I discovered, the more I had to give. So it meant I had to change my career. So I left teaching and tried to find an outlet for the knowledge that I had gained. And I found it very difficult to find an acceptable profession where I could pass on my truths without it being too strange. So the best I could do was to look into alternate methods and hypnotherapy which gave me a label that meant people could relate to me under that sort of banner. And once that happened, I was able to use my gifts which I feel were a result of that near-death experience. Everybody thought I'd gone quite peculiar because I'd left the security after fifteen years teaching, and I felt quite lost myself while I was redirecting my energy. So my parents thought I was quite irresponsible and my husband and children didn't understand what I was doing.

Only two respondents, Cass and Janet, described an improvement in their relationship with their spouse following the NDE. Cass said this followed an initial period of strain, but in Janet's case it was immediate. Janet, who was told during her NDE to share it with her husband, said:

> Our relationship has really strengthened through the NDE. I think because of the fact that we both became aware that we had a job to do.

Shana was engaged to be married at the time of her NDE, but afterward she called the engagement off. She said:

> Well, after that I didn't want to get married anymore.

I mean, I didn't want to live that life. I came back and I didn't know *how* to be, but I didn't want to be how I was. It was a case of "I don't know what I want but I don't want this."

Tessa's case is interesting since she married following her NDE, but her divorce was still precipitated by NDE after-effects. The problems began when she told her husband about her NDE and, as she said: "I got the wrong answer." She tried to pursue a more spiritual life but constantly faced his opposition. She said:

When I started going to yoga he said it's all mumbo-jumbo, and I was going around with those nutty friends, which I really wasn't at all. I mean, gosh, you can go to an adult education class on yoga, can't you, and nobody says you're all a lot of nuts going there. [So] I dropped it. It was hard to sort of keep things like that when you've got kicks and knocks at home, and being told you were nutty. Nobody likes to be told that sort of thing. And that's when I think I just sort of rebelled against it. Eventually I just thought, well, I've got to live my own life, and if someone doesn't like it, they're not going to stop me.

Twenty-four of thirty-eight respondents said they experienced strain in their relationships with other family members following their NDE. Barbara, who had her experience as a child, described her relationship with her family following her NDE:

After that I always felt, always felt with my family that my family were there and I was over here. Always. I suppose that was coming back from where I'd been. I never felt part of the family. . . . I didn't like being different, but I was and I knew I was.

Olivia recounts the difficulty she had in sharing her experience with her brother:

> My brother is a brilliant man, he's a mathematician. But [after the NDE] when he was younger, he couldn't understand the concept at all, because he's so logical. I went over [to New Zealand] last year and we sat up talking for four nights till between two and three in the morning, and he said, "Explain it to me, I want to understand, I want to feel it, I think I need to feel it, explain it to me." And I can get through to so many people, but I couldn't get through to him. It was very exasperating.

And Patrick said:

> I think when you have these experiences, you don't actually fit into the mold of everybody's thinking. You're sort of released from the common mind, if you like. But if you meet someone who's had one of these experiences you have a direct brother/sister approach immediately, which you sometimes haven't got with blood relationships. My brother was very dear to me, but in this sort of thing we were poles apart.

In terms of relationships with friends, twenty-seven of thirty-five respondents experienced strain, and this resulted in twenty-one cases in major changes in friendship networks. A few mentioned how lonely this could be. For example, Kate said that there was strain in relationships with friends:

> In the sense that suddenly you grew, you know, to be about twenty times bigger than you were, and so that your whole attitude and knowledge and everything, is just so increased that you leave people behind.

And it's hard because it's lonely. But I couldn't help it, and I certainly wasn't turning back.

And Anthea said:

I found that a lot of the friends that had been very necessary for me were no longer necessary so I just stood away. Also, now I find it very lonely, because I can't have really close relationships with people.... It's just that all of my energies go into the work I'm doing and what's left over I have to give to my family. So I have an isolated life in terms of friendship, which is very sad in a way, but I get a lot of loving support from the people I work for.

Bill, Lou and Virginia all said that they had no friends at the time of the NDE, but that now they each have a network of close friends who are on the same path. Others made similar comments about their new friends. For example, Ursula said she made different friends following her NDE, who are "more in step" with her ongoing spiritual development. Moira noted that before her NDE she never felt good enough for anyone. She said she used to think:

Why would anyone like me? But [the NDE] has given me an inner strength, and now I've built wonderful friendships and that's a very strong part of my life, wonderful friends.

Janet recounted that after the NDE

We changed our whole direction and our mode of living. We lost a lot of friends for a while there because they thought we'd gone religious or something, until they found that we weren't really out there Bible bashing or going to church, but we were living something that they were quite amazed about. . . .

So, interestingly, a lot of our older friends who thought we had gone a bit funny at first are gradually coming back. And they are actually quite interested in what we do.

It is clear, then, that relationships with spouses, family and friends can undergo a lot of strain following an NDE. It appears that the personal strength and sense of purpose gained during the experience can propel the experiencer into a way of life that is totally unanticipated in their closest relationships. In addition, there can be an associated sense of urgency that transcends any previously established personal bond. Obviously this can be a shock to the person "left behind" but it can be almost as disturbing and overwhelming to the near-death experiencer. It seems that the person who "comes back" after an NDE is often not the same person who "departed." Quite apart from the experience itself, the changed attitudes, beliefs and priorities of the experiencers mean that their daily lives are deeply affected.

ATTITUDE TO LIFE

Kenneth Ring found that near-death experiencers appreciate life more fully and have little interest in impressing others or accumulating material wealth for its own sake. To test this result, some of Ring's questions from the *Life Changes Questionnaire* were included in the initial interview.

The answers showed a marked shift away from materialistic values and impressing others, and toward greater appreciation of life and interest in spiritual matters.

Material Success

Thirty-eight of the forty-two respondents who answered this question noted that their interest in material success had decreased since their NDE. Four people reported no change. This is a stronger trend than in Ring's results, where thirteen reported a decrease in interest in material success and thirteen reported no change.[14] In another question Ring asked about "concern with the material things of life." His results here are more comparable with mine: nineteen reported a decrease and seven no change.[15] Since my questions were open-ended, both aspects of "materialistic attitudes" were usually touched on by my sample.

Following their NDE, several experiencers left lucrative careers to fulfill themselves in other ways. For example, Alexandra said:

> Although it was a bit hard at the beginning, it was such a relief to get out of medicine. I didn't have my former ambition, my whole ambition to be comfortable and well-off. I mean, that was just turned upside down, and I don't know whether it had to be but it was, it happened.

And Edwina said:

> If I wanted material success I wouldn't have given up law. I mean, I could earn hundreds of thousands of dollars a year, in about four or five years, in the corporate law scene I've been in, but I know it would kill me. As you can tell, I'm not really into possessions, more into a lot of old junk [laughs], but not material possessions.

Others are similarly unconcerned by material things. For example, Martine said: "I'm not motivated by money as long as I don't have to starve and have enough to buy my books, these sorts of things." And Mary remarked: "I've given away all my material things. I would work hard for money only for a specific purpose, like going overseas." And Ursula said:

Material success is not important. The financial situation will always right itself. We will always have what we want. I don't live a lavish lifestyle but everything is provided that we need. If life unfolds the way it should, all will be provided.

Lou reflected on his past attitude. He said: "In the past I always wanted to be wealthy and well known, but that was just fantasies. Now that's not important."

It is interesting, in view of their lack of attachment to material goods, to note how comfortably most near-death experiencers live. It seems that, as they often say, their needs are abundantly fulfilled. They appreciate the abundance in their lives whether it be material or spiritual, yet there is no attachment to material possessions. If the need arises, they are able to leave it all behind. Olivia described her experience:

I'd always had lovely homes, and they were very important to me. The material things in life were very important to me, up until my experience. After this I literally, within five years, walked away from everything, and I left everything behind. The funny thing was that most of it came back to me later anyway, but it didn't matter. It was a wrench on the physical level, but another part of me knew it didn't matter. Even things that had been given to me, that had sentimental value, they weren't important. Other things were far more important.

And Kate described how, after her NDE, she found her attitude had changed. She said:

I do remember lying there, thinking, and saying to everyone who came to see me, "Whatever I think, I have not thought of a *thing*, I have thought only of people." It's only relationships. If I never walk into the house again, I have not thought of a *thing* about it. And I think in that sense I was fortunate to have had the NDE so I really knew what was important.

As Ring notes: "Matter is not what matters."[16]

Desire for Fame

Seventeen out of twenty experiencers in my sample said they had a decreased desire to be well known following their NDE. The other three claimed no change. Once again this is a stronger effect than is shown in Ring's sample, where twelve said they had a decreased desire to be well known, twelve claimed no change and two claimed an increase.

Martine said:

I'm not interested in fame, no. I was recognized when I did my pottery but I must not have wanted it somehow because I never pushed it enough. I seemed to back away from it. As soon as I came to a certain stage I backed away from it. It's like, that's not the answer.

Nature and Ordinary Things

There was a strong increase in appreciation of nature and the ordinary things in life. Thirty-seven out of forty-five respondents claimed an increase in appreciation of nature and nineteen out of twenty-four reported an increased enjoyment of the ordinary things. Ring's findings are similar, with twenty-three out of twenty-six claiming increased appreciation of nature and twenty-four reporting increased appreciation of ordinary things.[17] Bill, when asked whether he had an appreciation of nature, said:

Oh, I never stop appreciating that one!

(Is that different from the way it was before your NDE?)

> Oh, my word, it is! Going underwater in the Barrier Reef recently, and seeing the most beautiful fish, I thought, "This is incredible!" And seeing things grow, and how life is going on in clams!

Paula said:

> Now I feel very peaceful when I'm with nature. I have a very strong bond there, to the point that I feel I communicated with a tree once, a tree that was in desperate need of watering. It was like mental telepathy with that plant. I went out there and it was desperate for water. I just feel so close to animals and nature.

Several others mentioned this ability to communicate with nature. Christina spoke of her communication with birds and animals and Moira found she had a particularly strong bond with trees. She said:

> I have a great affinity with trees because my grandest, most wonderful experience was with trees. I'm aware that every plant, every tree, everything has a consciousness of its own, and that we are one with it, if we only knew. And we can communicate in a way with them. I mean, we're self-knowing, the tree isn't self-knowing, but we are one.

And Shana said:

> I think I always had an appreciation of nature, but after [the NDE] I became much more conscious of it, much more conscious of the living world, that everything is all conscious.

Shana has found that she can communicate with dolphins

and is in the process of setting up a center on the coast of New South Wales to work with them. She described how she became involved with them:

> Well, six years ago [1983] they came into my head in a dream, thousands of them. I mean, I didn't have a clue, and every time I closed my eyes they'd come into my head. And within a week people'd given me all sorts of information. And I thought, warm-blooded, air-breathing animals just like us, with a bigger brain, and all that sort of stuff, so I became quite interested. And then I went to New York and dolphins kept coming into the work I was doing, and I thought this was really bizarre. And on the way back I saw a dolphin and thought, "What's this all about?"
>
> So now I'm setting up a center on the coast at Sandy Beach, a giant undertaking but it's all going smoothly. There's always enough money to cover what is needed there. . . . Through working with dolphins in Florida I found that the autistic and hospice people are helped by them.

Michael described his close affinity with the natural world:

> Now I go bushwalking a lot by myself because I tend to get the same feeling as when I was above the surf. I feel sort of, you know, at one with everything. I can get that same feeling in the bush by myself. It's only sort of very brief, but it's worth it. . . . I can communicate on a feeling level. It's sort of hard to explain but, I don't know what it is.

And Mary said:

> Oh, I do appreciate nature, and people, in fact the whole of life. To look at somebody's garden, or just

to smell a rose. I've always been pretty much in tune
with nature, but it's deepened since the NDE.

Olivia noted that since her NDE she has had "a greater appreciation of nature and beauty and peace, definitely." And
finally, when Anthea was asked whether her appreciation
of nature had increased since her NDE, she answered:
"Oh, absolutely yes, definitely! And a real appreciation of
how everything is so intricate and so valuable and so beautiful."

Interest in Spiritual Matters

Thirty-six out of thirty-nine respondents reported an increased interest in spiritual matters since their NDE. The
other three reported no change. This shift in values would
already be obvious from the results presented earlier.

Robert described the way in which his spiritual awareness had increased and enhanced his understanding of
himself since his NDE. He said:

There's a spiritual awareness of, I mean, it's not a religious feeling, there's just a more spiritual awareness of yourself, and it seems to build. It gets
stronger each day. It's something you can't describe,
but you feel you're getting stronger in it every day.
It's just as if you're growing again, you know. I feel
as if I'm spiritually growing where before I'd
stopped, if you understand what I mean. Don't know
if I sound silly or not, but that's how it is for me.

LIFESTYLE CHOICES

Further changes in life direction are evident in the choices
near-death experiencers make about their lifestyle. As already suggested, an improvement in self-image, changes in

relationships and general changes in attitude to life all provide a context within which these choices are made.

Diet

Thirty-four out of forty respondents noted that they were more conscious of their diet since their NDE, and the other six reported that there had been no change. Three of them commented that their change in diet was not related to the NDE as such, but to their heart complaints. However, the majority saw their change in awareness of what they ate as being related to the greater respect they felt for their physical being as the vehicle of their soul, following their experience. Four of them are now vegetarian. For example, Grace said:

> I hate animals being killed, because every time an animal is killed for food, it's murder. There's no doubt about it. It *is* murder. To eat the flesh of another creature—I'm very against it. I used to go fishing, but I can't even do that anymore.

Several others reported that they rarely ate meat at all these days and had cut out red meat in particular. For example, Juliet commented that she never ate red meat but admitted ruefully to a weakness for cakes and sweets. And Bill said:

> I used to eat steak nearly every day. Now I eat tuna, deep-sea fish. I relate to the oils in the fish that are so good for you. Lots of salads, fruit and vegetables—just everything in balance.

Anthea noted:

> I found myself through no conscious will eating less meat and it wasn't something I set out to do. I just

found that I couldn't tolerate meat in the same way. Especially red meat.

Several remarked that the changes were noticeable but had been gradual. For instance, Alexandra said: "The NDE started me and it continued gradually." And Cora said: "There have been gradual changes to diet, major changes. My whole life is completely different now."

Moira recounted:

I am paying much more attention to what I eat, much more attention. I eat good food now. I'm still a devil with cream cakes though [laughs]. But I don't eat all the rubbish that I used to eat and I'm very careful, you know, I don't cook with fat and I don't bother with gravies, and I really have taken a step there.

Janet summarized a common feeling: "I think that really our whole lifestyle is just being totally conscious of living the very best we know how—not to abuse our bodies."

Alcohol Use

Twenty-five out of thirty-eight respondents claimed a decrease in consumption of alcohol since their NDE. Thirteen reported no change, although four of these were already nondrinkers. Patrick said: "Now I drink very little. I used to, I used to be a sop." And Olivia said:

My alcohol consumption's cut down enormously. I was never an alcoholic, but my husband unfortunately was, and I drank along with him. I'm a lot more aware now of my body as something that needs looking after and nurturing.

Of those whose drinking had decreased since the NDE,

most said they now drank very little. For example, Moira's response was typical:

> I drink very very rarely. Sometimes I might have wine with dinner if I'm going out, but otherwise on a daily basis I wouldn't drink alcohol. I'd go for weeks without alcohol.

Nine were now nondrinkers. Virginia commented:

> No alcohol, no cigarettes—I smoked for twenty-three years! No alcohol, no cigarettes, no drugs, no sex or rock 'n' roll! [laughs] Maybe a little bit of rock 'n' roll.

Tobacco Use

Seventeen out of thirty-nine respondents noted that their use of tobacco had decreased since the NDE. The other twenty-two claimed no change—but they were all already nonsmokers. In fact, there are only two out of thirty-nine who still smoke and they are both trying to give it up. Cora said she has only one cigarette a day, and Robert said:

> I'm now trying to give up smoking and I'm very annoyed with myself as a matter of fact, because I gave up for five weeks at Christmastime, when I was in hospital. I didn't even feel like one. But I've cut down, as I said. I've had three packs of cigarettes in the last fortnight, so I'm not going too bad.

Drug Use

Twenty-two out of thirty-eight respondents said that there had been a decrease in their use of prescription drugs since their NDE. Two claimed that there had been an increase due to a decline in their health—Albert with heart disease and Kate with cancer. There were fourteen who claimed that there had been no change in their drug use, although it should be noted that eight of these were already drug-free.

Of the twenty-two who said there had been a decrease in their use of prescription drugs, eleven said that they took none at all, and felt quite strongly about it. For example, when asked whether she took any prescription drugs now, Paula said: "*No!* [laughs] No way! *Nothing!!*" Olivia said: "No. I don't even like taking antibiotics—I'd rather take garlic or horseradish." And Anthea noted:

> Well, as a matter of fact, I was on medication for high blood pressure and had been for about four years, but after this [the NDE] I'm totally free. I don't take any drugs of any kind.

Others reported making minimal use of drugs. Mary said: "I suppose I take a headache pill about once every three months."

Media

Nineteen out of thirty-four respondents said there had been a decrease in their watching of television following their NDE, and fifteen claimed there was no change. Of those nineteen whose television watching decreased, four owned no television set, and nine claimed to watch it very seldom. As Alexandra said: "I just didn't want to see the world in that way anymore."

Of those fifteen who reported no change, all were television watchers but only two claimed to watch it a lot. Anthea said:

> I find myself very bored with TV. However, sometimes, especially if I've had a pretty hectic sort of day and it's all heavy stuff, like if I've been seeing

very sick people, I can just sit and unwind and watch rubbish on television and quite enjoy it.

Eighteen out of thirty-two respondents reported a decrease in use of newspapers following their NDE. Eleven claimed there was no change and three claimed an increase in newspaper reading. For example, Evan said that he made a point of reading the newspaper "every day from front to back." By contrast Martine said:

> I don't read newspapers. That's a very strange thing that's happened to me. I used to read all those newspapers and get very angry. People now talk about terrible things happening in the world and I have to say, did it happen? I feel a bit odd that that could have happened to me. But they talk only about this horrible stuff and I feel . . . it's not that I deny it's happening, I know there's earthquakes and things like that, but if I concentrate on things like that, it takes all my energy.

Exercise

Seventeen out of thirty-seven respondents reported an increase in exercise since their NDE, another seventeen reported no change and three claimed a decrease in exercise since their NDE due to ill health. Some people remarked on the change in their exercise pattern over the years since their NDE. For example, Kate said: "These days I really rest, because of the cancer, but before I became ill I was really thin, I played squash and cricket and all sorts of things."

Of those seventeen who claimed no change, eight were already regular exercisers. Among those who exercise regularly, walking was most popular, closely followed by swimming and yoga. Paula described a newfound love of diving:

I dive with a snorkel and mask, it's an incredibly relaxing feeling just to be in the water. I haven't done much of it yet, I've only just completed a course in diving but it's, oh, such a peaceful feeling. It's beautiful, it's a completely different world and also I love the communication with the fish.

Mel is more active in his exercise program, which has increased dramatically since his NDE and physical recovery. He said:

These days I run about twenty-five to thirty miles a week, I swim one or two days a week, I go to the gym two or three days a week and I do t'ai-chi and meditate.

Alternative Therapies

Since the NDE, it appears that there has been a shift away from traditional medicine toward alternative healing methods, including self-healing. Twenty-three out of forty respondents reported an increased use of alternative therapies following their NDE, and eighteen out of forty reported a decreased use of doctors. A wide range of alternative therapies is used by experiencers, although the most popular are acupuncture (used by nine), herbalism and naturopathy (used by eight), and homeopathy (used by seven). Others frequently mentioned were osteopathy, reflexology, aromatherapy and hypnotherapy.

Almost equal to the increase in use of alternative therapists was a decrease in the use of doctors. As Ben said: "I would only ever see doctors socially." There was a general feeling that doctors were a last resort. Five women noted that they only ever go to the doctor for gynecological checkups, and six other experiencers remarked that they go very, very rarely—that there could be years between visits. For example, Bill said:

I try and do without doctors now. It's that long since I've been to one. I've got an open mind toward it—I know that we need them. But I'm also aware how powerful the mind is on one's own self as well. I can change so much in my own body. It's unbelievable now that I never realized it was possible. I can switch the headache off if I wish to, or I can sink into it.

Cora said: "I never go to doctors. I use homeopathic and herb healing or whatever. I would go to a doctor only if I had to."

Martine noted:

I know more or less when something is happening in my body why it is happening, so if I work on that emotional thing I can fix it. I go to the doctor only to have skin cancers removed and that sort of thing.

And Virginia said:

Doctors—really, I wouldn't see them unless I had something chopped off, or something really obvious. It's good to be able to use the medical profession, but the main healing, say if I got the flu or anything like that, I'd heal myself.

It can be seen from the above that near-death experiencers demonstrate, overall, an increased attention to the care of their physical bodies. Abuse of their bodies, whether through use of food, alcohol, tobacco or prescription drugs, has decreased markedly. Their use of television and newspapers has also decreased, due to an underlying feeling that these are not particularly healthy ways to view the world. There is also an associated shift toward keeping health care in their own hands by using the body's own energies for healing, or at the most to use the most natural and least intrusive therapies. Although it is recognized that doctors can be useful for major problems of a physical level, a preference is shown for self-healing.

When asked to describe their present lifestyle compared with their lifestyle before the NDE, the answers were highly positive. For example, Al said: "My lifestyle is much more naturalistic. It's helped me to get rid of materialistic shackles, being owned by things."

Lorenzo noted: "The biggest change for me—I am more peaceful. Before I worry a lot."

Ursula described her present lifestyle as "comfortable."

> I feel that I've got a direction now, that there's a certain amount of order. I feel that any problems that come up are only just little tests and they will be overcome.

Harriet said:

> Life's more meaningful, it's been a long time but I've always felt that since then. I think it [the NDE] made me more caring, it made me deeper. Put it this way, up until then I really didn't think a great deal about anything. I felt after that there was a reason for me being here—whether it was because of all the stray boys, or whether it was . . . there's no way of knowing. But life's more meaningful. And another strange thing too—I don't know how you feel about it, but I feel in my way, and I only started feeling it around that time, that you, that I get out of life only what I put into it. Do you feel like that?

When Anthea was asked how she would describe her present lifestyle, she said:

> *Extremely* fulfilling! *Unbelievably* fulfilling! *Totally* rewarding! I had no idea that fulfillment at this level

was a possibility. I'm totally contented, very re-
warded in what I do and I'm just so happy.

(How does this compare with your lifestyle before the
NDE?)

Oh, I shudder to think! Oh, look truly, when I compare myself today with the person I was before this
experience, you just can't compare. Really I'm a different person totally. I'm just another person altogether.

CHANGES IN INTERESTS

As can already be seen from the preceding sections, priorities and interests can change dramatically following a
near-death experience. These changes can cover a wide
range of areas. However, two recurring themes are the
near-death experiencers' determined search for knowledge
and their frequently expressed desire to utilize newly
awakened talents they had previously undervalued or did
not know they possessed. As Ring notes:

It seems that what the NDE does, at least in some
cases, is enable the individual to . . . actualize inner
potentials to a sometimes astonishing degree.[18]

It is important to note here that any search for knowledge
and any attempt to utilize newfound talents takes place
within a particular social context. For example, the possibility of attending college is diminished for those living on
farms distant from an urban center, especially if they are
women with children or a low level of formal education.
Demographically, the fifty experiencers of this study were
widely distributed geographically throughout the eastern
states of Australia in both rural and urban areas.

In addition, their level of educational attainment varied widely. Even taking into account that there were ten respondents under the age of seventeen, there was a disproportionately high percentage of the sample at the lower end of the educational ladder at the time of their NDE. By the time of the interview there had been a slight move up the ladder, although there were still only six university graduates. However, this tends to belie the actual activity of respondents in terms of "learning," since the pursuit of knowledge did not always take them to formal educational institutions. Neither did their geographical location seem to hinder them unduly. Their ability to maximize their abilities, whatever their geographical or educational situation, appeared to be a feature of their post-NDE lives.

Omitting the ten who were seventeen years or younger at the time of their NDE, thirty-two of the remaining forty respondents said there were major changes in interests following their NDE which they directly attributed to the effect of the experience on their lives. Eight said there had been no particular change in interests attributable to the NDE.

Many specifically mentioned that their entire attitude to learning had changed. For example, Bronwyn said, "I see learning much more broadly—just about everything is learning." And Christina said she had noticed "whatever I need to know, the information comes from some direction, whether it's about painting, painting dolls, dressmaking, whatever." Anthea explained her view:

Before that experience I'd always considered learning to be of the academic nature. And now I feel that that is very valid but there is another type of learning which to me seems to be even more valid, and that is a learning of spiritual matters gained not so much through what other people can tell you but through what you can decipher for yourself.

Similarly, Cora said that she now valued experiential learning above the academic kind. And Olivia said that since her NDE her whole attitude to learning had changed because she had become "aware of how much there is to learn." Ben noted:

> Any curriculum is very limited. [After the NDE] I wasn't interested in getting a degree, getting recognition from an institution or other people—I wanted to *know*.

The studies they tended to engage in reflect their eagerness, as Ben said, "to *know*." This "knowing" generally had three purposes—to find out more about themselves, to develop newly awakened personal gifts or talents and to help others. As Moira said: "The experience was the underlying basis of everything. Without that I don't think I would have done any of the things I have done." Martine found that after the NDE.

> I wanted to find out how I ticked. I'm fascinated by the way people tick, how it goes together, how it fits together. I have an incredible amount of patience for this sort of thing. I look at all the facets of a problem. I have more and more the feeling that when it comes to that, I go higher and higher and the circle gets bigger, so I see more and more and more until what is down there is not important anymore. I read all those books now, it's a joy. I make notes and then I feel I can pass it on. At the beginning I had to start right at the bottom because I didn't know anybody who was thinking like that. My lifestyle today is definitely not the lifestyle of a woman of my age, I suppose. I'm still very aware, very outgoing and try to find out what's going on in the soul.

Helen, who lives in a country town, related how her inter-

est in music and art began after her NDE. She admits that
sometimes she tends to take on too much, but she feels
driven to learn. She said:

> I love art, I love it, that's what I'm doing at the mo-
> ment, because once you start doing art you can see
> things in a much brighter beautiful light, you know.
> As I say, you look at the leaves ... but I want to
> learn languages, I want to learn Italian and I'd love
> to learn a few languages. If anything, I probably take
> on a bit too much—I'm learning the violin at the
> moment, I'm also doing singing lessons, I'm doing
> art classes, as well as being the [music] teacher of
> thirty students. But there's a lot of things I still want
> to do [laughs] and I think there's not enough time in
> the day to do them.

Barbara's case is interesting since she had her experience
as a ten-year-old. Her father was an atheist and she said
that at the time it was clear that there was no way she
could tell her parents what had happened to her. She told
nobody and the experience was put out of her mind until
seven years before the interview, when it came back to her.
At that time she shared it with her daughters. Within four
years her eldest daughter had died of cancer. She believes
now that the experience was returned to her because she
was in need of it to help her through her daughter's death.
Thus the changes in interests in Barbara's case date from
the time of the "retrieval" of her experience. From that
time she found a new direction. She said:

> I read a lot. I did a course in acupuncture, I did a
> rebirthing course, I did Elisabeth Kübler-Ross
> seminars—things I would never have thought of
> doing before.

Harriet lives on a farm and never finished high school.

Some years after her NDE she found she had a gift for craft work and eventually realized that she could share this gift with other lonely women on farms in her district. Harriet was able to transcend the limitations of her situation, while developing her own talent and helping others. She described how it happened:

It all started because a lady saw my spinning wheel and said, "I've always wanted to spin," and I said, "Well, come along." This happened a couple of times and then I started to wonder if there was room for a social group. I was told, "Oh, it'll never work." I'd never done anything like this in my life before, so I typed up a notice and put it on a bulletin-board and forty-two women turned up! They were out on farms, so there *was* a need for it, you see, and it's been going ever since. We met here [at home] for eight or nine months before I hired the hall. And it was pretty hard to get because in the country they're set in their ways, I suppose, and they weren't sure whether they'd let me hire the hall, because they thought we might make a mess. So now there are fifty-two people who make use of that day.

Yet recently we were down to $2 in the bank, and I'd made about twenty phone calls to get funding. In desperation someone told me to try the lady from Rural Women's Affairs, so I did. She met me the next day and she rang the shire and told them they should be paying me for what I was doing. It finished up they were ringing me and asking me to come in, and out of all that, the shire took over the $500 insurance for the hall and gave a $200 donation and we were back in business again.

So I go to the library and I look up books and I go to workshops and I learn things and then I in turn bring it back to them, and we have a lovely time. I try all those things, things I never thought I'd ever

do. I've been doing lots of things, I've been spinning, and weaving, a lot of fabric crafts, or lamp-
shades, all sorts of things. Beads is just one of the
latest things I've been doing, I just try anything now.

Finally, Anthea related how the strongly felt need to develop her newly awakened gift changed her interests dramatically, and led to her ability to help others. She said:

Well, the first thing was I enrolled at college to take
psychology and I found myself being very dissatis-
fied with it because to me it didn't seem that that
was the way really that we are, that people are. So
after six months I left school because I became more
and more disgruntled the more I attended. I couldn't
accept it, I felt there was so much more. So then I
padded around for a bit and wondered what I should
be doing. Eventually I was led to enrolling in the
course of natural therapies that was so much more
valid for me, and I was able to relate to that so much
better than the formal, academic-type situation. But
as I was studying that, I was actually told in a dream
that I was going to become clairvoyant, and that I
would be in the kindergarten stage. So three weeks
after that dream I in fact had my first clairvoyant vision and I didn't know if I should trust that but more
and more situations came up when I was telling
strangers truths about themselves. Then I realized
that the dream was in fact a direction. And so I
started to give readings to the lecturers at the college
where I was studying. They could see the gift I had
because I was giving diagnoses as well. I was ad-
vised by a couple of them to get out of studying, to
get out and into life and use my gift. So I did. I followed up the natural therapies course with hypnotherapy and found that very interesting too, but I've
worked ever since and that's about eight years now.

(So you left your job as a teacher, started this whole new field of study and actually started work again as a hypnotherapist?)

Well, after seeing about two or three people as a hypnotherapist, I couldn't just hide behind that. So as soon as I started seeing people for healings and readings on their life, the whole thing just took off and people come to me now either as somebody who needs to see me as a clairvoyant, or hypnotherapist, or psychic healer.

Anthea's major career change is not an isolated example. Omitting the ten near-death experiencers who had their experiences as children, twenty-eight of the remaining forty had a major career change attributable to their altered interests following their NDE. However, it should be noted that even some of the "childhood" experiencers have made career choices and changes which they attribute to their NDEs. For example, Michael, who had his experience as a fifteen-year-old, said:

One of my main interests now is horticulture [laughs]. I sort of had no idea what I was going to do, but after that [the NDE] I signed straight up for horticulture, which, I mean, I had never thought about it, I had no idea what horticulture was.

And Edwina, who had her experience as a sixteen-year-old, said:

After the NDE I took a year off, and I'd been so nurtured and so controlled by my father, I had my whole law career mapped out for me. So I just sort of slipped back into that. I achieved but I sort of took it a bit tongue in cheek. . . . But now, of course, I look at all the spiritual development from that point

> [the NDE] and I think, yeah, it's part of that understanding that I have to use my psychic gift. I've been given a very intellectual mind for a reason too, but I'm getting out of law, I'm going to change jobs, I'll do editing in a publishing company for a while, just to think, and work it out. I know it will become clear what I have to do, but I need more time to make it clear.

There have been a number of career changes already mentioned in previous sections, such as Alexandra's departure from medicine to work as a Jungian psychotherapist and run wilderness retreats, and Anthea's abandonment of teaching for psychic healing. It has already been noted that Janet left a dry-cleaning business in an affluent suburb of Sydney to establish a spiritual retreat center in the Snowy Mountains, and that Eileen chose to leave nursing to earn her income as a cleaner and establish a welfare bureau for the Irish people of Melbourne. It should not be thought that these people are exceptional among the sample. Many others followed similar patterns. Even among the retired people of the sample, there is still a movement toward helping others. For example, Barry, who had very little formal education as a child (due to ill health), is now a volunteer teacher of adult literacy. And Al delights simply in wandering the wilderness areas of the world with a pack on his back, sharing his love of nature and life with anyone he meets. This makes a big change from his previous career. He said:

> I'm not interested in power anymore and that's important because I had positions of extreme power in the past—powers that the Defense Department in the United States had given to me. I had freedom to issue delegations of pure authority throughout the federal government. I had this enormous freedom of

power. So I've had that, I've been able to get rid of
that, and feel very good about it, the freedom of it.

Bronwyn noted that after her experience, for the first time
she had sought work teaching English to speakers of other
languages. And Cass left a career in television production
to become a nutritionist. She said:

> I couldn't get out of show business quickly enough.
> I just didn't want any part of something so material,
> so phony. I didn't want to be mixed up with those
> people anymore. I mean, I've got lots of friends in
> TV who are like us, you know, and I still see those
> people. But my old TV friends—they were so ambi-
> tious, so hard, you know. I was just so glad to get in
> my car and get away from all this bitchiness, all this
> nothing. And I thought, it's almost like having a se-
> cret that you can't pass on to somebody else. . . .
> Now I'm in health and nutrition, and we care for
> people and help people. I mean, it's a business, but
> it's wonderful to see someone losing weight or some-
> body gaining weight, or somebody's blood pressure
> coming down. And, you know, there's a lovely feel-
> ing of respect for people. I'm studying and training
> all the time, and that's been fantastic for me.

Cora described how her NDE, especially the life review,
strongly influenced her choice of career afterward. She
said:

> I became very interested in children and childhood
> experiences, and that had a lot to do with the learn-
> ing from that stored memory. My initial work was
> taking a course at Sydney University on childhood
> development—I became involved in alternative edu-
> cation for children, and then learned to be a mid-
> wife. The experience was the motivator as it touched

on baby/mother life issues. The experience gave me tremendous faith in being able to contact babies inside the uterus.

Finally, Sue revealed that she now does two jobs.

I work now with my second husband doing all the office work for our business. But I've also taken up nursing old people, looking after those who can't care for themselves. I do this every weekend for the whole weekend, sleeping overnight on the premises. I love old people, I feel totally devoted to them. I really relate well to them.

Leisure

In terms of leisure pursuits and entertainment, the experiencers of this sample tended once again to follow similar patterns. For example, twenty-five out of fifty nominated "being with people" as their preferred pastime. This was followed by listening to music (fourteen respondents), going to the theater (ten), going to movies (nine), reading (eight), eating out in restaurants (six) and going to the opera (three) and ballet (three). They also enjoyed a number of outdoor pursuits such as bushwalking, going to the beach, fishing, riding, walking and gardening. It is noticeable that most of the above tend to be rather peaceful pursuits.

Jennifer has an unusual way of spending her leisure time:

I work with the "historical flight." It's entertainment enough for me. I'm the only woman who works on restoring vintage aircraft. I get there and get the rust out of the old aircraft. I've always been interested in flying, but never did any when I was younger, I couldn't afford to do it. But now . . .

On the other hand, Alexandra expressed a fairly typical range of leisure interests. She said:

> Oh, well, I love music, and I see an occasional good film, or play, depends a bit on where I am. But my real entertainment is to get out and watch people [laughs]—take a ferry ride or play with kids, or you know, do something like that. I do love people, and getting together or planning a party or things like that—seasonal festivities and celebrations, simple things. And gardening is one of my big entertainments if I have the time.

Politics and Social Issues

A diminishing interest in politics and an increased interest in social issues was widely reported by the near-death experiencers of this sample. Of the thirty-five people who answered this question, twenty-one reported decreased interest in politics and only five an increased interest. On the other hand, thirty-five out of forty said they now had more interest in social issues and none had become less interested.

It is intriguing to contemplate the responses of the minority, who said their interest in politics had increased since their experience. For example, Albert noted that although his interest had increased in recent years, it had nothing to do with his NDE, but rather related to his status as a pensioner. Christina remarked that although she was now more aware of politics, she doesn't actually participate in any activity since "there is no political party worth joining." And Mary said that although she is interested in politics, "I'm in despair over our present politics and politicians."

Claire had her NDE experience as a child, but her comments about her attitude to politics at the time of the interview are informative. She said:

> I believe that most political movements need a spiritual base otherwise they become very self-righteous and hate-filled—really sick! That's why I have an ambivalence politically.

Thus, even among the minority, whose interest in politics had increased since their NDE, there is no approval evident. Among those whose interest has decreased, much the same attitude is expressed. For example, Charlotte noted that she had been an involved member of a political party but was now disillusioned and no longer participated. Similarly, Grace noted:

> I'm a member of a political party, but the only reason I joined was to make business contacts. But I never go! I hate it! I just think the whole hype and stuff is all nonsense, it's all very cynical.

And when Jennifer was asked if she was involved in any way politically, she said: "Oh, no, oh, no, I hate it, they're such liars."

Alexandra described her change:

> I had a modest flush of political things as a student, that were connected with Vietnam and abolishment of capital punishment, which I really did throw myself into, but now my political interests have decreased. But political issues do come up in therapy and I don't sidestep them as I think some therapists might.

Olivia revealed that she felt quite cynical about politicians. But she said:

> I do wish we could get them all together and make them understand the theory of reincarnation. So that if they think they're getting away with things, it's

okay, because they're not getting away with anything.
They would be so much more responsible if they believed in that concept and applied it.

And Edwina, a childhood near-death experiencer, said of
her present attitude: "It's totally useless—people fighting
and battling over political issues ... it's irrelevant, it's just
playing games, silly men's games."

Barry said that his interest in politics had not changed
since his NDE—he'd always thought of politicians as
"gangsters." Finally, Virginia noted that there had been no
change in her interest in politics either. However, she did
reveal the different way in which her interest now manifests. She said:

> I was always interested in politics. I was brought up
> in a political household. My grandmother was going
> for federal Parliament herself. So I was always inter-
> ested. I did the rounds of the political parties, check-
> ing them all out at one stage, but I never formally
> joined. I don't have any actual contact now, but in
> my morning meditation I always send white light to
> the main politicians around the world that I can re-
> member so that anything that is carried forward can
> go through in the right conditions, and is not inter-
> fered with by negative forces.

In terms of interest in social issues, Virginia said:

> There are many social issues that concern me. There
> are certain areas within the world and certain areas
> in Australia too that do concern me. The whole legal
> system needs reform. And peace. In my younger
> days I used to march. I don't feel we can have peace
> in the climate that exists in the world today. You
> can't possibly hope to have peace while materialistic
> views still exist in the world. We have to have gen-

uine change before peace can happen. How can you think about peace when all around us in our own city there are things like homeless children? We can work best for peace from the inside out. Education is our work toward peace. Teaching people to appreciate that there is more to life than a three-dimensional view of things, that there is more to life than football. That there is more to life than that narrow frame of reference—to widen their horizons. I don't wish to sound airy-fairy about this because I genuinely believe that it will happen.

Virginia was not alone in her belief that change had to start from within. Mel said:

I'm a member of a conservation foundation, I was very active in that, but I found it was dissipating all my energies, instead of focusing on my own stuff. Because it all starts with yourself, there's no question about that. You can't change the universe, you change yourself. I'm pro the peace movement but I don't want to go marching because I don't know what it achieves. I absolutely support the equality of the sexes but a lot of feminists out there are damaging themselves. They are coming from "There's you and me" rather than "There's us."

And Janet said:

I'm concerned about our earth. Therefore we've made Oakdale into a wildlife sanctuary and endeavor to do everything organically. We try not to pollute our earth any further in our own lives. So we're talking as much as we can to all the people who come here to try to raise their consciousnesses as to what's going on.

I'm not working for the peace movement but I

think on the level of inner peace I'm working full
speed ahead, because that's where I believe it really
stems from. If you can get people to really acknowledge that sense of needing to be totally at one and at
peace with God and themselves, then obviously that
has to flow out into the universe.

Alexandra said:

I have in fact in the last year or two done more peace
activists' training than I've ever done before. It's become more introverted. It's really designed for them
to know themselves, to know whether the conflict is
within themselves. . . . I'm also very involved in the
ecology movement, but again it's all based, like the
wilderness trips, on getting everyone to be responsible for their own personal ecological situation.

Christina talked about her concerns. She said:

In their unawareness, people do very destructive
things to other people and the planet. I have no involvement in the peace movement, but I think that
though they are well intentioned, it won't have much
effect until the general awareness of people is
brought up.

And Ursula said:

The ecological and peace movements are very worth-
while. People should be aware of these issues, especially the peace movement. But that all starts in
yourself. You can't tell another person "Be peaceful,"
"Don't do this," "Don't do that." The only thing is—
you can be peaceful.

Michael had an interesting view on the peace movement:

I was in the Wilderness Society, that's a branch of the peace movement. I'm not for violence, but I'm not actively seeking peace. I understand that the violence is a part of where we live, it's a part of this world, it's something we have to come to grips with, that we have to accept. I tend to think it's another vehicle for learning.

As would already be evident, there are a number of respondents who actually work full-time in their areas of social concern, and these concerns range far and wide. For example, Michael is a horticulturalist, and conservation issues concern him greatly:

Logging wilderness areas is an emotional issue for me. I feel strongly because I know how much is left, and doing horticulture you know how fragile it is.

Cora is deeply involved in the areas of women's rights and health, and children's rights. And Denise, who is now the director of a psychiatric hospital, said:

To me the quality of life is what is important, whether the issue be euthanasia, abortion, suicide or what. I hate to see abused children. I don't go too much on the "greenie" issues, my issues are more in the welfare areas. I feel very strongly that the law is geared toward men, especially with rape, contraception, even to have your tubes tied. . . . I'm concerned for the psychiatric population. They are discharged into the community but the community is uncaring and they end up on the streets. I'm also concerned that nurses' rights are starting to be overbalanced by patients' rights.

There is concern about the abuse of drugs in our society that has already been reflected in the personal choices near-death experiencers have made in their own lives. In addition, Mary works in support of the Life Education program run in schools, Claire works with women and their children in a residential drug and alcohol rehabilitation center and several others are strong supporters of the Twelve-Step programs such as Alcoholics Anonymous and Narcotics Anonymous, along with the sister programs for families, such as Al-Anon and Nar-Anon.

Although there is strong general support for the "human liberation" movements, at the same time there was in some cases an ambivalence or caution expressed that the extremes of these movements are, as Mel said "damaging themselves." Janet felt: "There's a lot of anger in those people, but it's a stage in their lives that they've got to go through." And Martine said:

> What I feel is there is so much anger behind those movements and it's not with anger that we can do anything. Annihilating the other one is not going to help. There is more strength in passive resistance. I can change more in changing myself and my attitude. They can't do anything to me because I have changed.

Moira noted:

> I am a feminist and believe in the things they believe in, but I don't believe in burning my bra and all those stupid things, being militant about it. I'm much more a believer in people liberation, everybody needs to be liberated to be themselves. There shouldn't be a struggle between the sexes.

Olivia revealed that she'd like to break down intolerance of all kinds:

> I see in people a very nasty degree of intolerance, and it makes life very unpleasant. There's a lot of ra-

cial and ethnic intolerance in Australia, and it's a very ugly thing. And it's ridiculous because, you know, at the end, if you believe in reincarnation, the soul knows no barriers, so we don't know where we were before or where we'll be next time, so intolerance . . . I'd love to break down some of those barriers.

And Shana said that although over the years she had been involved in the ecology movement, now she said: "I decided I could be more effective in doing what I'm doing now—working on the communication thing, working for no separation."

Finally, Ruby discussed her view of "the wider picture:"

I think if mankind is on its path, things are going to happen and I should not and cannot judge the way other people live. I think that all people have a right to survive, to speak, to work for what they want. I don't think anybody should take anything from anybody. The Aboriginals are black people, they've got different-colored skin but they still feel the same as us. . . . I think possibly my total outlook on life has changed [since the NDE]. How can I put it, oh . . . if you think of the ocean and it comes up and it hits the land and it puts out puddles. The source is the ocean and all the puddles and pools are people. And each of them have different things, some of them are there longer than others, but eventually in time they all work their way back to the source. . . . If you believe in reincarnation, you sort of say, I'm not their judge.

Thus, overall, with regard to politics and social issues, there is a strong sense that politics as we know it, and politicians, are regarded with little respect. Near-death experiencers view a wide range of social issues with grave concern, and most of them work in some way to ameliorate the situations that cause them most distress. However, there is a noticeable tendency to look beyond the usual materialistic methods of approaching these problems. There is a fairly widely accepted acknowledgment among this sample of experiencers that, as Virginia said, "we can work best for peace from the inside out," or, as Mel said, "You can't change the universe, you change yourself," or as Alexandra suggested, everyone needs to be "responsible for their own personal ecology." This is not a sample of people who feel powerless in the face of overwhelming social ills. Rather, there is a strong sense of personal power in recognition of their place in the whole, but there is also an awareness of the lessons to be learned from the larger flow, and the need, beyond a certain point, not to "push the river."

As Aldous Huxley wrote in an introduction to *Mystics as a Force for Change:*

A population trained to make use of such "other kinds of seeing" as the aesthetic, the visionary, and the mystical would be unmanageable by the traditional methods of narcotizing or inebriating propaganda. In the eyes of the politicians and generals who control our destinies, it is most undesirable that the mass of humanity should be trained to see the world as beauty, as mysteriousness, as unity. It is in a culture-conditioned world of utilitarian values, dogmatic bumptiousness, and international dissensions that our rulers have come to the top; and that is the kind of world they would like their subjects to go on being conditioned to create for themselves. Meanwhile let us derive what comfort we may from the thought that other kinds of seeing are always there, parted from the normal waking of consciousness (in William James's words) "by the filmiest of screens."[19]

As we can see, remarkable changes take place in the life directions experienced by the near-death experiencers. In no area investigated could this change be considered marginal. Overwhelmingly, the subjects in my research sample now consider themselves to be more worthy and capable, with a strong sense of purpose in their lives. They are more at peace, and have a deeper understanding of themselves.

This change in attitude to self quite naturally overflows into their approach to others. This is particularly evident in their loving disposition, their desire to help others, their compassion and insight into the problems confronted by people they meet. It is intriguing, then, to note a frequent breakdown in the close personal relationships that had been established before the NDE. This breakdown perhaps provides one of the clearest measures of the depth of the changes that take place following an NDE. Accommodating post-NDE priorities to pre-NDE relationships was shown to be acutely problematic in many cases.

Their interest in material success declined sharply, whereas their interest in spiritual matters increased. The choices they made about lifestyle, such as drinking alcohol, smoking, eating and using prescription drugs, reflected their commitment to respect for their bodies. Overall they described their lifestyle as more meaningful, peaceful, purposeful and fulfilling.

Their changes in interests were equally dramatic, and manifested in observably practical ways such as changes in study direction and career. Once again these changes followed the same pattern, and were based on greater self-understanding, development of personal talent and helping others.

The Near-Death Experience in Context

When attempting to understand any social phenomenon, it soon becomes clear that even the most objective analysis is carried out from a particular point of view by a researcher unavoidably in-situation. In the same way, the near-death experiencer is also unavoidably in-situation. For instance, in an earlier chapter it was revealed how participation in this research project and contact with the researcher became, at times, a significant part of the context within which they continued the process of weaving the NDE meaningfully into their lives. However, the respondents' interaction with the researcher is only one of many interactions with their context. In order to understand the experiencers' post-NDE attitudes, and discover the way in which their interpretations and meanings become integrated into their lives, both the epistemological and social context of their "life-affirming" and "death-accepting" response to the NDE must be explored and taken into account.

The procedures and techniques used for the qualitative analysis in this chapter are those of the "grounded theory" approach. These are designed to develop a set of concepts that provide a thorough theoretical explanation of the social phenomenon being studied. The theory that emerges should be thoroughly grounded in the data and have not only descriptive but explanatory power. Anselm Strauss and Juliet Corbin note that for them, grounded theory is "a transactional system, a method of analysis that allows one to examine the interactive nature of events."[1]

Before their experience, near-death experiencers each live within a particular set of conditions—a biographical, social, cultural, historical context, creating meaning in their daily lives through their interaction in that world. However, after the NDE, although to all outward appearances the wider context has not changed, the experiencers find that the meaning they had created is no longer sufficient. The experiencer has undergone an ontological shift. Although the world would generally be said to be the same, their perception of it, and their being within it, has changed. In order to maintain coherence in their lives, meaning has to be re-created, renegotiated within the context of this changed world view. Thus the conditions provided by context, the strategies used to deal with them, the interactions that result and their consequences are all fundamental to an understanding of post-NDE life.

This chapter first examines some general epistemological and social components of the conditional matrix within which the NDE itself occurs. It then presents a theory for the integration process—the "integration trajectory"—and examines the conditions, interactions, strategies and consequences that give it shape.

THE WESTERN SCIENTIFIC PARADIGM

At a general level, perhaps one of the most salient features of the NDE context is the Western scientific paradigm which, despite the advent of quantum mechanics early in this century, is still today widely based on classical Newtonian physics.

Physics, along with the rest of Western science, had its beginnings in Greece in the sixth century B.C. in a tradition antithetical to present classical theory. At this time, the sages of the Milesian school of Ionia were concerned with discovering the essential nature of things they called "physis," but they made no distinction between animate and inanimate forms of existence, since they believed that all were endowed with life and spirituality.

By the time of Isaac Newton's birth, Western thought had been for two thousand years deeply imprinted with Aristotle's materialistic, atomistic scientific system. In a few short years Newton had initiated modern mathematics, modern astronomy and, above all, modern physics. He had then gone on to studies in areas such as theology and alchemy, which he personally saw as far more important. Nevertheless, a mechanistic world view continued to dominate most scientific thought.

It is little recognized that Newton himself blamed Descartes for this outcome, since the Cartesian view of nature was based on the fundamental division into mind (*res cogitans*) and matter (*res extensa*), which permitted scientists to treat matter as completely separate and independent of themselves. Obviously Descartes' perspective was extremely influential in the development of classical physics, but his influence did not end there. His famous statement, *Cogito ergo sum*—"I think, therefore I am"—and its acceptance by Western men and women has led to the strange split between body and mind (already foreshadowed by the early atomists) becoming entrenched as a fundamental "reality" in Western lives. As with all dichotomies, its systematic association with other hierarchically valued phenomena or qualities increased its seeming inevitability and led to its establishment as "natural law." Science became increasingly materialistic, atomistic, reductionistic and either agnostic or atheist, but most significantly, it was widely seen to be successful.

Largely seduced by the successes of this model of science, and in order to be seen as truly "scientific," some new sciences such as psychology and sociology began to copy the methods. This situation is ironic when it is realized that at that time, within physics itself, the discovery of quantum mechanics was already posing a serious challenge to the Cartesian-Newtonian world view. As Sir Arthur Eddington wrote in 1929:

> We have learnt that the exploration of the external world by the methods of physical science leads not to a concrete reality but to a shadow world of symbols, beneath which those methods are unadapted for penetrating.

Sir James Jeans was also aware of the limitations of scientific theorizing:

> Physicists who are trying to understand Nature may work in many different fields and by many different methods; one may dig, one may sow, one may reap. But the final harvest will always be a sheaf of mathematical formulae. These will never describe Nature itself... [Thus] our studies can never put us into contact with reality.[2]

Even much more recently, certain elegant experiments in physics by Alain Aspect have shown decisively that the whole class of realistic local theories of the universe (including materialism) are untenable. Yet, in most fields of scientific endeavor life continues as though quantum mechanics never existed, as though no doubt has ever been thrown on the validity of a Cartesian-Newtonian worldview that is materialistic, dualistic, reductionistic, etc. For that minority of scientists who have become aware of

quantum mechanics, many use it as a recipe book that
works, without examining its philosophical implications.
And among the widespread nonscientific community
quantum mechanics, if noticed at all, is still perceived as
a piece of esoterica that has no direct relevance to reality.
The firmly entrenched nature of this Cartesian-Newtonian
worldview has immense and obvious consequences for
near-death experiencers seeking to understand their experience. As the transpersonal psychiatrist Stanislav Grof
notes in an interview with Saniel Bonder and Ron Boyer:

> By and large, the scientific community still holds to
> the mechanistic viewpoint in which consciousness is
> seen as an epiphenomenon that mysteriously devel-
> oped after billions of years of blind, mechanical, ma-
> terial processes. This is the way of looking at the
> world with which transpersonal experiences [such as
> NDEs] and quantum physics are both incompatible.[3]

Near-death experiencers are confronted by this incompati-
bility of worldview not only when reviewing their own
previously held assumptions but also, and especially, when
seeking corroboration outside of themselves. These beliefs
are still widely taught and held, and are defended vocifer-
ously against the onslaught of individual NDE accounts.

There seems to be a breakdown of communication between the adherents of opposing paradigms and apparently
no room for compromise. From the viewpoint of scientists
stuck within the current Cartesian-Newtonian paradigm,
the reality of NDEs has to be dismissed as impossible, or
at the very least explained away. Anthropologist Michael
Harner describes this wholesale rejection of other forms of
reality as cognicentrism, a counterpart in consciousness to
ethnocentrism between cultures. He writes:

> In this case it is not the narrowness of someone's
> *cultural* experience that is the fundamental issue, but

the narrowness of someone's *conscious* experience. The persons most prejudiced against a concept of nonordinary reality are those who have never experienced it.[4]

Generally, within Western culture there is a considerable lack of knowledge about other states of consciousness, and cognicentrism is rife. Thus the social organization of knowledge in our society, especially the Western scientific party line, *ensures* that there is a conspicuous societal silence about mystical experiences of any kind. However, for near-death experiencers an additional layer of taboo is imposed on their experience since it concerns death.

THE WESTERN "DENIAL OF DEATH"

All cultures, whether primitive or modern, have always had their own ways of dealing with death, which can be highly ritualized and complex. However, their individual cultural attitudes to death can be quite distinct. E. Mansell Pattison noted in 1967 that societies fall into three main types: "death-defying," "death-denying" and "death-accepting." In our widespread acceptance of modern Western societies as death-denying, it is often forgotten that, as he reminds us:

> Traditional Western civilization, rooted in the Judaeo-Christian heritage, has in large measure been a death-defying culture. In *1 Corinthians 15:54–55,* the keynote is sounded: '. . . death is swallowed up in victory. O death, where is thy sting? O grave, where is thy victory?'[5]

In such a tradition, embedded in the "mythical-membership" level of consciousness,[6] the individual is subsumed in the group. There is social organization and social control. As one of a group, the individual can envisage a social future beyond individual death. In return for the sense of belonging, however, service to the group is implicit in this contract. Even today, on certain occasions and in certain organizations the cry can still be heard—"My country, right or wrong!" As Pattison suggests: "Those who fight for causes, ideologies, families, or country may do so in defiance of the fact that they die in the doing."[7]

An astonishing example of death defiance taken from anthropological literature is that of the Dinka, a cattle-herding people of the Sudan. Clive Kessler recounts that the Dinka are organized in camping groups. The head of the senior group in each area is known as master of the fishing spear, and is recognized as an important ritual and political leader. Spearmasters are said to be in touch with the life force itself and represent the life of Dinka society and the Dinka people as a whole. The problem is, how can a mortal person hope to continually embody the life force? How does he die? Kessler notes that

> Quite simply, spearmasters do not die—or, rather, are . . . not taken from those they represent by death. Dinka society cheats death, fashions a social triumph over mortality as it is ordinarily encountered—by burying the spearmaster, in a protracted and deliberate ritual exercise of terrible solemnity, while he is still alive! . . . Rather than being taken from his people by death, the spearmaster would instead (as they put it) "go to the earth" in their midst, "sitting erect" rather than prone in a conventional grave. . . . His burial, then, is somehow a social defiance of death and an affirmation of the continuing vitality, the collective immortality, of those whom he symbolized. In this exertion of control over mundane death, Dinka fashioned a triumphant celebration of themselves and of their society's values and continuity.[8]

Death defiance requires a notion of belonging to something more powerful than the self, whether it be a society, an army, a political party, a religion or a football team. However, once the rational level of consciousness is reached, there is an awakening perception of in fact being alone. The existential worldview of "man as a futile passion" whose life is essentially meaningless is symptomatic of this consciousness. As Ken Wilber writes, "An absolutely unprecedented cry of anguish, guilt, and sorrow screams out from the world's myths, narratives, and records" once mankind is faced with awareness of its own mortality and isolated existence.[9]

So today in modern Western societies the notion that we deny death is a familiar one. Ernest Becker in his well-known treatise *The Denial of Death* notes that his whole book is based on the assumption that there is a universal terror of death. He writes:

> The idea of death, the fear of it, haunts the human animal like nothing else; it is a mainspring of human activity—activity designed largely to avoid the fatality of death, to overcome it by denying in some way that it is the final destiny for man.[10]

According to Becker, death is ever-present at a subconscious level. However, he maintains, life is made bearable by our obliviousness to this fear in our conscious life. As he notes, repression takes care of the complex symbol of death for most people.[11]

Arnold Mindell approaches the subject from a different angle, since his personal interest lies in working with patients in comatose states. However, he also observes that cultural taboos inhibit our interest in death and dying. He writes that, for some, death is unmentionable, and for others it is too painful to contemplate. However,

... for most of us, regardless of our beliefs, the ever-present threats of loss of our loved ones and confrontation with our own mortality are reasons enough to avoid the topic.[12]

Denial can appear in many different guises and settings, the most spectacular of which is probably the cryonics industry, which, for a considerable sum of money, can freeze a dead person's body with the hope that sometime in the future medical science will advance to a point where the body can be reanimated and cured of its disease. However, it can also appear in more mundane situations, from the common usage of social niceties to cushion us from reality—euphemisms such as "he just passed away," to an inability to contemplate the impact of major disasters unless personally involved, when tens, hundreds or thousands of people are killed. And when one *is* personally confronted by death, the situation is socially "managed" to limit its impact, not only for the dying or dead individual, but also for the benefit of any bystanders, whether family, friends, health-care professionals, ministers of religion or strangers such as a person delivering flowers.

Thus, unlike in earlier times, when death was an unavoidable feature of life, in modern Western societies—as Kessler notes—death is

> ... technologized, euphemized, managed by specialists, all out of ordinary sight. It is made altogether alien: doctor, undertaker, and ritual officiant all manage it for us, by dressing themselves up to do so in various garbs that are not ours; by managing it through languages and jargons that are often not ours; by making it, under the aegis of their own jealously guarded expertise, *their* specialized business, which is to deny that it is any of ours.[13]

To return to such a death-denying environment from a near-death experience can be, at the very least, disconcerting for the near-death experiencer, since as a result of their experience they have *no* fear of death. In fact, near-death experiencers form a strongly "death-accepting" group in our society, and this "death acceptance" is not merely based on belief, but rather is founded on deep personal experience. Having reached the "astral," "psychic" or even "subtle" level of consciousness[14] during their NDE, they have transcended the mental-egoic fear of ego dissolution commonly believed to be at the basis of death fear and its ego defense—death denial. Then they find, often to their dismay, that it is in the medical setting that the "Western scientific paradigm" and the "denial of death" come together and present a human face.

THE MEDICAL SETTING

At some time or other, either before, during or after their NDE, most near-death experiencers find themselves in a medical setting. Indeed, in many cases it is because of recent scientific advances, especially advances in resuscitation technology, that they were able to survive their near-death episode at all. When examining the medical setting, there are three main levels of attitudes that have a profound impact on experiencers: the institutional, the interactional and the personal.

At an institutional level, it has been suggested that the dedication to thwart death indicates a belief on the part of the medical profession that death is never appropriate. Death is seen as the enemy. Michael Sabom, a cardiologist, notes that this attitude is vividly illustrated in a bas-relief on the facade of a major American medical center that depicts modern medicine, in the form of a man, doing battle with death, portrayed as the "grim reaper." Is it any wonder, with such a negative representation of death, that, as a society, we avert our gaze?

Sabom further suggests that medicine's institutional attitude to death and dying is reflected in the lack of training in this subject given to medical students. He quotes a report that found:

> In the American medical school, death is often regarded as a personal failure, an affront to a physician's power or a threat to his rescue fantasies. One recent survey of 107 U.S. medical schools . . . showed that only seven had a full-time course on thanatology.[15]

Reflecting on her own medical training, Sandra Marshall, a final-year medical student in South Australia, wrote in 1991:

> During my short medical career I have always managed to avoid dying patients, as I think most of my colleagues have. I think this is because we have not been expected to know how to cope with dying patients since our medical officers generally are also terribly insecure about death and feel that since they are unable to deal with the situation adequately, we shouldn't be expected to try. . . . It is no wonder that students feel inadequate talking to dying patients, for when our medical course is examined, it is found that palliative care is an infrequent topic for discussion. Medicine is notorious for denying failure of treatment. . . . If someone dies, it is because they have "failed to respond." We have been trained to cure people. . . . Hence accepting that patients won't get better is completely alien.[16]

There is a similar lack of training evident in nursing education. Certainly, in their professional lives, nurses are trained to care for the terminally ill. They are also instructed in particular routines for postmortem care. Yet, although they are taught how to physically care for the bodies of their patients, this is very different from being taught how to psychologically handle death and dying. In the medical setting, as several studies have revealed, doctors and nurses are just as uncomfortable in personal confrontations with dying as anyone else, whether it be telling a patient of their impending ·death, or confronting their own mortality. For example, Pattison notes that

> ... observation of nurses' reactions to call lights on a terminal care ward revealed that the closer to death the patient became, the slower the nurses were to answer the call light.[17]

In fact, the dying are much more difficult to deal with than the dead, since they cannot be so easily objectified. The dying require care and attention. They ask direct or indirect questions, express fears and other feelings. Yet these questions and fears are often left unanswered due to a lack of skills in this area of interpersonal relationships. As Avery Weisman and Thomas Hackett point out: "Physicians, as well as others close to the patient, sometimes do not respond to veiled inquiries simply because of their own anxiety." They also note that quite frequently, even dedicated physicians adopt what appears to be an impersonal professional manner simply as a means of coping with daily disaster.[18] However, whatever the reason, this attitude has important consequences for the doctor-patient relationship. Sabom quotes one of his respondents as saying "I'll be damned if I share my feelings about death and dying with anyone who makes two-minute U-turns at the foot of my bed."[19]

Weisman and Hackett believe that in fact many patients would be willing to discuss their death if only the doctor were able to overcome his own guilt or anxiety enough to permit it. Thus the doctor-patient relationship, inhibited as it is by an institutionalized lack of training in this area, is also very much affected by the individual physician's personal attitude to his or her own death.

Near-death experiencers are another case altogether since they force the health-care professional to confront the reality of the other side of death, the aspect that is avoided more than any other. As a number of my sample made clear: "Doctors can't handle that sort of thing!" Despite the powerful position of physicians in the doctor-patient relationship, their legitimacy as the gatekeepers of reality and knowledge is undermined in the eyes of their patients by their predominantly negative responses to NDE accounts. But from the viewpoint of the doctor thoroughly trained in the Western scientific paradigm and a product of our society's death denial, such a negative response could only be expected. Michael Sabom revealed his own initial response to NDE phenomena: "My indoctrinated scientific mind just couldn't relate seriously to these "far-out" descriptions of afterlife spirits and such." However, when he investigated the situation for himself, the third patient he approached revealed an NDE. Sabom wrote:

> To my utter amazement, the details matched the descriptions in [Moody's] *Life After Life*. . . . At the conclusion of the interview, I had the distinct feeling that what this woman had shared with me that night was a deeply personal glimpse into an aspect of medicine of which I knew nothing.[20]

Thus, in summary, the wider context within which a near-death experience occurs, especially the Western scientific paradigm, the denial of death and their conjunction in the Western medical setting, is of central theoretical and analytical relevance since it is overwhelmingly characterized by an inability to accommodate such a phenomenon. This obviously has significant consequences for experiencers, both immediately and subsequently, as they attempt to make sense of the experience in their daily lives for years to come.

THE "INTEGRATION TRAJECTORY"

The preceding chapters have already provided ample evidence of the changes that occur in the lives of those who have had an NDE. However, there is little in these results to suggest exactly how this experience is woven into the fabric of their lives. Does it happen smoothly or does it happen in fits and starts? Does it happen quickly or does it take a long time? Are there any commonalities of pattern or do individuals follow their own unique paths to integration, or nonintegration, of this major event? Do near-death experiencers actually cast off their old identities and assume new ones or do they simply trim around the edges, take a tuck in here, let a seam out there, in order to accommodate their new selves a bit more comfortably?

In attempting to answer these sorts of questions, I returned to the data once again and found, after extensive recoding, theoretical sampling and analysis that experiencers appear to follow what I have called an "integration trajectory" beginning immediately after the NDE and continuing until they feel the experience to be an integral part of their lives. However, integration should not be seen as an end point, one point in time, but, rather, like death itself, it is actually a process that eventually finds itself completed. And the completion represents not an end, but a new beginning. Neither should integration be seen only as an internal process. Although some experiencers do readily accept their NDE privately, there is still a need to test it and have it accepted socially before they experience it to be truly integrated.

In the following theoretical schema it will be suggested that integration can be said to have occurred when the trajectory and biography of the near-death experiencer are congruent. That is, there comes a time when the experiencers recognize (often in retrospect) that their NDE is now a part of their lives, congruent not only with their attitudes but also their actions. One aspect of this congruence is presented by Greyson and Harris when they write: "The therapeutic work is complete when the individual has found a way to actualize in daily life the love he or she received in the NDE."[21]

In this presentation of the integration trajectory, the emphasis will be on integration as an interactive process that happens over time. That is, it will be advanced as a social rather than solely psychological process. It will be seen that integration can be facilitated or hindered by a wide variety of social interactions, from the most intimate to the most impersonal. The notion of trajectory has been deliberately chosen to describe this process, since it suggests an ongoing dynamic process constantly being negotiated and managed by the individual within a particular social, intellectual, historical context. It should be noted that a trajectory can encompass many transitions along its path, for example, change in marital status, employment, education and religion, as well as life crises such as the death of a loved one. It is at such points that trajectory and biography intersect most powerfully. Any of these transitions may trigger a change in trajectory direction as well as a speeding up or slowing down of passage along the trajectory path.

A trajectory has both duration and shape. That is, different trajectories take place over different periods of time, and each type follows a different pattern. For instance, as the name would suggest, an accelerated trajectory is characterized by a fairly direct path to a speedy integration, whereas an arrested trajectory is characteristically found among people who put their experience on hold for a time, until something triggers further passage toward integration. The arrested period of time can be quite lengthy. In an extreme case among my sample it was forty-five years!

Some Important Variables

In the case of each near-death experiencer, it appears that there are certain events or interactions which, depending on their outcome, can be critical in directing them onto a particular trajectory. Although the variables possible are many, there are several that reappear regularly in accounts of post-NDE lives. This discussion will focus attention on these, while others will later be referred to in passing as they arise in interactions.

For some experiencers, even interactions *during* the NDE can provide a starting point for their trajectory. For instance, whether they choose to come back or are forced against their wishes can make a big difference in acceptance of their situation when they return. Thus reluctant returnees are unlikely to find themselves on an accelerated trajectory (at least not until they overcome their anger, disappointment or sense of rejection), whereas those who chose to return may soon find themselves with a strong sense of purpose moving rapidly toward integration and beyond. That is, the manner of the "homecoming" can be of central importance in whether or not experiencers accept that they are back. This acceptance is a precondition for progress toward integration along any trajectory. Another acceptance is also necessary—acceptance that the NDE is meaningful, whether or not they yet know what to make of it.

Many experiencers also comment on a shift in their awareness of context. After an NDE things look different. Patrick Gallagher suggests that this process somewhat resembles what anthropologists experience. When they first enter a new society they experience culture shock and when they later return to their own society they become aware of a counter shock. This comes about since the homecomer has no expectation of such a shift. Alfred Schutz notes:

The homecomer expects to return to an environment of which he always had and—so he thinks—still has intimate knowledge and which he has just to take for granted in order to find his bearings within it.[22]

Therefore this context awareness shift can come as something of a shock. Schutz writes:

Yet the change in the system of relevance . . . is differently experience by the absent one and by the home group. The latter continues its daily life within the customary pattern. . . .[23]

They have little idea of what the experiencer has undergone, or, even more significantly, what its impact has been. At the same time, experiencers suddenly find themselves aware of many features of their environment that had previously gone unnoticed, for example, the cognicentrism of their family, their doctors, nurses or ministers of religion. As Lyn Richards notes:

The webs of "reality" presented to us are invisible, until we run into them by defying them. . . . [This] experience may work for ideology the way dew does for spiderwebs, by highlighting the threads against the social scenery.[24]

In Schutz's terms, the "thinking as usual" that includes the "of-course" assumptions relevant to any social group simply breaks down and can no longer function for the near-death experiencer. It can be a bitter lesson to find that the taken-for-granted world is not as secure as it once seemed. The experience, which is unacceptable within the present Western worldview, leaves the experiencers floundering on the outer, without any defined status in their social group. They have left the security of their former status, they have undergone the experience and now they return to find they cannot truly go back to their former status, and yet there is no new status to receive them. This is one reason for the experiencer's need for corroboration and validation of their experience. They need a legitimate starting point for taking their bearings in a once-familiar world that has been stripped of its markers.

In his essay *The Stranger* Schutz writes:

> Strangeness and familiarity are not limited to the social field but are general categories of our interpretation of the world. If we encounter in our experience something previously unknown and which therefore stands out of the ordinary order of our knowledge, we begin a process of inquiry. We first define the new fact; we try to catch its meaning; we then transform step by step our general scheme of interpretation of the world in such a way that the strange fact and its meaning become compatible and consistent with all the other facts of our experience and their meanings.... If this process of inquiry succeeds, then this pattern and its elements will become ... a matter of course, an unquestionable way of life, a shelter, and a protection.[25]

The first step is to define the new fact, to catch its meaning. The process of disclosure is perhaps the key factor in defining and legitimizing the experience for most near-death experiencers—a precondition to further attempts at catching its meaning. There are many possible disclosure scenarios, each having its own impact on the integration trajectory of the experiencer. However, for example, at the most positive extreme, if immediately after an NDE the experiencer tells the doctor and is listened to attentively and reassured that it is an experience known to happen; if the experiencer then tells the nurse, who says she has had other patients recount similar episodes; if the experiencer then tells a family member who also knows of the experience and promises to bring in a book on the subject—then this person is off to a good start, probably along an accelerated trajectory to integration. Yet there are many possible interactions in life, and the passage to integration is unfortunately rarely so smoothly initiated.

Unprotected by mundane social identities, experiencers are extremely vulnerable at this early stage yet, naively, many are eager to tell others what happened. Frequently it is in this act of disclosure, sharing the experience with another person, that the experiencer first becomes aware of context—especially the pervasiveness of death denial and the unacceptability of mystical experiences in Western society. This can be puzzling and upsetting and might soon lead to a decision subsequently to keep the experience private. At the other end of the spectrum, for others, already aware of this context, or doubtful about the reality of what happened, nondisclosure is often the direct result. A silence on the experience can last for many years until something triggers further exploration. Typically, although not necessarily, this takes the form of corroborative information, such as a magazine or newspaper story, a book or, more rarely, a meeting with another known experiencer.

Once the context has been recognized, however inchoately, the process of context adaptation begins. The strategies employed by experiencers in adjusting to what they perceive to be a context hostile to NDEs are many and varied. For example, at one extreme, they may, in Goffman's terms, attempt "to pass"—remain inconspicuous, their identities as near-death experiencers hidden—rather than be stigmatized or have the experience challenged. One experiencer recently wrote to me:

It was several years before I could tell anyone about it, as I feared no one would believe me, and that the memory of such an experience would be spoiled for me, and make only nonsense to anyone else.

Silence is one of the most widely used coping strategies. Somewhat in the middle of the scale, some might make attempts at normalization of the experience, that is, to make it seem ordinary, to give the impression that they are not particularly attached to the experience as a way of protecting themselves from scorn. These experiencers tend to strip their account of emotional content and simply catalogue the elements of their experience: "I left my body, went down the usual sort of tunnel, saw a light, etc."

At the other extreme, experiencers may attempt to bypass mainstream societal values by creating for themselves new social networks that do meet their needs. Thus, they might actively seek out people who do approve of such things. They may link up with New Age social movements that give permission to talk about mystical experiences, and which, indeed, often have an indiscriminate appetite for any unusual phenomenon. Or they may try joining a spiritualist church or an Eastern religion to be in contact with others they believe might be familiar with otherworldly experiences.

There are many other strategies used for seeking meaning and following their vision, despite the context. One fairly recent and powerful facilitator for overcoming the silencing is the International Association for Near-Death Studies. This organization creates the conditions under which near-death experiencers can come together and seek affirmation from each other. The interaction that takes place within such a context varies markedly from interaction in the society outside the group, since all members are at the very least interested in the phenomenon even if they have not had an NDE themselves. IANDS also acts as an information resource for experiencers and others such as health-care professionals. As a consequence of making available such resources, running conferences, arranging public talks and providing speakers for media interviews, true "context subversion" can occur. For example, some doctors and nurses are now interested in changing the way they work with people in comatose states, with those resuscitated from near-death crisis situations and the recently deceased. In addition, as an earlier chapter has shown, experiencers themselves frequently retrain and work in this area—once again spreading information about NDEs and acting, whether intentionally or not, to undermine the predominant paradigm, to subvert the context.

Thus, the trajectory followed by any experiencer will in large part be influenced by a number of key variables: choice to return, acceptance of being back, acceptance of the experience as meaningful, change in context awareness, disclosure of the experience, context adaptation and/or context subversion. The manner in which these variables are negotiated gives preliminary shape to their trajectory. Both the time required to do this and the resultant trajectory patterns are varied.

The Trajectory-Biography Interrelationship

It has already been suggested that integration can be said to occur when the trajectory and biography are congruent. That is, a distinction is made between trajectory (the path taken to fit the NDE into the daily life of the experiencer) and biography (the life into which it is to fit). Obviously there is a close relationship between the two, but they are not initially inseparable.

Metaphorically, the NDE could perhaps be seen as an extra thread of wool of particularly bright hue that is to be woven into a piece of macramé. The life of the experiencer (the biography) is the unfinished macramé and the trajectory is the path traced as this bright new thread is woven into the overall design. However, in order to accommodate this extra piece of brightly colored wool, the original design has to be revised. Some will find this revision too daunting and put aside the new thread until they can work out what to do with it; some may try to disguise its brightness by weaving it under other colors or even dying it so others won't notice its unusual brightness; some will see it as an opportunity to look at the entire macramé afresh and develop a new, more vigorous, more beautiful pattern with the new thread as inspiration.

Thus, it can be seen that however the "thread" is perceived, trajectories do not simply happen. Trajectories require management—in Strauss's terms they are "work," and so are biographies. A significant aspect of the structural conditions within which this trajectory work is carried out are the biographies of others with whom the experiencer interacts. For instance, most experiencers are at some time in interaction with the biographies of doctors, nurses, and sometimes psychiatrists, psychologists and clergy. They also interact with the biographies of family members and friends. And as Wiener et al. suggest, it is not only people who have biographies—in a very real sense so do hospitals, medical specializations and intensive care units, since they all have histories and futures.

For example, despite many common features, hospital biographies can be quite individual. The level of resources for equipment and trained personnel will differ from small rural to major city institutions. Even in major cities, resources can be severely strained depending on the needs of the community being serviced. Thus a major city hospital could have its resources overtaxed by a wider social context—the poverty of the local community, the AIDS epidemic or the widespread use of crack.

The financial support for particular medical specializations will also vary from institution to institution, and over time. Often this will interact with what has been called a "machine biography." For instance, well-funded research has led to development of increasingly sophisticated technology that permits intervention in the dying process, enabling medical personnel to save the lives of patients formerly certain to die. Within the hospital setting there is a wide range of possible staff biography interactions. Staff responsible for administration, cleaning and catering all interact on a daily basis, as do physicians, nurses and their patients.

Using the case of an early disclosure scenario, it is possible to see how a near-death experiencer's trajectory and biography can interact with other biographies around them. For the sake of simplicity, the example will principally deal with the interaction of two biographies—those of the physician and the experiencer. The hypothetical scenario takes place in a hospital setting, thus is embedded in a context that has its own well-established institutional routines and practices. The experiencer is attended by a male cardiologist whose biography (professional and even personal) will provide some of the conditions for the interaction. Perhaps, as suggested by Michael Sabom, as a consequence of medical training, this cardiologist has a strongly held belief in science and has chosen this particular medical subspecialty because it is a precise technological discipline utilizing measurable physiological data. Perhaps he feels more comfortable interpreting measurements than counseling patients. This doctor's response to the experiencer could perhaps also be colored by whether or not the crisis is expected and whether he judges it to be self-inflicted. In many years of practice he has never heard an NDE account firsthand, and any mention of them in the media he has dismissed as unscientific and farfetched. With regard to his own mortality, he has never given it much thought, expecting that when the body dies, obviously that is that.

The experiencer's biography has not prepared him for an NDE either. He is middle-aged, works at a trade, smokes and is overweight. He has not been to church since childhood and holds no afterlife beliefs. He has never given dying much thought and has never encountered anyone who has had an NDE. During his NDE he experienced a "life review," and was told "it was not his time yet." He chose to return.

When he regained consciousness sometime later, his doctor happened to be present and the somewhat over-whelmed experiencer told him what he had experienced. As could be expected from the doctor's biographical details, he greeted such an affront to his belief system with discomfort and a "rational" explanation. Due to the unequal nature of doctor-patient relationships, the doctor's rationality inevitably governed the interchange to the detriment of the experiencer's own account. The experiencer could have responded in a number of different ways. Perhaps he was puzzled, and a seed of doubt was planted regarding the reality of what happened. That is, perhaps he accepted the doctor's explanation. However, he could also have used the strategy of outward compliance to the doctor's explanation while inwardly rebelling, determining to find out more. That is, in the first case, the experiencer's trajectory could have been arrested by this interchange. Or, in the second case, the meaning seeking and reality testing could have continued by means of further disclosures to other staff, family or friends.

At this early stage of post-NDE life, physical recovery from the near-death crisis often has the highest priority. Depending on the severity of the crisis, this biographical work may take up most of the energy of the recovering experiencer. However, for many experiencers, the NDE is immediately accepted as meaningful, whether or not there has been a helpful response to disclosure, and the trajectory work has already begun.

Trajectory Work and Biography

For the purposes of this analysis, trajectory work is that activity (action/interaction/strategy) that manages and controls the integration process and directly furthers progress on a particular trajectory path. Trajectory work and biography are always interrelated and often intersect. Indeed, the biography of the near-death experiencer provides one of the most important contextual conditions for trajectory work. The fact that an experiencer is young or old, female or male, single or married, educated or uneducated, middle class or working class, employed or unemployed, creates a particular biographical context within which the trajectory work will be done.

The relationship between trajectory work and biography can be complex. At times it is the trajectory work that is given priority over biography maintenance. For instance, Barbara Harris describes how, despite her husband's increasing opposition, she became involved in volunteer work at a local hospital, and later felt impelled to begin training as a respiratory therapist. On the other hand, at different times for other experiencers, it may be the trajectory work that is overtaken by the exigencies of biography. For example, depending on life-cycle stage, being a mother can be an important biographical detail that requires work in terms of interaction with children, schools or child-care organizations. If the mother is employed, it can also involve fatigue and the juggling of work hours, and emotions as diverse as frustration, guilt, resentment, satisfaction and pleasure. A biographical detail such as "mother work" can, by its overwhelming time-consuming nature, temporarily act to impede trajectory work.

Biography and trajectory work can intersect at various points to provide intervening conditions that may either hinder or facilitate the next stage of integration activity. For instance, when "mother work" is in crisis after the death of a child, an abrupt shift in trajectory path can be triggered, with an awakening of interest in the NDE and an enhanced commitment to change. For example, Martine recounted the story of her daughter's death and the aftermath:

Because of my experience, I could help my daughter when she died. She went into a coma and when she came out again she just looked at me and she said:

"Mommy, take me home." I just said, "I will." And at that moment I realized something happened in me. I knew she was not asking me to bring her home to our little house, but to take her home where she was going. I knew she was dying and I knew where she was going. So somehow I just stood next to her, I was just there with her, I held her hand and we "walked" over there. And she came out absolutely gleaming, aglow. So I felt yes, she is seeing what I have seen years and years back, where I was going years and years ago. A few hours later she went into a coma and never came out.

The experience helped me a lot. I was grieving for myself but I knew where she was, and I could not be sorry for that. It is beautiful where she is. I knew there was no pain there. There is no pain where she is. It helped me a lot. It does still help me somehow. When I think of her it is not a sad thing. . . . After Sylvie died I started to be aware there were other things, in a tangible way, but I couldn't talk to my husband about it. It took me still a couple of years before I heard of meditation. Against my husband's wishes I went with my youngest daughter and took a course at the Self-Transformation Centre. More and more I meditated and it became a joke with my husband—"Here she goes again!" I slowly kept it up. When I started to meditate I think he thought I was starting to escape him. And I was!

Meaning seeking is probably the major component of trajectory work. It begins early and provides much of the impetus for continued movement along the trajectory path. After the NDE, one of the first kinds of trajectory work involves a subcategory of meaning seeking that I have called reality testing. Often the experiencer feels the need to check out the reality of what happened. This can be risky, since they are vulnerable and disclosure leaves them open

to possible discredit. Thus some choose initially to keep
the experience to themselves, and do this reality testing as
best they can, reflectively. Some choose to quietly seek out
information on "that sort of thing" by going to libraries or
bookshops. Some give hints of what happened and observe
the response. Others reveal all. Whatever their choice, the
process of reality testing reveals an important feature of
trajectory work—that it can be of two kinds, inner and
outer.

Inner trajectory work is made up of at least three
subcategories: intellectual work, identity work and inner
spiritual work.

Intellectual work involves developing a clear understanding of all the information (inner and outer) bearing
on the NDE—including the experiencer's own actual experience of it, and the response to it by others, whether written, spoken or unspoken.

Identity work is largely an ego-strengthening exercise
for experiencers, including development and consolidation
of self-confidence and self-esteem. This work can be as-
sisted by reflection on their own experience during the
NDE—especially the sense of being a worthy person, unconditionally loved and accepted. Some engage in identity
work through participation in therapy, or personal development, communication or self-awareness training courses.
This work facilitates a reorientation of values, a reordering
of priorities, and can give a focus to their strong sense of
purpose.

Inner spiritual work typically involves the transcendence of the ego through prayer and the practice of meditation with the aim of maintaining a conscious contact
with the Light, Higher Power or God (however that being
is understood), seeking and taking guidance.

All three can best be seen as being in a dialectical relationship with aspects of outer trajectory work such as relationship work, career work (paid or unpaid) and study
work, although at different times the focus may appear to

settle more on one than on the others. Both inner and outer trajectory work are avenues of meaning seeking, and all make their contribution to the shape and duration of the integration trajectory followed.

Trajectory Types

Using my data, I have discerned four clear integration trajectory types, most of which have either two or three subcategories that distinguish differences within the major types, and give some indication of the complex nature of the thrust toward integration. These are arranged in order from most rapid integration to nonintegration.

Type 1: Accelerated	i) confirmatory
	ii) accelerated
Type 2: Steady	iii) steady-accelerated
	iv) steady
Type 3: Arrested	v) arrested-accelerated
	vi) arrested-steady
	vii) arrested
Type 4: Blocked	viii) blocked

Type 1: Accelerated Trajectory
Both forms of accelerated trajectory are characterized by their speedy path to integration.

The *confirmatory trajectory* is the most extreme form of accelerated trajectory, and leads to the most rapid integration. This type of trajectory is typically followed by near-death experiencers whose life experiences have already prepared them for such an episode. Prior to their NDE, these people were already on a spiritual path and had had other experiences of nonordinary reality in one form or another.

Experiencers who follow a confirmatory trajectory are

already accepting of psychic phenomena and death. For these people the NDE *confirms* already strongly held beliefs based on personal experience and intellectual exploration. Their NDE has the effect of giving them absolute confidence in, and tends to add depth to, these beliefs. Since they have no doubts about its reality and legitimacy, disclosure is not a problem for them, although their awareness of context leads them to discriminate between those they can share it with, and those they can't. This is not difficult for them since these experiencers are generally already structurally situated within a network of like-minded others who have had similar experiences and/or are similarly accepting and interested.

Prior to the NDE, their awareness of social context with regard to mystical experiences and nonordinary reality in general is already high. Thus there is little change in this important aspect of context awareness afterward. Nevertheless, the experience itself adds a new contextual condition within which they must re-view and reorder their lives. Context adaptation for this group of experiencers will of course require some trajectory work, but this work, whether inner or outer, is not seen as problematic because the path to be followed is familiar and already much appreciated rather than a journey into the unknown.

Mary is typical of experiencers who follow the confirmatory trajectory to integration. At the time of her NDE, she had already been working as a healer for many years and had experienced a wide range of psychic phenomena. She said that before her own near-death episode she already had some understanding of NDEs but admitted that it was an understanding based mainly on her reading of Elisabeth Kübler-Ross, and theosophical literature. She said:

> Any book you read is just purely intellectual. It cannot possibly resemble the experience—it's so intimate and so personal. . . . I mean, you can

understand something intellectually but it doesn't have any impact.

She had a similar intellectual acceptance of death.

Well, I knew intellectually that my inner being, my spirit, would not die, it would just go into another dimension, which was great, but it was all in the head.

During her deep NDE (which scored twenty-four on Ring's WCEI scale), she had a profoundly moving experience of love, and was given the knowledge that she had further work to do in this lifetime. Therefore she chose to return to her body. She had no difficulty in accepting the meaningfulness of the experience and had no doubt as to its reality. Although she knew her doctor to be a caring man, she was very aware of his orthodoxy and did not disclose her experience to him, since she felt sure he would have dismissed it "as hallucination or some other fancy name." She had friends she could tell and soon found that she was sharing it with the dying people with whom she worked.

Soon after her recovery from the near-death crisis, she was asked to work in a hospice, which she regards as the "further work" she had to do. She said:

That experience meant a lot. When you're dealing with people who are dying, it helps them to know that you know what you're talking about. It's all very well reading a book about it, but face-to-face, with physical contact, and eye contact, it makes all the difference to have been there.

Thus, in looking at these few aspects of one person's trajectory, it can be seen that rather than having to chart new territory, change tends to follow and deepen already established patterns. It is therefore not long before the NDE is well integrated.

• • •

The standard *accelerated trajectory* is also characterized by a swift passage to integration. However, in this case there is far more trajectory work to be done along the way since there is generally no preparation for such an episode in the life experience of these experiencers. Although the actual constellation of trajectory work can be extremely complex and vary greatly from case to case, one feature of the accelerated trajectory is overridingly clear—the NDE is recognized as an event of primary significance in the lives of these experiencers and is held as a focus for further development. The impulse to understand and somehow live up to this vision remains paramount, and provides the energy that drives the experiencer so rapidly along this path.

In many ways Janet is typical of those who follow the accelerated trajectory. Her NDE occurred during surgery (hysterectomy) when she had a cardiac arrest. She had a deep experience (measuring twenty-two on Ring's WCEI scale) during which she said, "I felt the presence of extreme love . . . and saw a review of my whole life." She said that the greatest shame she felt about her life was that she had totally rejected the concept of God. She said:

> I'd totally given no acknowledgment to God, I really didn't believe in God. And I was incredulous that I could ever have doubted that God existed because He was so real and tangible. I say "He," but that's my conditioning. God was just this essence, this total essence of love.

She was told that it wasn't her time to go on because she still had her life's work to do. She said:

> I remember asking what my life's work was. And I was told you'll not know at this time but you

will be shown.... I was also told to come back
and to tell my husband and children what had happened.

She did not regain consciousness until a couple of days
later. At that time she felt "a bit shattered" that she
couldn't be where she'd been during the experience. Yet
she said:

It felt pretty good to be in my body. But I noticed
that there'd been a change in me. There was a complete change in my attitude to the people looking after me. I'd brought back with me a touch of that
love, and it's stayed with me. I think it's always remained, that sense of peace.

She thus accepted that she was back and had no doubt
about the meaningfulness of the experience.

For Janet, early disclosure was not a problem, since she
had been told to share her NDE with her husband and children. Her husband was surprised but accepting, and
through later difficulties was to provide her greatest support. She also told the surgeon what she'd seen and heard,
and described the conversation with the Light. He was
startled and didn't say much except to warn her against
having operations that involved an anaesthetic. Despite the
surgeon's response, Janet *knew* that her NDE was real
and important, and believed that, literally, she still had
her life's work to do. The problem was to find out what
that life's work was, so that she could get on with it. For
the next eighteen months she continually questioned what
it had all been about. She spoke to various ministers of religion and was warned against delving into such dangerous
things. By contrast, her friends thought she'd gone "all religious" and began to drift away. Her mother was also worried about her change in behavior. Finally "by accident"
she met a Jungian analyst who, she said,

... totally believed me and related to what I'd gone through, and suggested I look at mysticism. He said, "You're not odd, just trust it . . ." So that was like a ray of sunshine beaming in at a time when I was starting to question whether or not there was maybe a problem.

During those months she said her "logical mind was chipping away at it," but she found she couldn't share it with many people. Changes in attitude had already happened, but only enough to be disturbing to others. What she really felt she needed was some sort of acknowledgment of what it was she was to do. Soon after, "the guidance" began. She said:

I was standing there, cooking, stirring a sauce, and being introspective and thinking, "What is it, God, that you want me to do?" At that point I just heard the same inner voice that I'd been confronted with when I left my body during the NDE. That presence of love came back there . . . and I was told that we were to go to the mountains in the south to make a place of rest and solace for many in the future. . . .

After that, every time I wanted to ask something, there was the answer. And I knew it was coming from something external to myself, but within myself, if you can understand. I had answers of a spiritual depth that I knew wasn't me. And I really wondered how I was going to explain this to my husband and children. I shared it with him and he believed me. So we kept asking questions. . . . And there was this terrible tension in me to know what it was we had to do, and it was almost like an obsession for a few months. But, of course, that was my lesson—to learn patience and obedience and learn to be led.

When we look at it now, from that first time to when we moved here to Oakdale was exactly nine months, and it was the period of gestation. And for us it was a total rebirth of our lives. We changed our whole direction and mode of living.

For Janet, the disclosures to her spouse and to the Jungian analyst were the most helpful, and provided strong enough support to enable her to override the hostility and doubts of others. In adapting to the new context, the trajectory work was complex—a combination of intellectual, identity and especially spiritual inner work, along with much relationship and career work. The outstanding feature of this and other accelerated trajectories is the speed with which so much change comes about, and integration is completed. In Janet's case, within twenty-seven months of her NDE her life had been turned upside down and she and her husband had given up their comfortable suburban lifestyle and business for a simple hut in a remote area of the Snowy Mountains. Within that short period of time Janet was living her vision, and that, of course, was only the beginning.

Type 2: Steady Trajectory

Unlike the accelerated trajectory, with its associated urgency, the *steady trajectory* is characterized by the unhurried yet consistent rate at which change comes about. Despite many small changes, the steady trajectory may proceed over many years before the NDE is integrated fully into the lives of experiencers.

Those following this type of trajectory typically have no preparation for such an episode and no basis from which to judge it. Privately, they readily accept the meaningfulness of the experience, but publicly they are cautious in their disclosures and tend initially to keep the experience to themselves while they consider its implications. On the other hand, for some near-death experiencers, it will have been an unfavorable response to an early disclosure that led them to follow the steady trajectory path in the first place. Thus, in the early stages, an inability to talk about the experience with others or a self-protective desire to keep it private is another important characteristic of this group of experiencers.

Some of those following a steady trajectory will quietly but unremittingly go about discovering what their NDE was all about, by whatever means they can. But others tend to engage more in passive meaning seeking. That is, they maintain an interest in the experience, will keep an eye out for articles about it but will not generally actively seek out information and groups on their own. Before the recent publicity about NDEs, many experiencers followed the steady trajectory and engaged in passive meaning seeking simply because they were unaware, due to our societal silence on such matters, that others had had similar experiences. Today this problem is not as acute.

Over time they become aware of differences in their own attitudes but tend to keep a low profile so they can be true to the NDE yet integrate it into their lives without too much disruption, that is, without "rocking the social boat."

Moira is typical of experiencers who follow the steady trajectory. She had her experience thirty-seven years ago. During her NDE (which scored fourteen on Ring's WCEI scale) she was drawn toward and found herself enveloped in a beautiful golden light. She wanted to stay in that environment of warmth and love, but a voice told her that she was too early, and she then found herself drawn back to her body.

From the time she awoke, "with all these faces over me and everybody working on me," she knew that the experience was important for her, and that she would no longer fear death. She said:

> After that, the feeling stayed with me for such a long while, and even now I can get back in it at a moment's notice. I can get back in it and experience it. And I knew from that moment on that there isn't any death—it's just a different state of consciousness. We

close our eyes in this room and we wake up in another room, sort of thing.

She was very aware of context and thus didn't consider disclosure to be an option at that time. She kept the experience private for many years, although never doubting its reality or significance. She said:

No, I didn't talk about it in those days. I mean, thirty years ago you were considered a crank. I didn't talk about it for many years because I just knew it was true. I knew it was the truest, most honest thing that had ever happened to me. I didn't for a moment think, "Oh, I'm going around the bend," or "There might have been something gone wrong in my brain." I just knew that that was the truth, and that was the true reality.... I finally told a couple of girlfriends many years later. They had been rather worried because they had had experiences—seeing visions and hearing voices. They didn't know what that was all about, and then I told them my experience, and went on from there.

The positive response at her first disclosure only added further validity to her own well-established view of the experience. After the NDE, over a period of many years, she began the complex process of context adaptation and trying to discover the meaning of it all. She became especially interested in the spiritual side of life:

I started investigating. I knew there was some underlying God or intelligence, but I felt that the churches had it all wrong [laughs] and I could never find the answers there. I'd read ordinary books on Christianity which always left me very much doubting. So after that I started experimenting. I went to spiritualist groups, and all those sorts of things, and I went

through all that spiritualism and psychism stage, and
gradually moved on to other religions and so forth. I
investigated all sorts of religions—Mormonism,
Christian Science, all sorts of things. And gradually
I developed my own philosophy—I knew there was
a God, and I knew that I wasn't separate. I knew that
I didn't need a priest or a minister between me and
God. I was a part of God.

In those days I think people believed all the or-
thodox stuff even more than they do now. I felt like
an inner rebel really. I listened to what everybody
said and nodded my head, but inside I thought, "Oh,
no, I can't accept that, that's not right." So I with-
drew from the ordinary church.

She also went through a stage of exploring her new psychic sensitivities, but only with people of like mind. Even
at the time of the interview she noted that she still experienced psychic phenomena but would no longer "go out
looking for it, or doing it on purpose." Over the years her
self-confidence and sense of self-worth had developed and
she found that her attitudes had changed along the typical
lines described in previous chapters, that is, she became
nonmaterialistic and more loving. She found that she
needed to be helpful to others and finally, some twenty
years later, made it her career, training as a welfare worker
and becoming welfare director of a mission society.

Thus it can be seen that a steady trajectory can be
quite long. In Moira's case it took over twenty years for
the NDE to be integrated comfortably, not only into her
attitudes but also into her life activity. Although the NDE
is acknowledged as meaningful from the beginning, it is
typically (but not necessarily) kept private for a long
time. Many of the changes that come about are therefore
achieved without any social support for their raison
d'être.

• • •

For some near-death experiencers on the steady path, the sudden achievement of social support and validation can be so significant that it will swing them out of their steady trajectory onto a more accelerated path to integration. Other triggers could also act in a similar way For example the trigger could be biographical (such as the death of a child), or it could be a fortuitous meeting with another experiencer, or it could come as a result of trajectory work (such as beginning work in a hospice). Whatever the source, a sudden speeding up of a previously steady trajectory path can transform it into a *steady-accelerated* trajectory.

The time spent in the steady phase of the trajectory can vary widely. For example, in the case of Martine, earlier cited, it was twenty years before the death of her daughter triggered a change over to the accelerated phase of her trajectory. In Gary's case it was five years.

For Gary the highlight of the NDE (rated seventeen on Ring's WCEI scale) was being in a state of luminous presence. He was absolutely convinced of the meaningfulness of his experience but had no idea at all what to make of it. He was wary of telling anyone about it. He said: "I didn't want to say anything to anyone because I thought I'd automatically be labeled crazy." However, four weeks after his NDE he found some corroboration in a Buddhist text. Being only sixteen at the time, he found it rather hard to deal with the Buddhist teachings, but he felt sure they could help him understand what had happened to him:

> For quite a while there, trying to grapple with all those things really made me feel quite disturbed, and the NDE fell a bit into the background. But I'd lay in bed at night and go through the visual imagery, and wonder whether I should say anything to anyone, or whether I was going crazy.

Nevertheless, he continued to change his attitudes and make changes in his young life:

> The whole experience really catapulted me into something quite different. I mean, I became quite different from the rest of my family as far as the way I think is concerned, really quite different.

Five years had passed before he made the first disclosure:

> I finally talked about it with some friends. When I was twenty-one I went to a Buddhist community in Queensland and it was then that it occurred to me that I could talk about it. In actual fact I was surprised that they were quite accepting of it even though they hadn't had experiences like that themselves.

The success of this disclosure was the turning point for Gary that gave social recognition to the NDE and provided him personally with enough confidence to make further disclosures, and to continue development along his own spiritual path. Other changes quickly followed.

Type 3: Arrested Trajectory
An arrested trajectory is characterized by the way in which integration of the NDE is stopped in its tracks by contextual conditions. Those in this situation value the experience but don't know what to make of it. They are unable to share it with anyone, either because it has consistently been rejected by others or because of a fear that it will be. Near-death experiencers on an arrested trajectory typically lack the confidence to undertake trajectory work alone, without some form of social support. Some are aware of this need and seek out that support, but others simply put the experience on hold until some future time when they feel they will be better able to deal with it.

Evan is typical of experiencers who follow an *arrested*

trajectory. During his NDE (rated eight on Ring's WCEI scale) Evan experienced a joyous out-of-body experience but had no interaction with other beings, heard no voices and made no choice to return. He simply woke up back in his body with the staff working on him. He was pleased to be back and very impressed by the experience but had no understanding of what had happened. Even at the time of the interview, nine years later, Evan was still intrigued by the experience but had no clearer idea about it. In the intervening years he had made three attempts at disclosure that were all rebuffed. Initially he told the doctor who "just looked up but was not very interested." When he told his wife, he said: "She just shut off, didn't say a thing and hasn't mentioned it since." Sometime later he returned to work, and Evan describes what happened when he told a work friend: "He said, 'Ah, pull the other bloody leg!' and stormed off. So after that I couldn't tell anyone."

Sometime after the interview I wrote to Evan, along with all the other experiencers, asking whether his participation in the research process and my going to see him had had any effect on the way he perceived his experience. Evan replied that it hadn't changed his views on the experience but, he wrote:

> Relating my experience to you was very much appreciated. I would be grateful if any further research on the subject could be forwarded to me, just out of curiosity.

Experiencers on an arrested trajectory have not closed off the possibility of integration. Their acceptance of the significance of the experience always leaves this possibility open, even though their inability to begin the necessary trajectory work halts proceedings for a time. There is always the potential for them to move to a steady or accelerated trajectory path when they feel they are ready or when something triggers a more active response. Both of these latter patterns are frequently found among childhood experiencers. For example, Barbara had her NDE at the age of ten, was unable to talk about it with anyone and forty-five years passed before she retrieved her experience and embarked on an accelerated path to integration. Similarly, Hal had his experience as a fourteen-year-old. Rebuffed in all attempts to talk about his NDE, he said:

> I thought I was the only person in the world to have such an experience. It wasn't until about thirty years later that I heard Elisabeth Kübler-Ross on TV and realized that other people have had it too.

This realization reawakened his interest in the experience and led him also to embark on an accelerated trajectory.

Cora provides us with an example of the *arrested-accelerated trajectory*. She was in her late twenties when she had her NDE (rated fourteen on Ring's WCEI scale). Her experience was interrupted by the resuscitation effort and she was brought back suddenly. This precipitous wrench out of the depths of the experience left her feeling shocked for some time after:

> I felt deep shock and I was bewildered. I didn't feel joyous or happy to be back or to have my life saved, because I had gone away in that experience. . . . I felt like I came back through my lungs, but that was because I was so interfered with physically.

Despite the shock, she had no doubt about the significance of the experience, but any attempts she made at disclosure were unhelpful and in some cases even hostile. With a strong sense of abandonment she stopped talking about it. Nine years later she started seeing a psychiatrist, who gave her "wonderful support" that encouraged her to look into it again. Other helpful disclosures further aided this process:

> I had that gap of not sharing it with anybody at all. So it's like there was this gap, but then the NDE transcended that gap in a way. It's like the experience was here, and then there's this gap, and then I took off into my more conscious life that I've lived in the last few years.

Now she says she can see that "the actual experience was something to be used, and given to other people in life, through my work."

Once the gap of the arrested phase of the trajectory was passed, Cora quickly entered the accelerated phase, involving both inner and outer trajectory work and bringing about many life changes in a short space of time.

Denise is typical of the *arrested-steady trajectory*. She had her NDE (rated twenty-one on Ring's WCEI scale) at age seventeen. During the experience she heard a voice that she took to be the voice of "God or St. Peter or someone of religious significance" that told her that she was too young and had a life of service ahead of her. She returned to her body with great regret. She accepted the importance of the experience but did not know what to make of it:

> It was a very significant experience. But it also seemed a peculiar sort of experience, seeing as I was a child at the time and unaware of anything sort of similar. I was quite embarrassed about it and thought, you know, I must have been losing my mind. I just couldn't understand it. I didn't discuss it with anyone. I was embarrassed. I thought well, perhaps a blow on the head has left me confused. I didn't discuss it.

It was not until fourteen years later that she made her first disclosure, triggered by coming across an article about NDEs in *Reader's Digest*. She recounts what happened:

> I read this thing in *Reader's Digest* at work, and I was just so stunned that I said to the people in the room, "Oh, but that's just what happened to me!" It was sort of an involuntary reaction. And we started talking about it, but even then I didn't say a lot. Working in psychiatry, I thought maybe it was some sort of an enzyme reaction or some chemical imbalance related to shock or stress. But also because of the importance to me—it was important to me and I didn't want anyone to belittle it. It was to me a pleasurable, moving and very intense experience.

This incident started her thinking about the experience again and relating it to her life. However, she never did tell her husband ("I thought he'd take it as foolish nonsense") and it was some years before she mentioned it again. By the time of the interview she still had told only three or four people. She said: "It doesn't disturb me to talk about it, it's just to me it's a personal thing. It's not that I am ashamed of it, it's just something private."

Denise has engaged in much trajectory work, both inner and outer, over the twelve years since the NDE was so unexpectedly brought back into her life. This process of context adaptation and meaning seeking was consolidated and given a final push to integration by meeting other near-death experiencers at the first IANDS meeting in my home last year. With regard to that meeting she later wrote to me:

> Now I am able to accept the experience as normal and relatively common. . . . I think the advent of IANDS is great. A "coming out" perhaps. I hope it continues. I now feel confident to spread the word.

Thus, the arrested trajectory may last many years, but there is always a potential for it to pass into a more active phase. Part of that potential lies in the experiencers' early acceptance of the significance of their experience and their willingness to embark on the necessary trajectory work. This is not the case for NDErs on a blocked trajectory.

Type 4: Blocked Trajectory

A *blocked trajectory* is typically followed by that minority of experiencers who deny that the experience has any value, and who therefore show no willingness or interest in its integration. There is no acceptance of the experience as meaningful, and if there is any attempt at disclosure, the response tends to corroborate this meaninglessness. There is no attempt at meaning seeking and there is a resolute belief that nothing has changed, so context adaptation and trajectory work is seen as irrelevant.

Albert is an experiencer who followed the blocked trajectory. Even during his experience (rated eight on Ring's WCEI scale) there was a denial of its importance for him, since when he was out of body observing the commotion around his body he did not recognize that it was himself. When he recovered, he said, he thought to himself:

> That's strange, that was me up there and why didn't I know that was me down there? I've never been able to relate the two, I knew quite clearly that everything was going to be all right, but I didn't know it was me.

At that stage it seems that he was still possibly open to working with the experience. However, after two disclosures he seemed reassured that the experience was not important and that he could forget about it. The next day he told his wife, who made no comment at all, although in later years referred to it, along with Albert himself, in a jocular fashion. A few years later he went to a psychiatrist "for depression." He said:

I've spoken to my psychiatrist about it and he made no real comment about it one way or the other. It helped me for him not to make anything of it. It minimized it in my mind and so I still feel that it was just a funny thing that happened to me "on the way to the theater," you know.

He said that before his experience he had heard that some people had traveled out of their bodies but was very skeptical—"It sounded ridiculous to me." Even after his own NDE he maintained his skepticism. He said: "I think it's a bit foolish. You know, I can't see there's any reality to it."

In contrast to the majority of near-death experiencers, in the years since his experience he did not regain a sense of well-being but suffered ongoing health problems and depression. He maintained: "Nothing's altered since that period of time." He died a year after the interview.

Overall, it should be clear, even from this general overview, that integration is not a process that happens uniformly. The many conceptual features interwoven in the integration trajectory theory enable distinctions to be made on several dimensions. For example, *time:* The accelerated trajectory carries the experiencer to integration more quickly than the steady trajectory. The arrested trajectory can reflect a delay of many years and the blocked trajectory can represent an unwillingness to engage in any trajectory work at all.

It would appear that *depth* of NDE as measured on Ring's WCEI scale could be a predictor of trajectory path. That is, on the basis of my limited data, it seems that those experiencers with the highest WCEI scores tend to follow accelerated trajectories at some stage, whether immediately or after an initial arrested period. Only those with the lowest WCEI scores tend to follow an arrested or blocked trajectory. Overall, there appears to be some correlation, although this needs to be further investigated before any firm claims for such an effect can be made.

On the other hand, the process of *disclosure* definitely is a key feature in determining trajectory path. The structural conditions under which this occurs (or does not occur), the strategies used by experiencers in these interactions and the consequences that result all contribute to the determination of the trajectory path to be followed and provide the conditions for further trajectory work. In some cases, notably the steady-accelerated, arrested-steady and arrested-accelerated trajectories, successful disclosure can be a key variable in moving the experiencer from one trajectory path to another, hastening integration.

The processes of meaning seeking and context adaptation are also extremely complex but can be identified and traced more easily with the use of conceptual categories such as inner and outer trajectory work (with their many subcategories), by means of which the conditions giving rise to them, the strategies used by experiencers and others, their interactions, and the consequences for the interactants can also be followed. And as earlier noted, further complicating the picture, biography and trajectory path can intersect at any number of points, often with profound implications for the near-death experiencer and the ultimate integration of their experience.

The next chapter concludes the study by providing a summary of the major findings with regard to the lived experience of near-death experiencers following their NDE.

Conclusion

One recurring theme in the near-death accounts is the difficulty experiencers have in talking about their NDE. This was examined in some detail in Chapter 5, where it was reported that near-death experiencers were more likely to tell family and friends of their experience than doctors, nurses or anyone else. It was found that a positive response was most likely to be received from a friend, whereas almost half of the family members who were told about the experience responded negatively. Not many disclosures were made to doctors and nurses by this particular group of experiencers. However, it was found that the nurses to whom the experience was disclosed tended to respond more positively than the doctors.

As discussed in Chapter 10, this response by health-care professionals is understandable in terms of the predominant Western attitude of death denial, a widespread belief in the Western scientific paradigm and lack of adequate training in this area. However, it is not in any way helpful to experiencers, who are frequently confronted by negative responses ranging from silence and discomfort to outright hostility. Nevertheless, it is within this context of general societal ignorance that experiencers live their lives, while grappling, often privately, with a wide range of aftereffects.

AFTEREFFECTS

My study found that attitudes to death changed markedly after an NDE. A belief in life after death was universal in this sample and this belief was firmly based on personal experience. There was also a well-established movement toward a belief in reincarnation, with eighty percent of experiencers claiming to believe in it following their NDE.

Attitudes to suicide were complex. There was a deeply held conviction among the sample following the experience that they would not personally take their own lives, further strengthening similar findings by other researchers. Although strongly against suicide for themselves, there was nevertheless an overriding compassion and sadness expressed for anyone who did commit suicide.

Following their experience, the entire sample of fifty near-death experiencers said they no longer had any fear of death. Quite apart from the beneficial effects on their own lives, this loss of fear was also instrumental in changing their attitude to the situation of others. For example, they commonly expressed a desire to work with one of the most avoided groups in our society—the grieving, the elderly and dying.

Many changes were also reported by this sample of experiencers in terms of religious beliefs, attitudes and practices. They overwhelmingly considered their experience to be spiritual rather than religious in nature. They also clearly rejected the religious label, preferring to describe themselves as spiritual. This perception was borne out in their religious affiliations, where over eighty percent of the sample claimed to have no religion. Overall, there was an established shift away from organized religion and church attendance and toward private nonformula prayer, meditation and a quest for spiritual values. There appeared to be a general feeling among this group that during their NDE they had had a direct contact with God, or a Higher Power, and they therefore had no need of any intermediary in that ongoing relationship.

An enhancement of psychic sensitivities was reported. Although prior to their near-death episode this sample was found to be normal when compared with a general population (in terms of their experience of psychic phenomena), following their NDE there was a notable increase in a wide range of psychic sensitivities. Overall, there was reported to be a significant increase in the incidence of episodes of clairvoyance, telepathy, precognition, out-of-body experiences and supernatural rescues. Intuition and healing ability appeared to be enhanced. There was a greater awareness of dreams, and an increase in the perception of auras and contact with spirits. Only the incidence of déjà vu was not found to be statistically significant.

However, there was a wide variety of responses to these increases in psychic sensitivity. Some experiences, such as enhanced intuition and clairvoyance, were often readily accepted as normal and absorbed into everyday life, whereas others, such as out-of-body experiences, telepathy or contact with spirits, were for some at times seen as disturbing. Almost every experiencer interviewed was aware of this increase in psychic sensitivity, although, interestingly, in view of the impact this had had on their lives, not one of them cited it as the most significant change to come about as a result of their experience.

Changes in life direction were found to be well established among this sample. In terms of attitude to themselves, there was a definite shift to a more positive view of self, a firm commitment to an inner life and a strong sense of purpose. Perhaps as a corollary of this higher self-esteem, there was a noticeable shift away from concern with what others thought of them. These major changes in attitude to self seemed to overflow quite naturally into changes in attitude to others.

•   •   •

In most cases, near-death experiencers tended to become much more loving, accepting, compassionate and tolerant of others. In addition, it was found that these experiencers tended to show greater sensitivity and insight following their experience, and their often-expressed desire to help others was enacted in a wide variety of ways.

In view of their positive loving attitudes and actions toward others, it is interesting to note how many close personal relationships, such as engagements and marriages, collapsed under the strain of post-NDE life. It was found in over half of those who were involved in such relationships at the time of their experience that it was extremely difficult to fit post-NDE priorities into their pre-NDE relationships. Frequently cited causes of dissension in relationships were changes in priority, such as a lack of interest in material success and a strong move toward spiritual development. A similar level of strain was experienced in relationships with friends, often resulting in experiencers creating friendship networks more appropriate to their new life direction.

Improvement in self-image, a commitment to spiritual growth, changes in relationships and general attitudes to life provided a context within which this sample of experiencers made many other choices about the way they wanted to live their daily lives. Overall, they became much more conscious of the sort of food they ate, they drank less alcohol, became nonsmokers and steered clear of prescription drugs whenever possible. They tended to watch less television and read fewer newspapers. There was also something of a shift away from the use of traditional medicine toward alternative healing methods, including self-healing. In all, there appeared to be a commitment to taking more responsibility for their own physical and mental well-being, as a complement to their developing spirituality.

Experiencers reported major changes in interests, which they attributed directly to the effect of their NDE. There was a widespread eagerness for knowledge, but this was not restricted to learning in a formal educational setting. The knowledge they sought tended to fulfill three main purposes: finding out more about themselves, developing newly awakened gifts or talents and helping others. Almost three-quarters of the adult experiencers made a major career change that they ascribed to their changed interests following their NDE. Many of these new careers—whether paid or unpaid—involved helping others. For instance, many reported an increased interest in social issues, and, by the time of the interview, a number of experiencers were actually working full-time in their area of social concern, and others were training or retraining in order to do so.

Finally, the grounded theoretical analysis discovered a pattern in the way near-death experiencers managed to integrate the experience into their lives, and this was named the integration trajectory.

Thus, by the time of the interviews this population of near-death experiencers was generally well-established on a spiritual path. They had a strong belief in an afterlife and no fear of death. They had generally managed to accommodate their increased psychic sensitivities. They had a healthy level of self-esteem and were deeply loving and compassionate toward others. Their heightened spiritual awareness and enhanced intuition appeared to suffuse much of their interaction in the social world which, over the years, had encompassed many difficult changes in relationships, study interests and careers. However, the changes considered by the experiencers themselves to be most significant were their growth in spirituality and love, knowing God and a profound sense of inner peace, and their loss of fear of death.

The implications of having a population of people with no fear of death are significant in a society such as our own, fraught as it is with death denial. When death is no longer feared, it is possible, as has been shown by these experiencers, to engage in meaningful relationships with the dying, to abandon immortality projects and to see attachment to immortality vehicles such as money, fame, and heroism as ultimately illusory. Such crucial changes in attitude provide a fundamental challenge to the widely accepted norms of Western society.

When it is realized that millions of people worldwide have had this experience—eight million American adults alone—it can be seen that the potential force for positive social change is enormous. These people *know* that death is not the end. They have encountered the "light" and experienced a depth of peace and love previously unimagined. Almost all of them are changed by the experience and through their interactions with others these changes move beyond the personal, beyond the lives of individual experiencers into the social realm, presaging a profound transformation of great benefit to society as a whole.

A Further Note on Method

THEORETICAL BACKGROUND TO THE STUDY

In *The Discovery of Grounded Theory,* Barney Glaser and Anselm Strauss write:

> To be sure one goes out and studies an area with a particular sociological perspective, and with a focus, a general question, or a problem in mind. But he can (and we believe should) also study an area without any preconceived theory that dictates, prior to the research, "relevancies" in concepts and hypotheses.[1]

Working in a nontraditional area of sociology, as I am in this study, there *is* no existing theoretical framework to provide relevancies in concepts and hypotheses in this particular substantive field. Despite the fact that the work done studying the near-death experience has been worldwide and strongly interdisciplinary, there has as yet been little participation by sociologists, and the theory developed so far has been scant. In addition, there has been no study such as this conducted in Australia at all.

This is not to assert that the project was begun free of

a sociological perspective or without a general guiding question. Based on my reading of American and British studies, my expectation was that there would be many similarities in an Australian population, certainly with respect to the content of the near-death experience itself, and possibly also with respect to the aftereffects. A number of suggestive results concerning aftereffects were found in the psychological literature (Kenneth Ring's 1984 study in particular) and provided the starting point for the investigation in terms of establishing some of the areas to be explored. One of the early aims was to verify whether, in a population of Australian near-death experiencers, there was indeed a pattern of change, and to establish its magnitude. However, from the outset the central issue of interest to me was the profoundly existential nature of the dilemma faced by experiencers after their experience.

Qualitative or Quantitative, or Both?

From the earliest days of sociology, qualitative research has often been characterized as unsystematic, leading to overly impressionistic findings lacking in rigor and theoretical backbone. Unfortunately this characterization has often had an element of truth about it, and was attributable in part to the image of the typical qualitative researcher, overwhelmed by vast quantities of unstructured data and faced with the massive task of making sense of it all. This very real problem was also exacerbated, until recent times, by an almost total absence of information about how exactly such data could be analyzed. The several texts that did deal with qualitative research tended to focus their attention on the pleasures of gathering data, leaving its analysis almost entirely to the imagination, while all the time waving the carrot of emerging themes and theories before anxious readers.

On the other hand, quantitative research, based on the

natural sciences (physics in particular), was early developed to a point where the rigorous testing of theory and verification of hypotheses were feasible, and therefore, it was thought, sociology's scientific credentials established. As a result, qualitative method tended to be relegated to the role of exploratory study with the aim of providing a few substantive categories and hypotheses on which to base the "more serious" scientific work of social surveys. However, as Alvin Gouldner notes, giving primacy to quantitative method in this way soon became "not simply a logic but a morality,"[2] with this "proper" scientific view of reality tending to take up all the available conceptual space. Opposing quantitative to qualitative, as the objective hard scientific approach versus the subjective soft fuzzy approach, has not been helpful to sociological endeavor, since in so doing, the grave shortcomings of the former and advantages of the latter are both obscured in a caricature. Ken Wilber writes:

> The empiric-scientific world view is unbelievable because it is partial, and in pretending to be total, it lands itself in incredulity. For, among other things, the empiric-scientific method is virtually incapable of dealing with *quality*. . . . Once you have translated the world into empiric measurement and numbers, you have a world without quality, guaranteed. Which is to say without *value* or *meaning* . . . In short, says [Huston] Smith, "values, life meanings, purposes, and qualities slip through science like sea slips through the nets of fishermen."[3]

It seems clear that quantitative and qualitative methods should not be in opposition to each other since they are both appropriate for different tasks in different realms. For example, quantitative method is appropriate in the physical world, which is characterized by *extension,* whereas qualitative method is appropriate in the mental world, which is characterized by *intention*. For example, on one level the length and breadth of this page can be measured, and the number of pages in this appendix can be counted, yet the meaning of the words on these pages cannot be quantified in the same way. On a more complex social level, the number of people claiming religious beliefs can be surveyed and the number who attend church weekly can be noted. However, it is not possible to assess quantitatively the consequences of holding such religious beliefs, or the importance of such beliefs in the lives of those holding them. It is not possible to quantify insight, memory or purpose in this way, for what characterizes such phenomena is their *intention,* their meaning and value.

Glaser and Strauss maintain that, at times, both forms of data can be helpful or even necessary as a supplement to each other, a means of mutual verification, providing different forms of data on the same subject, which, when compared, can facilitate the generation of theory. Due to its exploratory nature, this study makes use of both. Quantitative analysis is employed in the calculation of frequencies of individual items, and later, in the evaluation of their relevance to the hypotheses, by the use of chi-squared tests. However, overall there is a primary commitment to qualitative methods and data.

In a sense the focus of this project could be seen as a Rorschach blot, the depth of color and dimensions of which will be measured by quantitative methods, whereas the meaning and significance must be interpreted through a qualitative process of investigation.

COLLECTION OF DATA: INSIGHTS FROM FEMINIST RESEARCH

Insights from feminist research were fundamental to the way this project was conceived. For example, in one kind of feminist research there is a commitment to women doing research *for* rather than *on* other women. That is, first, there is a recognition that the researcher is part of the research process—the researcher *is* one of the researched; and second, the researched is not simply perceived as an object to be examined and scrutinized but as a subject with certain concerns that are to be taken into account. In addition, there is a reciprocity in the relationship that goes beyond the participation in dialogue that is central to such an undertaking. It is not simply the role of the researcher to take, but also to give. Finally, it is amid this engagement of researcher and researched that the data is generated.

In this project, as a near-death experiencer myself, I am one of the researched population and there was a commitment from the outset to present myself as a fellow experiencer. In fact, this turned out to be a major advantage at many stages of the project. As an interviewer, the fact that I was a fellow experiencer was instrumental in breaking down the barrier between researcher and researched. Due to my own status as one of them, they believed that I would understand what they were talking about, that I would take seriously their accounts and accept the validity of their experience-in-the-world. For many near-death experiencers this represented more than they had previously encountered, and their responses were at times highly emotional.

In the many methodology texts that exist it is rare to see any mention of such a situation. Generally sociologists are cautioned to avoid or discourage any reciprocity of relationship between interviewer and interviewee. Jack Douglas disagrees strongly with such caution and colorfully describes the scientific interviewer fleeing "from intimacy with lowly 'subjects' as if they were infected with the bubonic plague."[4] My own approach emphasized the personal contact.

The belief that any person can enter a situation such as an interview, interact with the interviewee and leave without having contaminated that interchange, whatever the precautions, appears to me to be fanciful. Even in physics it has been found that any observation disturbs the observed system. How much more complex is a human interaction. I agree with Ann Oakley, who writes:

> The mythology of "hygienic research" with its accompanying mystification of the researcher and the researched as objective instruments of data production [needs to] be replaced by the recognition that personal involvement is more than dangerous bias—it is the condition under which people come to know each other and to admit others into their lives.[5]

ANALYSIS OF UNSTRUCTURED AND SEMI-STRUCTURED DATA: THE "GROUNDED THEORY" APPROACH

Over the last decade there has been an increasing interest shown in developing a qualitative research process that can be demonstrated to be every bit as rigorous as quantitative researchers claim their method to be. However, this is not as straighforward as it may at first seem. It is simply not appropriate to apply the version of rigor associated with quantitative data (the realm of extension) to the much more complex domain of qualitative data (the realm of intention). Ken Wilber notes in a contrast between empiric science and phenomenology:

> Empiric science rests upon a community of facts—if you get bad facts, you get bad science or at least partial science. Just so, real . . . phenomenology . . . depends in large measure upon the quality of the community of interpreters. Good interpreters, good thinkers, ground good phenomenology. They discover those truths that apply to the subjective realm, and in that sense the truths are subjective truths. But

that doesn't mean mere individual whim. First of all, a bad interpretation will simply not mesh with general subjective consensus. It is rebuffed by a reality that is subjective but very real and very lawful, just as a bad empiric fact is rebuffed by other facts. Second, a phenomenological truth ... must be tested in a community of like-minded interpreters ... just as an empiric fact ... must be tested against the community of other facts. It's no mere wishful thinking and subjective license. The hermeneutic test is just as stringent and demanding as the empiric test, but of course the empiric test is easier because it is performed by a subject on an object, whereas phenomenology is performed by a subject on or with other subjects. Much more difficult.[6]

Glaser and Strauss write that the practical application of grounded theory demands just this sort of rigor, in that it requires a close fit with the substantive area in which it will be used, it must be easily understandable by any interested person, and it must be general enough to be applied to more than one specific situation within this substantive field. Overall, they exhort researchers to provide clear statements of theory and description so that it is possible for any reader to decide upon their credibility and they caution against seeking rigor through the indiscriminate application of quantitative method, whatever the context.[7]

Glaser and Strauss originally developed their grounded theory approach as a response to what they perceived to be an unfortunate emphasis on verification of theory to the detriment of its generation. They emphasize that grounded theory is about a purposeful discovery of theory from data that have been systematically collected through social research. Grounded theorists set out to generate new theory through a process that is as painstaking and rigorous as it is creative. It does not happen by accident. That is, the emergence of theory is central to the endeavor, not a chance occurrence. It also does not just happen at the end of the project—there is a strong emphasis on "theory as process."

More recently, Anselm Strauss notes that rather than being a specific method or technique, grounded theory is

a *style* of doing qualitative analysis that includes a number of distinctive features, such as theoretical sampling, and certain methodological guidelines, such as the making of constant comparisons, and the use of a coding paradigm, to ensure conceptual development and density.[8]

He writes that "the grounded theory style of analysis is based on the premise that theory at various levels of generality is indispensible for deeper knowledge of social phenomena" and that "such theory ought to be developed in intimate relationship with data, with researchers fully aware of themselves as instruments" for its development.[9] He advocates a highly self-conscious approach to the work of research that corroborates much of what has already been referred to earlier in the section on insights from feminist research. He writes:

The researcher, if more than merely competent, will be "in the work"—emotionally as well as intellectually—and often will be profoundly affected by experiences engendered by the research process itself.[10]

Both Glaser and Strauss have emphasized that despite the necessity of following certain guidelines, there is no one right way to do grounded theory. They believe that personal pacing and what they call "experiential data" are crucial to the way in which any project is carried out. This experiential data may range from technical knowledge such as research skills to actual personal experience related to the research topic that might inform the researcher's theoretical sensitivity and provide ideas for comparisons and theoretical sampling. Strauss encourages researchers to develop their own style, to use their own gifts and mine their own experience for maximum effect. However, he does note that this is

> linked with the understanding that this is not license to run wild but is held within bounds by controls exerted through a carefully managed triad of data collection/coding and memoing. This triad serves as a genuinely explicit control over the researcher's biases.[11]

How Is It Done?

Basically, grounded theorizing relies on three main processes, each of which are intimately connected: data collection, coding and memoing. It is difficult to outline sequentially how analysis proceeds, since many of its processes are carried out concurrently, or at least interdependently. For example, from the very earliest stages, the collection of data, whatever its form, is strategically guided by the emergence of conceptual categories, their conceptual properties and hypotheses or generalized relations among these categories and properties (however provisional these initially might be). These concepts cannot simply be imposed from outside, but have to earn their place in the analysis by being systematically generated from the data. At all stages, data collection and analysis is informed by theoretical sensitivity—an ability to recognize indicators of theoretically relevant concepts present in the data. In addition, at all stages, data collection is driven forward by a combination of constant comparison and theoretical sampling. That is, the process underlying the generation of theory involves, as much as possible, joint collection, coding and analysis of data.

Coding is central to this entire process. As Strauss and Corbin note: "Coding represents the operations by which data are broken down, conceptualized, and put back together in new ways."[12] Each incident in the data needs to be coded into as many analytical categories as possible. As this proceeds, comparison can be made with all previous incidents coded in the same category, with the aim of generating the theoretical properties of those categories. In doing this, the analyst is forced to acknowledge the diversity in the data, and can begin to see not only the development of an individual category but also the changing relations between categories. It is essential, while doing this, to record these insights in memos, since such insights, to be useful, must be transformed into more theoretical categories, properties and hypotheses, and must be available for perusal as the analysis proceeds.

The point is to organize ideas about the data rather than the data itself. These ideas will in turn guide the analyst in further theoretical sampling. Unlike statistical sampling, in theoretical sampling there is no claim to randomness since, as the name suggests, it is a direct inquiry, a purposive search for categories, properties and interrelationships, controlled by the needs of the emerging theory. That is, a decision is made on analytic grounds about which data to collect, and where.

As Strauss and Corbin note, the aim of theoretical sampling is to sample events or incidents, not persons *per se*. They write:

Our interest is in gathering data about what persons do or don't do in terms of action/interaction; the range of conditions that give rise to that action/interaction and its variations; how conditions change or stay the same over time and with what impact; also the consequences of either actual or failed action/interaction or of strategies never acted on.[13]

Theoretical sampling increases in depth of focus as the analysis proceeds through open coding, and axial coding to selective coding.

Strauss notes that the excellence of a piece of research depends in large part on the excellence of its coding. In qualitative research there are a number of ways of coding. For example, Matthew Miles and A. Michael Huberman code primarily for retrieval, to find patterns and test theory. Whereas Strauss makes clear that for the purposes of grounded theorizing it is not enough to simply summarize the data by applying descriptive labels indicating instances of particular categories. In order to overcome this type of coding pattern, he suggests the use of what he calls a "coding paradigm." This involves coding data for relevance to a particular category in terms of conditions, interaction, strategies and tactics, and consequences. Strauss even goes so far as to say that ''without inclusion of the paradigm items, coding is not coding."[14] Immediately after this is done, the analysis begins to develop complexity and conceptual density.

For example, in my own project, for the purposes of my quantitative analysis I made note of, and coded, incidences of various psychic phenomena occurring in the lives of near-death experiencers following their NDE, such as incidences of precognition. However, in the qualitative analysis I had a category, "reality expansion," in which precognitive events formed an incident. In coding these events using the coding paradigm, I could note the varied conditions affecting the incidence of particular precognitive events such as whether they occurred during a dream, in waking moments, in the form of a vision or were just a feeling. I could further note whether the person was a child, an adult, had had previous such experiences, believed such things were possible, found them a nuisance or found them intriguing. I could note what action/interaction took place. For example, whether the person acted in response to their precognitive insight, whether they told anyone about it (what the response was, and how they felt about that response) or whether they kept it to themselves. I could note the diversity of their strategies or tactics, for example, whether they blocked their particular ability, denied that the experience had any meaning, or actually acted on it. I could then note whether this action involved giving a warning to the person concerned, or not giving a warning, or giving a general warning without revealing that the source of information was a precognitive event, or secretly waiting to see if it was fulfilled. I could note the consequences of this action/inaction such as the fulfillment of the prophecy and feeling of horror that the warning was not given or not heeded (or gratitude that it was) or the consequences of its nonfulfillment. I could note the puzzlement of some experiencers as to why such a gift was given to them and as to how such a gift should be handled. I could note that some experiencers sought information from books, other persons or courses to learn more about their particular facility (which related to another category, "meaning seeking"). All the above conditions, interactions, strategies and consequences are actually taken from my interview transcripts. It can be seen even in this brief review of some of the possibilities concerning one set of incidents in one category how dense the analysis can become when following the coding paradigm, and how the complexity of human existence is revealed to a much greater extent by this method than by my simply stating that eighty-nine percent of my sample experienced precognition after their NDE.

At the beginning of a research project, for example, after having collected one or two interviews, the researcher uses open coding. Strauss emphasizes that the aim of this sort of coding is to literally open up the inquiry and provide suggestions for the next steps to be taken. He notes that open coding is done by close scrutiny of the transcript, line by line, "to produce concepts that seem to fit the data." At this stage, however, every interpretation is tentative. Concepts generated in this process may or may not work or be ultimately useful to the analysis. As the theory develops, these early concepts will gradually be modified or elaborated and any false leads generated at this point will eventually be canceled out by further data collection and coding.

Although open coding is always begun early in a research project, it is often a lengthy process. In addition, it can be initiated at any point if the inquiry needs opening up again. However, overall, as the project proceeds and the theorizing develops, the focus of coding and sampling narrows, with an emphasis on increasing complexity and conceptual density.

The second type of coding is axial coding, so named because it involves an intense analysis done around the axis of one category at a time in terms of the coding paradigm items—conditions, action/interaction, strategies and consequences. This type of coding typically begins even while open coding is still in progress. However, its more specific aim is to discover and establish relationships between categories and subcategories, on the basis of which the researcher will make a commitment to one or more core categories and move into selective coding.

In selective coding the focus is on the core category. As Strauss notes:

> To code selectively means that the analyst delimits coding to only those codes that relate to the core codes in sufficiently significant ways as to be used in a parsimonious theory.[15]

He further notes that at this stage it is the core code that guides ongoing theoretical sampling and data collection. Once again the analyst uses the coding paradigm, but this time to look for those conditions, strategies, etc., that relate specifically to the core category. Strauss writes:

> . . . the core category has several important functions for generating theory. It is relevant and works. Most other categories and their properties are related to it, which makes it subject to much qualification and modification. In addition, through these relations among categories and their properties, it has the prime function of *integrating* the theory and rendering it *dense* and *saturated* as the relationships are discovered. These functions then lead to theoretical *completeness:*—accounting for as much variation in a pattern of behavior with as few concepts as possible, thereby maximizing parsimony and scope.[16]

However, final theoretical integration is achieved only in the final writing up of the analysis. This can be much aided by the use of integrative diagrams and memos. As has already been noted, memos are written from the earliest days of the project to record and build up theoretical ideas. As the analysis proceeds, the memos become increasingly focused, with the ultimate aim of aiding in the theory's final integration. At any point, insights gleaned from the literature in the form of possibly useful concepts or hypotheses can be introduced for consideration into the memos, with the proviso that they will be checked out against the data, and will prove their relevance before earning a place in the analysis.

Memos are often sorted, and later memos tend to build on earlier ones. As Strauss emphasizes, memos are cumulative. A similar process occurs with diagrams—early diagrams becoming included in the more complex later integrative diagrams. That is, they also are cumulative and contribute to the final integration of the analysis. As a final note on integration, Paul Atkinson writes:

> This aspect—making it all come together—is one of the most difficult things of all, isn't it? Quite apart from actually achieving it, it is hard to inject the

right mix of (a) *faith* that it can and will be achieved; (b) recognition that it has to be worked at, and isn't based on romantic inspiration; (c) that it isn't like the solution to a puzzle or math problem, but has to be *created;* (d) that you can't always pack everything into one version, and that any one project could yield several different ways of bringing it together.[17]

In summary, as Strauss and Corbin write:

[To do grounded theory well] requires maintaining a balance among the attributes of creativity, rigor, persistence, and above all theoretical sensitivity.[18]

Interview Schedule

1. Date of interview
2. Name
3. Sex
4. Address
5. Telephone number

Interview

6. Approximate date of NDE?
7. Year of birth?
8. Country of birth?
9. Country of birth of parents? Mother _____ Father _____
10. Marital status at time of near-death experience?
11. Marital status now?
    [*If the same category, check if the same relationship.*]
12. Did you have any children at the time of your near-death experience? How many?
13. Have you had any children since then?
14. Educational level at time of near-death experience?
15. Educational level now?
16. Occupation at time of near-death experience?
17. Occupation now?

• • •

Now I would like to ask you some questions concerning your near-death experience.
18. Could you tell me under what circumstances it occurred?
19. Could you describe for me what happened during your experience?

[*Probe to clarify points not clearly made by the respondent. Use the following questions, depending on what the respondent has already said.*]

20.   i) Was this experience difficult to put into words?
      ii) [If yes:] Can you try to tell me why?
      iii) Was it like a dream or different from a dream?

21.   i) When this episode occurred, did you think you were dying or close to death?
      ii) Did you actually think you were dead?
      iii) Did you hear anyone actually say that you were dead?

22. Did you hear any unusual noises or sounds during the episode?
23. What were your feelings and sensations during this episode?
24.   i) Did you at any time feel as though you were traveling or moving?
      ii) What was that experience like?

25.   i) Did you at any time feel that you were somehow separate from your own physical body?
      ii) During this time were you ever aware of *seeing* your physical body?

    iii) Did you try to contact the people around your body (to touch them or speak to them)?

26.   i) During your episode did you ever encounter other individuals, living or dead?

    ii) [If yes:]Who were they?

    iii) What happened when you met them?

    iv) Did they communicate with you? What? How?

27.   i) Did you at any time experience a light, glow or illumination? Can you describe this to me?

    ii) [If yes:] Did this "light" communicate anything to you? What?

28.   i) When you were going through this experience, did your life (or scenes from your life) ever appear to you as mental images or memories?

    ii) [If yes:] Can you describe this to me further?

    iii) Did you ever feel judged while this was going on?

    iv) Did you feel that you learned anything from this experience? What?

29.   Did you at any time have a sense of approaching some kind of boundary or point of no return?

30.   i) Did you want to come back to your body, to life?

    ii) Did you eventually *choose* to come back to life, did you just find yourself alive again or were you *sent* back?

    iii) [If the last:] Was this against your will? How did you feel about this?

    iv) How did it feel when you found yourself conscious again in your own body?

    v) Do you have any recollection of how you got back into your physical body?

31. Is there anything else you'd like to add here about this experience?

32. i) Do you have any idea why you didn't die at that time?
    ii) In terms of your own understanding of your experience, would you say that it happened to you for a reason?
   iii) Do you know what that reason is?

33. i) After your experience did you try to talk about it with other people?
    ii) Whom did you tell it to?
   iii) How soon after the event?
    iv) What was their reaction?
     v) [If appropriate:] Have you at any time since your near-death experience sought help from professionals to deal with your experience (e.g., counselor, social worker, psychologist, psychiatrist, etc.)?
    vi) Has this been helpful? In what ways?

34. i) Before the experience we've been talking about, had you ever read or heard about the near-death experience?
    ii) Have you read or heard anything about it since your experience?

It is now ____ years since you had your near-death experience. One way to get at the significance of such an event is to try to determine whether it tended to bring about any changes in your life.

First, I'd like to ask you some questions concerning your attitude to death.

35. i) Before this incident occurred, what did you believe happened at death?

    ii) What do you now believe happens at death?

36. i) Did you fear death before your experience?

    ii) [If no:] Did you think about it at all?

    iii) Do you fear death now?

37. i) Before your experience, what was your attitude about suicide (for yourself, for others)?

    ii) How do you feel about it now?

38. i) Reincarnation is the idea that we come back to earth to live in a physical body again. Before your experience, how convinced were you that such a thing could happen?

    ii) Do you believe in reincarnation now?

39. i) Before your experience, did you have any interest in issues related to death and dying?

    ii) Has your level of interest changed since then?

    iii) [If applicable:] How do you express that interest?

Now I would like to ask you some questions about your religious affiliation and/or spiritual life.

40. Would you describe your near-death experience as predominantly religious or spiritual in nature, or would you describe it in some other way?

41. i) Before this experience, how religious or spiritual a person would you have said you were?

    ii) How would you describe yourself now?

42.   i) Before your experience, did you identify your-
         self with any particular religious denomination?
         Which one?
      ii) Do you identify yourself with any particular re-
         ligious denomination now? Which one?

43. Did your experience have any particular effect on your
    spiritual values or religious beliefs and practices?
    [*Checklist:*]

    . feelings about organized religion
    . effect on church, attendance, etc.
    . tendency to pray
    . practice of meditation
    . inward feelings or experiences of God or a Higher
      Power
    . quest for spiritual values/higher consciousness

Now I would like to ask you some questions about psychic
experiences. (Psychic phenomena refer to a wide range of
events in which people claim either to be aware of or able
to do things that normally are presumed to be impossible,
e.g., to "read" another person's thoughts or to separate
from one's physical body.)

44.   i) Before your near-death episode, what was your
         own attitude about these sorts of things?
      ii) What is your attitude now about these things?

45.   i) Have you ever had a psychic experience?
      ii) [If yes:] Could you give me some examples?

[*In each case, ask whether the experience had ever occurred before the near-death episode.*]

[*Checklist:*]

- *clairvoyance:* a term used to describe an awareness of an event that seems to come to you without your usual senses being involved. For example, a mother may suddenly just "sense" or "know" that her daughter, 2000 miles away, has been seriously injured in a car accident; several hours later she receives a telephone call confirming her "psychic" impression.
- *telepathy:* knowing what someone else is thinking without that person telling you.
- *knowing what people will say before they say it*
- *precognition:* knowing when something is going to take place that could not reasonably have been predicted from other information. For example, a person may claim that an airplane is going to crash somewhere on a specific date—and it does.
- *déjà vu:* a term used to describe an experience that seems like a reexperiencing of something that has happened before.
- *supernatural rescues:* Most people have found themselves in situations where things are going badly for them or where they are at a loss as to what to do, when suddenly something quite unexpected occurs and rescues them from their plight.
- *intuitive sense*
- *inner source of knowledge or wisdom*
- *sense of guidance*
- *awareness of dreams*
- *out-of-body experience:* one where your consciousness or mind seems to function independently of and outside your physical body. Sometimes during such an episode, you can actually see your own physical body as though a spectator to it.
- *spirits or guides*

. *healing powers*
. *seeing auras*

46. Would you say that since your near-death episode your psychic sensitivities have changed in any other way that we have not already covered?

Now I would like to ask you some questions regarding changes that may have occurred in life direction since your near-death experience. First, I'd like to ask you about your attitudes to yourself, your motivation and general outlook.

47.   i) Did your experience change your attitudes or feelings about yourself?
       ii) Could you describe in what ways these have changed?

   [*Checklist:*]
   . Feelings of self-worth
   . Interest in self-understanding
   . Search for personal inner meaning in life
   . Sense of life purpose
   . Feelings of personal vulnerability
   . Desire for solitude
   . Concern with what others think of me

48. Did your experience affect in any way your motivation in life?

   [*Checklist:*]
   . Ambition to achieve high standard of living
   . Interest in material success
   . Desire to become well-known person

49. Did your experience give you any kind of new outlook on life?

   [*Checklist:*]
   · Appreciation of nature
   · Appreciation of the ordinary things in life
   · Concern with spiritual matters
   · Sense of the sacred aspect of life
   · Involvement in family life

Now I'd like to ask you a few questions concerning your relationships.

50.   i) Did you experience any strain in your primary relationship (with your spouse, etc.) after your near-death experience?
       ii) Could you describe what happened?
       iii) Did that relationship survive intact?
       iv) [If no:] Were you eventually divorced (separated) from that person?

51.   i) Did your relationships with other members of your family come under any strain after your near-death experience?
       ii) Could you describe what happened?
       iii) Did those relationships survive intact, were they severed or did they change?

52.   i) Were your relationships with friends subject to strain after your near-death experience?
       ii) Could you describe what happened?
       iii) Do you still have active friendships with these people, have your relationships undergone some change or have you severed connection with them altogeth~~?

53. Have you at any time since your experience sought help from professionals to deal with these issues? (e.g., counselor, social worker, psychologist, psychiatrist, etc.)

54. Did your experience affect how you felt about or related to others generally?

   [*Checklist:*]
   . Desire to help others
   . Compassion for others
   . Empathy or understanding for others
   . Patience/tolerance for others
   . Ability to express love for others
   . Acceptance of others *as they are*
   . Insight into the problems of others

Now I'd like to ask you some questions about your interests, any study you might have undertaken and work in general.

55. Did your interests change in some specific way that you feel now might have been triggered by your experience?

56.   i) Did your attitude to learning change?
     ii) [If yes:] Could you describe in what ways?

57.   i) Did you commence study after your near-death episode?
     ii) [If yes:] For the first time? Or in a new area?
     iii) [If yes:] What area? Why did you choose that particular field of study?

58.   i) Did you seek work, change jobs or leave work as a result of your near-death experience?
     ii) [If yes:] Could you describe your reasons?

• • •

Now I'd like to ask you some questions about the priorities in your present lifestyle.

59.   i) How would you describe the priorities in your lifestyle today?

ii) How does this compare with your lifestyle before your near-death experience?

60. In your daily life, have you made any major changes since your near-death experience in the following:

. diet
. alcohol consumption
. tobacco use
. drug-taking (prescription or otherwise)
. television watching
. newspaper reading

61.   i) Today, do you do anything else specifically to care for your physical body?

[*Checklist:*]
. exercise
. alternative therapies (specify)
. medical profession
. other (specify)

ii) How does this compare with your practice before your near-death experience?

62. i) Since your experience, what sort of entertainments do you prefer? (e.g., theater, film, ballet, opera, football game, other spectator sports, picnic in the country, day at the beach, etc.)
    ii) How does this compare with your preferences before?

Now I'd like to ask you some questions concerning social issues.

63. i) Since your near-death episode, has your concern with political matters increased or decreased?
    ii) [If yes:] Could you explain this (or provide details if appropriate)?

64. i) Are there any social issues that particularly concern you?
    ii) [If yes:] What is your personal involvement with this issue/these issues?

65. Are there any other areas that you have been concerned with or involved in since your near-death experience that you would like to mention?
66. We've talked at some length now about your near-death experience and the changes that it may have helped to bring about in your life. Is there anything else that I haven't touched upon that you would like to raise with me at this point, either about the experience itself or its aftereffects?
67. Finally, what would you say is the most significant change that has come about for you as a result of your near-death experience?

NDE Knowledge
Questionnaire

Name: (optional)_____

Sex _____ Age _____

(If student:) Course _____ Year _____

(If trained nurse:) Department _____

Years of experience _____

This questionnaire is basically concerned with determining the amount known by trained/student nurses about the near-death experience, and whether it was learned from personal experience, personal contact or from some other source.

The near-death experience is now known to occur when a person is on the brink of death or in some cases actually clinically dead, and yet is successfully resuscitated or somehow survives to recount an intense experience. People who have had a near-death experience generally describe some or all of the following features: an out-of-body experience, the sensation of traveling very quickly down a dark tunnel toward a light, a feeling of peace, an encounter with a "being of light" and/or the spirits of deceased relatives or friends, an instantaneous life review and, for some, entrance into a "world of light".

1. Have you ever been close to death? Yes _____ No _____

2. If so, did you ever have a near-death experience? Yes _____ No _____

3. If so, please briefly describe the circumstances (e.g., accident, postoperative complications, childbirth, etc.) and the content of the experience.

4. Have you ever had someone describe such an experience to you? Yes _____ No _____

5. How often have you had a near-death experience described to you by a patient? Never _____ Once _____ 2–4 times _____ 5–10 times _____ More often _____

6. Have you ever had someone other than a patient describe this experience to you? If so, what was this person's relationship to you? (e. g. brother, parent, friend, etc.) _____

7. Have you heard about the near-death experience from any other source? Yes _____ No _____

8. If so, what was the source? (e.g., newspapers, magazines, radio, television, books, journal articles or other—please specify) _____

_____

9. How would you describe your level of knowledge about near-death experiences? Very limited _____ Low _____ Medium _____ High _____

10. Any further comments you would like to make?

Notes

Full details can be found in the bibliography.

Preface

1. Wilber, *Up From Eden,* p. 12.
2. Wilber, "Odyssey: A Personal Inquiry into Humanistic and Transpersonal Psychology," p. 89.

Chapter 1

1. Colgrave & Mynors, p. 489.
2. Smith, p. 16.

Chapter 2

1. Audette & Moody, pp. 1–2.
2. Sutherland, pp. 241–251.
3. Gabbard & Twemlow, "Explanatory Hypotheses for Near-Death Experiences," p. 69.
4. Blacher, p. 2291.
5. Sabom, "Near-Death Experiences," p. 30.
6. Jung & Pauli, p. 128.
7. ibid., p. 129.
8. Kletti & Noyes, p. 5.
9. Gabbard & Twemlow, "An Overview of Altered Mind/ Body Perception," p. 357.

10. Sabom, *Recollections of Death*, p. 176.
11. Carr, p. 126.
12. Ring, *Life at Death*, p. 216.
13. Schorer, pp. 111–113.
14. Pasricha & Stevenson, p. 169.
15. Evans-Wentz, p. 33–34.
16. Gallagher, p. 141.
17. Zaleski, p. 32.
18. Roberts & Owen, p. 612.
19. Wilson, p. 160.
20. Vicchio, p. 85.
21. Moody, *Reflections on Life After Life*, p. 111.
22. Gallagher, p. 141.
23. Harris & Bascom, p. 2.
24. ibid., p. 6.
25. Ring, "Near-Death Experiences: Implications for Human Evolution and Planetary Transformation," pp. 78–79.
26. Greyson, "Can Science Explain the Near-Death Experience?" p. 87.
27. Atwater, " 'Unofficial' After-Effects of the Near-Death Experience," p. 21.
28. ibid., p. 18.
29. Jung, p. 323.
30. Straight, pp. 114–115.
31. ibid., p. 118.
32. Harris & Bascom, p. 187.
33. Jung, p. 328.
34. Moody, *Life After Life*, p. 89.
35. Ring, *Heading Toward Omega*, p. 163.
36. ibid., p. 99.
37. ibid., p. 102.
38. ibid., p. 50.
39. Gallagher, pp. 140–141.
40. Moody, *The Light Beyond*, p. 33.
41. Flynn, p. 72.

42. Pennachio, p. 167.
43. Harris & Bascom, p. 36.
44. Ring, *Heading Toward Omega*, p. 134.
45. Harris & Bascom, p. 186.
46. Flynn, p. 5.
47. Ring, *Heading Toward Omega*, p. 145.
48. Flynn, p. 6.

Chapter 3
1. Moody, *Life After Life*, p. 151.
2. Greyson, "The Near-Death Experience Scale: Construction, Reliability and Validity," p. 375.

Chapter 5
1. Herzog & Herrin, p. 1074.

Chapter 6
1. Ring, *Life at Death*, p. 175.

Chapter 9
1. Sabom, *Recollections of Death*, p. 125.
2. Ring, *Life at Death*, p. 204.
3. Ring, *Heading Toward Omega*, p. 102.
4. ibid., p. 311.
5. ibid., p. 306.
6. ibid., p. 310.
7. ibid., p. 301.
8. ibid., pp. 301, 304.
9. ibid., p. 302.
10. ibid., p. 303.
11. ibid., p. 303.
12. Harris & Bascom, p. 150.
13. ibid., pp. 188–189.
14. Ring, *Heading Toward Omega*, p. 308.
15. ibid., p. 307.
16. ibid., p. 133.

17. ibid., p. 300.
18. ibid., p. 120.
19. Ghose, p. xv.

Chapter 10

1. Strauss & Corbin, p. 159.
2. Wilber, *Quantum Questions,* p. 8.
3. Bonder & Boyer, p. 35.
4. Harner, p. xvii.
5. Pattison, p. 32.
6. Wilber (1981, p. 9) describes consciousness as being structured in eight main levels ranging from the lowest level of matter to the highest level of ultimate spirit, with each level transcending and including the preceding ones. Thus, the levels are: (1) Nature: physical nature and lower life forms; (2) Body: highest bodily forms, especially typhonic, magical; (3) Early mind: verbal, mythical membership; (4) Advanced mind: rational, mental-egoic, self-reflexive; (5) Psychic: shamanistic; (6) Subtle: saintly; (7) Causal: sagely; (8) Ultimate: absolute.
7. Pattison, p. 32.
8. Kessler, pp. 148–150.
9. Wilber, *Up From Eden,* p. 36.
10. Becker, E., p. ix.
11. ibid., p. 20.
12. Mindell, p. 7.
13. Kessler, p. 150.
14. In a somewhat more detailed "map" of the transpersonal realm of the spectrum of consciousness, Wilber (in Meadow et al., 1979, p. 68) outlines six transpersonal levels. In this map he collapses lower levels into (1) the Gross realm; and follows with (2) the Astral realm: out-of-body experiences and certain occult knowledge; (3) the Psychic realm: psi phenomena such as ESP, clairvoyance and precognition; (4) the

Subtle realm: higher symbolic visions, light, higher
presences, and intense but soothing vibrations and
bliss; (5) the Lower causal realm: beginning of true
transcendence and the undermining of subject-object
dualism; (6) the Higher causal realm: transcendence of
all manifest realms; (7) the Ultimate realm: absolute
identity with the Many and the One.

15. Sabom, *Recollections of Death,* p. 142.
16. Marshall, p. 2.
17. Pattison, p. 36.
18. Weisman & Hackett, pp. 242–244.
19. Sabom, *Recollections of Death,* p. 141.
20. ibid., p. 4.
21. Greyson & Harris, p. 51.
22. Schutz, p. 106. Reprinted by permission of Kluwer
    Academic Publishers.
23. ibid., p. 113.
24. Richards, p. 107.
25. Schutz, p. 105. Reprinted by permission of Kluwer
    Academic Publishers.

Appendix I
1. Glaser & Strauss, p. 33.
2. Bowles & Duelli-Klein, p. 165.
3. Wilber, *Eye to Eye,* pp. 26–27.
4. Douglas, p. 93.
5. Oakley, p. 58.
6. Wilber, *Eye to Eye,* p. 187.
7. Glaser & Strauss, *The Discovery of Grounded Theory,*
   pp. 237, 232, 234.
8. Strauss, p. 5.
9. ibid., p. 6.
10. ibid., p. 10.
11. ibid., p. 11.
12. Strauss & Corbin, p. 57.
13. ibid., p. 177.

14. Strauss, p. 28.
15. ibid., p. 33.
16. ibid., pp. 34–35.
17. ibid., p. 214.
18. Strauss & Corbin, p. 58.

Bibliography

Alcock, J. E. "Pseudo-Science and the Soul." *Essence*, 5, 1 (1981), 65–76.

Aspect, A. "Experimental Tests of Realistic Local Theories via Bell's Theorem." *Physical Review Letters,* 47 (1981), 460.

Atwater, P. M. H. " 'Unofficial' After-Effects of the Near-Death Experience." *Metapsychology: The Journal of Discarnate Intelligence,* 2, 2 (1986), 7–23.

Atwater, P. M. H. *Coming Back to Life.* Melbourne: Collins Dove, 1988.

Audette, J., & Moody, R. "Denver Cardiologist Discloses Findings After 18 Years of Near-Death Research." *Anabiosis,* 1, 1 (1979), 1–2.

Australian Values Study Survey, 1983. Data collected by Roy Morgan Research Centre. Melbourne: Australian Values Study Steering Committee, 1984.

Barrett, Sir William. *Death-Bed Visions.* Northamptonshire: Aquarian, 1986.

Basterfield, K. "Near-Death Experiences: An Australian Survey." *A.I.P.R. Bulletin,* 9, 2 (1986), 1–4.

Bauer, M. "Near-Death Experiences and Attitude Change." *Anabiosis,* 5, 1 (1985), 39–47.

Becker, C. B. "The Centrality of Near-Death Experiences

in Chinese Pure-Land Buddhism." *Anabiosis,* 1 (1981), 154–171.

Becker, C. B. "The Failure of Saganomics: Why Birth Models Cannot Explain Near-Death Phenomena." *Anabiosis,* 2, (1982), 102–109.

Becker, C. B. "The Pure Land Revisited: Sino-Japanese Meditations and Near-Death Experiences of the Next World." *Anabiosis,* 4, 1 (1984), 51–68.

Becker, C. B. "Views from Tibet: NDEs and the Book of the Dead." *Anabiosis,* 5, 1 (1985), 3–20.

Becker, E. *The Denial of Death.* New York: The Free Press, 1975.

Blacher, R. S. "To Sleep, Perchance to Dream . . ." *Journal of the American Medical Association,* 242 (1979), 2291.

Blackmore, S. J. "Birth and the Out-of-Body Experience: An Unhelpful Analogy." *The Journal of the American Society for Psychical Research,* 77, 3 (1983), 229–238.

Bonder, S., & Boyer, R. "The Part and the Whole: Death and the Scientific World View: An Interview with Stanislav Grof, M.D." *The Laughing Man,* 2 (1981), 28–35.

Bowles, G., & Duelli Klein, R. (eds.) *Theories of Women's Studies.* London: Routledge & Kegan Paul, 1983.

Carr, D. B. "Pathophysiology of Stress-Induced Limbic Lobe Dysfunction: A Hypothesis for Near-Death Experiences." *Anabiosis,* 2 (1982), 75–89.

Carroll, L. "Through the Looking-Glass" in *The Complete Illustrated Works of Lewis Carroll.* London: Chancellor Press, 1984.

Clark, K. "Clinical Interventions with Near-Death Experiencers" in Greyson, B., & Flynn, C. *The Near-Death Experience: Problems, Prospects, Perspectives.* Springfield, Illinois: Charles C. Thomas, 1984.

Colgrave, B., & Mynors, R. A. B. (eds.) *Bede's Ecclesiastical History of the English People.* London: Oxford University Press.

Corbin, J., & Strauss, A. "Grounded Theory: Procedures,

Canons, and Evaluative Criteria." *Qualitative Sociology,* 13, 1 (1990), 3–21.

Counts, D. A. "Near-Death and Out-of-Body Experiences in a Melanesian Society." *Anabiosis,* 3, 2 (1983), 115–135.

Dobbs, B. J. T. *The Foundations of Newton's Alchemy.* Cambridge: Cambridge University Press, 1983.

Douglas, J. *Creative Interviewing.* Beverly Hills: Sage Publications, 1985.

Drab, K. J. "Unresolved Problems in the Study of Near-Death Experiences: Some Suggestions for Research and Theory." *Anabiosis,* 1, 1 (1981), 27–43.

Eddington, A. S. *The Nature of the Physical World.* New York: Macmillan, 1929.

Ehrenwald, J. "Out-of-the-Body Experiences and the Denial of Death." *The Journal of Nervous and Mental Disease,* 159, 4 (1974), 227–233.

Evans-Wentz, W. Y. *The Tibetan Book of the Dead.* Oxford: Oxford University Press, 1960.

Flynn, C. *After the Beyond.* New Jersey: Prentice-Hall, 1986.

Fremantle, F., & Trugpa, C. *The Tibetan Book of the Dead.* Berkeley, California, and London: Shambhala, 1975.

Furn, B. G. "Adjustment and the Near-Death Experience: A Conceptual and Therapeutic Model." *Journal of Near-Death Studies,* 6, 1, Fall (1987), 4–19.

Gabbard, G. O., & Twemlow, S. W. "Explanatory Hypotheses for Near-Death Experiences." *ReVision,* 4, 2 (1981), 68–71.

Gabbard, G. O., & Twemlow, S. W. "An Overview of Altered Mind/Body Perception." *Bulletin of the Menninger Clinic,* 50, 4 (1986), 351–366.

Gallagher, P. "Over Easy: A Cultural Anthropologist's Near-Death Experience." *Anabiosis,* 2 (1982), 140–149.

Gallup, G., Jr. *Adventures in Immortality.* Great Britain: Souvenir Press, 1983.

Ghose, S. *Mystics as a Force for Change.* Wheaton, Ill.: Theosophical Publishing House, Quest Books, 1981.

Gibbs, J. C. "The Near-Death Experience: Balancing Siegel's View." *American Psychologist,* 36 (1981), 1457–1458.

Gibbs, J. C. "Moody's versus Siegel's Interpretation of the Near-Death Experience: An Evaluation Based on Recent Research," *Anabiosis,* 5, 2 (1985), 67–82.

Giovetti, P. "Near-Death and Deathbed Experiences: An Italian Survey." *Theta,* 10, 1 (1982), 10–13.

Glaser, B. G., & Strauss, A. L. *The Discovery of Grounded Theory.* London: Weidenfeld & Nicholson, 1967.

Glaser, B. G., & Strauss, A. L. *Time for Dying.* Chicago: Aldine, 1968.

Goffman, E. *Stigma: Notes on the Management of Spoiled Identity.* Harmondsworth: Penguin, 1968.

Green, J. T., & Friedman, P. "Near-Death Experiences in a Southern Californian Population." *Anabiosis,* 3, 1 (1983), 77–95.

Grey, M. *Return From Death.* London: Arkana, 1985.

Greyson, B. "Toward a Psychological Explanation of Near-Death Experiences: A Response to Dr. Grosso's Paper." *Anabiosis,* 1, 2 (1981a), 88–103.

Greyson, B. "Near-Death Experiences and Attempted Suicide." *Suicide and Life-Threatening Behavior,* 11, 1 (1981b), 10–16.

Greyson, B. "Increase in Psychic Phenomena Following Near-Death Experiences." *Theta,* 11, 2, Summer (1983a), 26–29.

Greyson, B. "The Near-Death Experience Scale: Construction, Reliability, and Validity." *The Journal of Nervous and Mental Disease,* 171, 6, (1983b), 369–375.

Greyson, B. "The Psychodynamics of Near-Death Experiences." *The Journal of Nervous and Mental Disease,* 171, 6 (1983c), 376–381.

Greyson, B., "A Typology of Near-Death Experiences."

American Journal of Psychiatry, 142, 8 (1985), 967–969.

Greyson, B. "Incidence of Near-Death Experiences Following Attempted Suicide." *Suicide and Life-Threatening Behavior,* 16, 1 (1986), 40–45.

Greyson, B. "Can Science Explain the Near-Death Experience?" *Journal of Near-Death Studies,* 8, 2 (1989), 77–92.

Greyson, B., & Flynn, C. P. *The Near-Death Experience: Problems, Prospects, Perspectives.* Springfield, Illinois: Charles C. Thomas, 1984.

Greyson, B., & Harris, B. "Clinical Approaches to the Near-Death Experiencer." *Journal of Near-Death Studies,* 6, 1, Fall (1987), 41–52.

Greyson, B., & Stevenson, I. "The Phenomenology of Near-Death Experiences." *American Journal of Psychiatry,* 137, 10 (1980), 1193–1196.

Grof, S., & Grof, C. *Beyond Death.* London: Thames & Hudson, 1980.

Grof, S., & Halifax, J. *The Human Encounter with Death.* New York: Dutton, 1977.

Grosso, M. "Toward an Explanation of Near-Death Phenomena." *The Journal of the American Society for Psychical Research,* 75, 1 (1981a), 37–60.

Grosso, M. "Recollections of Death: A Medical Perspective." (Book Review). *Anabiosis,* 1 (1981b), 172–176.

Haraldsson, E. "Representative National Surveys of Psychic Phenomena: Iceland, Great Britain, Sweden, USA and Gallup's Multinational Survey." *Journal of the Society for Psychical Research,* 53, 801, Oct. (1985), 145–158.

Harner, M. *The Way of the Shaman.* New York: Bantam Books, 1986.

Harris, B., & Bascom, L. *Full Circle: The Near-Death Experience and Beyond.* New York: Pocket Books, 1990.

Hermann, E. J. "The Near-Death Experience and the Taoism of Chuang Tzu," *Journal of Near-Death Studies,* 8, 3 (1990), 175–190.

Herzog, D. B., & Herrin, J. J. "Near-Death Experiences in the Very Young." *Critical Care Medicine,* 13, 12 (1985), 1074–1075.

Holck, F. H. "Life Revisited (Parallels in Death Experiences)," *Omega,* 9 (1978–79), 1–11.

Honegger, B. J. "The OBE as a Near-Birth Experience" in Roll, W. G., Beloff, J., & White, R. A. (eds.), *Research in Parapsychology.* Metuchen, N.J.: Scarecrow Press, 1982.

Irwin, H. "The Near-Death Experience in Childhood." *Australian Parapsychological Review,* 14 (1989), 7–11.

James, W. *The Varieties of Religious Experience.* Great Britain: Collins Fount Paperbacks, 1979.

Jung, C. G. *Memories, Dreams, Reflections.* Great Britain: Collins Fount Paperbacks, 1978.

Jung, C. G., & Pauli, W. *The Interpretation of Nature and the Psyche.* New York: Pantheon Books, 1955.

Kellehear, S. A., & Heaven, P. "Community Attitudes to Near-Death Experiences: An Australian Study." *Journal of Near-Death Studies,* 7, 3 (1989), 165–172.

Kessler, C. "The Cultural Management of Death: Individual Fate and its Social Transcendence." In Crouch, M., & Hüppauf, B. *Essays on Mortality.* Australia: University of New South Wales, 1985.

Kletti, R., & Noyes, R., Jr. "Mental States in Mortal Danger." *Essence,* 5, 1 (1981), 5–20.

Kohr, R. L. "A Survey of Psi Experiences Among Members of a Special Population." *The Journal of the American Society for Psychical Research,* 74, Oct. (1980), 395–411.

Kohr, R. L. "Near-Death Experience and Its Relationship to Psi and Various Altered States." *Theta,* 10, 3 (1982), 50–53.

Krishnan, V. "Near-Death Experiences: Reassessment Urged." *Parapsychology Review,* 12, 4 (1981), 10–11.

Krishnan, V. "Near-Death Experiences: Evidence for Survival?" *Anabiosis,* 5, 1 (1985), 21–38.

Lee, A. " 'The Lazarus Syndrome': A Care Plan for the Unique Needs of Those Who've 'Died.' " *RN,* 41, 6 (1978), 60–64.

Lienhardt, R. G. *Divinity and Experience: The Religion of the Dinka.* Oxford: Clarendon Press, 1961.

Lindley, J. H., Bryan, S., & Conley, B. "Near-Death Experiences in a Pacific Northwest American Population: The Evergreen Study." *Anabiosis,* 1, 2 (1981), 104–124.

Lowental, U. "Dying, Regression, and the Death Instinct." *Psychoanalytic Review,* 68, 3 (1981), 363–370.

Lundahl, C. R. "The Perceived Other World in Mormon Near-Death Experiences: A Social and Physical Description." *Omega,* 12, 4 (1981/82), 319–327.

Marshall, S. L. "My Hospic Experience." *Hospress,* 5, 1 (1991), 2.

McLaughlin, S. A., & Maloney, H. N. "Near-Death Experiences and Religion—A Further Investigation." *Journal of Religion and Health,* 23, 2 (1984) 149–159.

Meadow, M. J. et al. "Spiritual and Transpersonal Aspects of Altered States of Consciousness: A Symposium Report." *The Journal of Transpersonal Psychology,* 11, 1 (1979), 59–74.

Merton, R. K. *Social Theory and Social Structure.* Glencoe, New York: Free Press, 1959.

Miles, M. B., & Huberman, A. M. *Qualitative Data Analysis: A Sourcebook of New Methods.* Beverly Hills: Sage Publications, 1984.

Mindell, A. *Coma: Key to Awakening.* Boston: Shambhala, 1989.

Moody, R. A., Jr. *Life After Life.* New York: Bantam Books, 1975.

Moody, R. A., Jr. *Reflections on Life After Life.* New York: Bantam Books, 1983.

Moody, R. A., Jr. *The Light Beyond.* New York: Bantam Books, 1988.

Morse, M. "A Near-Death Experience in a 7-year-old Child." *American Journal of Diseases of Children,* 137, 10 (1983), 959–961.

Morse, M., Conner, D., & Tyler, D. "Near-Death Experiences in a Pediatric Population: A Preliminary Report." *American Journal of Diseases of Children,* 139, 6 (1985), 595–600.

Morse, M., Castillo, P., Venecia, D., Milstein, J., & Tyler, D. "Childhood Near-Death Experiences." *American Journal of Diseases of Children,* 140, 11 (1986), 1110–1114.

Noyes, R., Jr. "The Encounter with Life-Threatening Danger: Its Nature and Impact." *Essence,* 5, 1 (1981), 21–32.

Oakes, A. R. "Near-Death Events and Critical Care Nursing." *Topics in Clinical Nursing,* 3, 3 (1981), 61–78.

Oakley, A. "Interviewing Women: A Contradiction in Terms," 1981. In H. Roberts (ed.) *Doing Feminist Research.* London: Routledge & Kegan Paul.

Orne, R. M. "Nurse's View of NDEs." *American Journal of Nursing,* 86, 4 (1986), 419–420.

Osis, K., & Haraldsson, E. *At the Hour of Death.* New York: Hastings House, 1986.

Palmer, J. "A Community Mail Survey of Psychic Experiences." *The Journal of the American Society for Psychical Research,* 73, 3 July (1979), 221–251.

Papowitz, L. "Life Death Life—During resuscitation, some patients face a life-or-death choice that no one else will know about—unless they ask." *American Journal of Nursing,* 86, 4 (1986), 416–418.

Pasricha, S., & Stevenson, I. "Near-Death Experiences in India: A Preliminary Report." *The Journal of Nervous and Mental Disease,* 174, 3 (1986), 165–170.

Pattison, E. M. "The Experience of Dying," *American Journal of Psychotherapy,* 21 (1967), 32–43.

Pennachio, J. "Near-Death Experiences and Self-

Transformation." *Journal of Near-Death Studies,* 6, 3 (1988), 162–168.

Plato *The Republic,* Harmondsworth: Penguin, 1973.

Raft, D., & Andresen, J. J. "Transformations in Self-Understanding after Near-Death Experiences." *Contemporary Psychoanalysis,* 22, 3 (1986) 319–346.

Rawlings, M. *Beyond Death's Door.* Sydney: Bantam Books, 1981.

Richards, L. *Nobody's Home.* Melbourne: Oxford University Press, 1990.

Ring, K. "Further Studies of the Near-Death Experience," *Theta,* 7 (1979), 1–3.

Ring, K. *Life at Death.* New York: Coward, McCann & Geoghan, 1980a.

Ring, K. "Psychologist Describes Near-Death Research Results." *Anabiosis,* 2 (1980b), 13–15.

Ring, K. *Heading Toward Omega.* New York: William Morrow & Co. Inc., 1984.

Ring, K. " 'Near-Death Experiences,' Implications for Human Evolution and Planetary Transformation." *ReVision,* 8, 2 (1986), 75–85.

Ring, K. & Rosing, C. J. "The Omega Project: An Empirical Study of the NDE-Prone Personality." *Journal of Near-Death Studies,* 8, 4 (1990), 211–239.

Ritchie, G. G., with Sherrill, E. *Return From Tomorrow.* New Jersey: Spire Books, 1978.

Roberts, G., & Owen, J. "The Near-Death Experience." *British Journal of Psychiatry,* 153 (1988), 607–617.

Royse, D. "The Near-Death Experience: A Survey of Clergy's Attitudes and Knowledge." *The Journal of Pastoral Care,* 39, 1 (1985), 31–42.

Sabom, M. B. "Near-Death Experiences." *Journal of the American Medical Association,* 244 (1980a), 29.

Sabom, M. B. "Commentary on 'The Reality of Death Experiences' by Ernst Rodin." *The Journal of Nervous and Mental Disease,* 168, 5 (1980b), 266–267.

Sabom, M. B. *Recollections of Death.* New York: Harper & Row, 1982.

Sabom, M. B., & Kreutziger, S. "The Experience of Near-Death," *Death Education,* 1, 2 (1977), 195–203.

Schnaper, N. "Comments Germane to the Paper Entitled 'The Reality of Death Experiences' by Ernst Rodin." *The Journal of Nervous and Mental Disease,* 168, 5 (1980), 268–270.

Schorer, C. E. "Two Native American Near-Death Experiences." *Omega,* 16, 2 (1985–86), 111–113.

Schutz, A. *Collected Papers II: Studies in Social Theory.* The Hague: Martinus Nijhoff, 1971.

Serdahely, W. J. "A Pediatric Near-Death Experience: Tunnel Variants." *Omega,* 20, 1 (1989–90), 55–62.

Serdahely, W. J. "Pediatric Near-Death Experiences." *Journal of Near-Death Studies,* 9, 1 (1990b), 33–39.

Serdahely, W. J. & Walker, B. A. "A Near-Death Experience at Birth." *Death Studies,* 14 (1990), 177–183.

Shakespeare, W. *The Works of William Shakespeare.* Great Britain: Basil Blackwell, 1947.

Siegel, R. K. "The Psychology of Life After Death." *American Psychologist,* 35 (1980), 911–931.

Smith, H. *Forgotten Truth: The Primordial Tradition.* New York: Harper Colophon Books, 1977.

Stevenson, I. "Comments on 'The Reality of Death Experiences: A Personal Perspective.'" *The Journal of Nervous and Mental Disease,* 168, 5 (1980), 271–272.

Straight, S. "A Wave Among Waves: Katherine Anne Porter's Near-Death Experience." *Anabiosis,* 4, 2 (1984), 107–123.

Strauss, A. *Qualitative Analysis for Social Scientists.* Cambridge: Cambridge University Press, 1987.

Strauss, A., & Corbin, J. *Basics of Qualitative Research: Grounded Theory Procedures and Techniques.* London: Sage, 1990.

Strom-Paikin, J. "Studying the NDE Phenomenon." *American Journal of Nursing,* 86, 4 (1986), 420–421.

Sullivan, R. M. "Combat-Related Near-Death Experiences: A Preliminary Investigation." *Anabiosis,* 4, 2 (1984), 143–152.

Sutherland, C. "Near-Death Experience by Proxy: A Case Study." *Journal of Near-Death Studies,* 8, 4 (1990), 241–251.

Vicchio, S. J. "Near-Death Experiences: Some Logical Problems and Questions for Further Study." *Anabiosis,* 1, 1 (1981), 66–87.

Weisman, A. D., & Hackett, T. P. "Predilection to Death." *Psychosomatic Medicine,* 23, 3 (1961), 232–256.

Widdison, H. "Near-Death Experiences and the Unscientific Scientist" in Lundahl, C. (ed.). *A Collection of Near-Death Research Readings.* Chicago: Nelson-Hall Publishers, 1982, pp. 3–17.

Wiener, C., Strauss, A., Fagerhaugh, S., & Suczek, B. "Trajectories, Biographies and the Evolving Medical Technology Scene: Labor and Delivery and the Intensive Care Nursery." *Sociology of Health and Illness,* 1, 3 (1979), 261–283.

Wilber, K. *Up From Eden.* New York: Doubleday Anchor, 1981.

Wilber, K. "Odyssey: A Personal Inquiry into Humanistic and Transpersonal Psychology." *Journal of Humanistic Psychology,* 22, 1, Winter (1982), 57–90.

Wilber, K. *Eye to Eye: The Quest for the New Paradigm.* New York: Doubleday Anchor, 1983.

Wilber, K. (ed.) *Quantum Questions: Mystical Writings of the World's Greatest Physicists.* Boulder, Colorado: Shambhala Publications, 1984.

Wilson, I. *The After-Death Experience.* London: Sidgwick & Jackson, 1987.

Zaleski, C. *Otherworld Journeys: Accounts of Near-Death Experience in Medieval and Modern Times.* Oxford: Oxford University Press, 1987.

Useful Address

IANDS (International Association for Near-Death Studies)
P.O. Box 502
East Windsor Hill, CT 06028

Index

Page numbers in bold type refer to main entries.

ABOUT THE AUTHOR

Dr. Cherie Sutherland, who has had a near-death experience herself, is a visiting research fellow in the School of Sociology at the University of New South Wales. Since beginning her near-death research, she has lectured widely on the subject and been involved in several film projects.

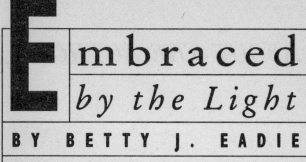